University of London Historical Studies

XX

UNIVERSITY OF LONDON HISTORICAL STUDIES

THE BISHOPS OF BATH AND WELLS, 1540–1640

This volume is published with the help of a grant from the late Miss Isobel Thornley's Bequest to the University of London

The Bishops of Bath and Wells, 1540–1640

Social and Economic Problems

by

PHYLLIS M. HEMBRY

UNIVERSITY OF LONDON

THE ATHLONE PRESS

1967

Published by
THE ATHLONE PRESS
UNIVERSITY OF LONDON
at 2 *Gower Street, London* WC1

Distributed by Constable & Co. Ltd
12 *Orange Street, London* WC2

Canada
Oxford   University   Press
Toronto

U.S.A.
Oxford University Press Inc
New York

© *Phyllis M. Hembry,* 1967

Printed in Great Britain by
WESTERN PRINTING SERVICES LTD
BRISTOL

PREFACE

WHEN an interest in Tudor Somerset led me into the study of the episcopal estates of Bath and Wells I soon realized that although some of the manuscript sources were rich in intimate detail most of them were scattered and fragmentary. No single collection has supplied the basic material or produced a chronological outline, so that many questions that one would like to meet about the bishops' activities are inevitably left unanswered. These lacunae are partly explained by the evidence of Nathaniel Chyles, the Restoration historian of the bishopric, that much material was destroyed during the civil wars: 'when the Bishop's Palace was plundered, the writings and records of the bishopric, of no advantage to soldiers, were seized on by some attorneys of the place and neighbourhood who, having made some small interest by them, as to their own practice, so confounded, embezzled and shifted them as impossible ever to be retrieved.'

So I have had to seek the pattern of the story in various places, and I have discovered that one of the many pleasures met in historical research is the selfless goodwill of the custodians of records. To the very many people who have answered my queries I give my thanks, and for research facilities I am grateful to the Institute of Historical Research; the Public Record Office; the British Museum; the Principal Probate Registry; the Bodleian Library; the late Very Rev. F. P. Harton, Dean of Wells; Mr H. J. Dodd, the Town Clerk of Wells; Mr C. W. Harris and his staff at the Diocesan Registry, Wells; the Somerset Record Office; Mr W. A. Seaby, formerly Secretary of the Somersetshire Archaeological and Natural History Society at Taunton Castle; and the Church Commissioners whose relevant records have since my visit been moved to Taunton. Dr R. D. Reid of Wells has most generously shared his local knowledge.

My thanks go also to Miss F. Bignell, Mrs N. Buzzell and Miss W. Moore for their gallant assistance in typing a rather tiresomely technical manuscript.

This book is derived from a thesis which was approved in December 1956 for the degree of Doctor of Philosophy of the University of London. I am greatly indebted to Mr Christopher Hill, now Master of Balliol, who urged me to attempt the task of rewriting the thesis for publication, to Sir John Neale whose memorable Tudor seminars have left so obvious an imprint on this book, to Mr T. F. Reddaway for interest and encouragement, and to Professor S. T. Bindoff, my guide and mentor, who generously read the manuscript and proofs in most exacting detail and gave valuable suggestions. Miss J. E. Hayward corrected my Latin and helped in countless practical ways.

Publication would not have been possible without a grant for which I have to thank the trustees of the Isobel Thornley Bequest Fund, and the Athlone Press has given me useful advice.

Cheltenham   P.M.H.
August 1965

CONTENTS

CONTENTS

MAPS

ABBREVIATIONS

B.M.	British Museum
Bull. Inst. H.R.	*Bulletin of the Institute of Historical Research*
Cal. S.P.D.	*Calendar of State Papers, Domestic*
Cal. S.P. Spanish	*Calendar of State Papers, Spanish*
C.P.R.	*Calendar of Patent Rolls*
Collinson	J. Collinson, *History of Somersetshire* (1791)
C.W.	City of Wells MSS
D.N.B.	*Dictionary of National Biography*
E.H.R.	*The English Historical Review*
H.M.C.	The Historical Manuscripts Commission
Linc. Rec. Soc.	The Lincoln Record Society
L. & P. Hen. VIII	*Letters and Papers of Henry VIII*
P.C.C.	Prerogative Court of Canterbury Wills
Phelps	W. Phelps, *The History and Antiquities of Somerset-shire* (1839)
P.R.O.	Public Record Office
Proc. Som. Arch. Soc.	*Proceedings of the Somersetshire Archaeological and Natural History Society*
S.R.O.	Somerset Record Office
S.R.S.	Somerset Record Society
T.C.	Taunton Castle MSS
Wells	*Calendar of the MSS of the Dean and Chapter of Wells*
Wells Cath.	Wells Cathedral Library MSS
V.C.H.	*Victoria County History*

Introduction

THE theological and constitutional aspects of the Reformation have not wanted their historians from Burnet, Fuller and Strype onwards. Whole libraries could be filled with general church histories and even more with the biographies of great churchmen. By contrast little attention has been paid to the sociological consequences of what was, in the event, a great act of nationalization halted half-way, the confiscation of church wealth. Only within the last decade has Mr Christopher Hill's study of the economic situation of the church in the half-century before the Civil War focused some interest in that direction, while more recently Professor Dickens has drawn attention to the Lollard origins of the attack on church endowment.[1]

How Henry VIII and his minister Thomas Cromwell managed parliament and people to effect a break with Rome, to establish an independent church in England in the 1530's, and to carry with them bishops whose attitudes ranged from enthusiasm to hostility, is generally known. When it was all over, the Pope's jurisdiction over the church in England was ended, no more English revenues were drained to Pope or absentee bishops, and the monasteries and nunneries, last bastions of Romish loyalty, had been abolished. Equally, church appointments now rested ultimately with the king. The bishops, that is the two archbishops of Canterbury and York, the fifteen English and the four Welsh bishops, had become virtually civil servants. The church in England had become insular, national.

What is not generally appreciated is that Thomas Cromwell's plan to rationalize the use of church wealth originally applied

[1] Christopher Hill, *Economic Problems of the Church from Archbishop Whitgift to the Long Parliament*; A. G. Dickens, *The English Reformation*.

not only to the religious orders but to all church estates. When his great survey of church property, the *Valor Ecclesiasticus*, was drawn up in 1535, a necessary preliminary to the redistribution of church wealth, it included both the land held by the monastic houses and that belonging to bishops and deans and chapters. There is evidence that plans were afoot to confiscate the lot, but to set aside some of it to create a fund to support salaried bishops. The bishops were to become paid servants of the state with a fixed income, no longer independent landowners, and there were to be more of them: an increase of thirteen on a county basis was suggested.

When one considers the map of the medieval bishoprics, the sprawling magnitude of the bishopric of Lincoln stretching from the Humber southwards to include Oxford, and the size of the diocese of Worcester out of which two other sees were soon to be carved, the logic of this proposed reform seems obvious. Ruthless in its efficiency, it went too far at the time: there was danger that it would provoke an extreme conservative reaction, perhaps even Catholic invasion by the Emperor, and so the 'grand design', almost certainly Cromwell's, was cut down. The monasteries were dissolved and their lands were confiscated, but the bishops were spared, and of the proposed thirteen new bishoprics only six, Bristol, Chester, Gloucester, Oxford, Peterborough and Westminster (briefly), were established. The Henrician proposal for augmenting the number of bishops, and putting them on a fixed stipend with central control of their estates, was too advanced, and it was shelved until the nineteenth-century reformers got to work with the setting up of the Ecclesiastical Commission.

This did not mean that the bishoprics were immune. Parliament had not given their dissolution legal sanction, but during the course of the sixteenth century the Crown, impelled by rising costs and the accumulation of debts from Henry VIII's wars, found the bishops easy prey. Pressure was brought on them to grant manors or long leases of estates to the Crown, sometimes by way of exchange, but nearly always on terms unfavourable to themselves. In the reign of Edward VI, with the extreme Protestants in charge, this depletion of the bishoprics became acute. Something was recovered in Mary's reign, but the Elizabethan church was established with only a part of its medieval endowment: in the bishopric of Bath and Wells more than half of the estates had been lost.

The task confronting the Elizabethan church was to become established on a permanent, solid basis after the confusing changes of the preceding half-century, but it was already weakened financially. The bishops complained that their revenues were insufficient: they had great demands of hospitality and charity to meet and a standard of living to maintain. Two other factors made their lot more difficult. Prices had risen markedly over the last two or three decades, and most bishops were now married and had families to support. The celibate churchman of high rank in the later middle ages had been able to live in princely affluence: his Elizabethan counterpart was a careworn father with perhaps only half his predecessor's landed capital.

Elizabeth I further aggravated the position of her impoverished bishops when in her first parliament, in 1559, an act was passed which allowed the Crown, during the vacancy of a bishopric, to help itself to episcopal temporalities (in effect manors) in exchange for parsonages and tenths, and also made it impossible for bishops to grant long leases to anyone except the Crown. This act gave the queen further control of the bishops: their appointment could be made conditional on a purchase price, namely a fat manor for Crown or courtier. The bishops had few defenders and were helpless against this act, for by now the courtiers, many of them enriched by monastic lands, were eager for other gains, the cathedral estates. Puritan attacks, too, on church ritual were alienating public opinion from the bishops. Cajoled and criticized, denied the firm support even of the queen, the Supreme Governor of the church, the bishops not surprisingly stiffened in their attitude in the last two decades of the reign. There was a refusal to compromise with their opponents, especially from 1583 under the disciplinarian archbishop of Canterbury, John Whitgift.

Then came a generation of weak Jacobean bishops and it was too late for episcopacy to save itself. Instructions to the bishops in 1622 and 1634 to conserve their estates and not to make ill-considered leases show that the Crown and the successive archbishops of Canterbury, Abbot and Laud, were alive to the problem of proper economic support for the bishops. But by now the Root and Branch movement, those who wanted to extirpate episcopacy entirely, had gathered momentum among the puritans, and it only needed William Laud's high-handed disciplinary measures after he became archbishop of Canterbury in 1633 to harden the opposition. Although for eleven years, from 1629, this opposition was impotent since there was no parliament to give it expression, with the calling of the Long Parliament in 1640 episcopacy was doomed. In 1641 the bishops were robbed of their political power, their seats in the House of Lords, and of their legal jurisdiction, their spiritual courts. Finally in 1646 the confiscation and sale of their estates began. The bishops fled into exile or circumspectly retired to rural quietude. The Root and Branch movement had gone far beyond the revolutionary schemes of Thomas Cromwell in 1535: it had temporarily abolished episcopacy in England.

The years from 1535 to 1646 are, then, a climacteric period in the history of the Anglican episcopacy, and this book is an attempt to examine in detail the social and economic consequences of these years for the bishops of one diocese. Bath and Wells has a double appellation, like Coventry and Lichfield or Sodor and Man. The bishopric had originally been based on Wells when it was created in 909 out of the diocese of Sherborne, but Bishop John of Tours (1088–1122) saw the opportunity to combine the see with the vacant abbacy of Bath, and he moved to Bath and made its church of St Peter, rather than the church of St Andrew at Wells, his centre. When he died he was buried there. The bishops were normally elected jointly by the monks at Bath and the canons at Wells, but following a disputed election at the vacancy occurring in 1242 Pope Innocent IV in 1245 settled the relationship of the two churches for all time: the election of bishops was to take place alternately at Bath and Wells and the bishop was to have the double style. This joint election continued until the dissolution, but the bishops tended to make Wells their centre. The last bishop's burial at Bath was in 1247. The funeral of Bishop Montague at Bath in 1618 was not a true revival of the Bath connection, for he had meanwhile become bishop of Winchester.

Bishops were then supported by rents drawn directly from their estates, and a monastic establishment with endowments of land in the vicinity had already existed at Wells since 766. After the establishment of the bishopric there, it was enriched by the accretion of the important manors of Banwell and Congresbury granted to Bishop Dudoco by Edward the Confessor in 1034. By the time of the Domesday Survey the solid core of the endowment which was to support the bishops, as distinct from the dean and chapter, right through the middle ages up to the Edwardian cataclysm, had already been acquired: the manors of Bishops Lydeard, Chard, Chew Magna, Compton Bishop, Evercreech, Kingsbury, Wellington, Wells, West Buckland, Westbury, Wiveliscombe and Yatton. Congresbury had been temporarily lost, but it was restored to the bishop in John's reign.

In the reign of Henry I the first manor outside Somerset was acquired, that of Dogmersfield in Hampshire: a convenient halt for the bishops on their long journeys between the west country and London. The Gloucestershire property of Pucklechurch, which at that date included the other two manors later differentiated as Westerleigh and Wyke, was brought in as an acquisition from the monks of Glastonbury, together with two more Somerset manors, Blackford and Cranmore.

Henry III's reign brought the manor of Cheddar and the borough of Axbridge to the episcopal endowment, and by 1291 at the latest the bishop's estates had become fixed at their greatest extent, except for the London property granted to Bishop Harewell by Edward III. There may have been from time to time some fluctuation of boundaries, especially in draining the marshy Somerset levels which reach to the very foot of the Mendip Hills, or there may have been some encroachment on the Royal Forest of Mendip, as when Bishop Burnell obtained a grant from Edward I to enclose some of his woods in Cheddar and Axbridge within the Forest of Mendip. Some separate estates were carved out of the original enormous Norman manors and granted away. The manor of Puxton is an example: it was detached from the manor of Banwell.

The grant of the London property, the Bath Inn, or Bath Place, in the parish of St Clement Danes to Bishop Harewell

(1366–86) was a necessary rounding off of the estates. It provided a metropolitan residence, a very necessary appendage to the west country estates in an age when bishops were also statesmen and in constant attendance on the king and council at Westminster. But the 'middle ages' for the bishops of Bath and Wells was the period of consolidation from 1291, the date of the great taxation of Nicholas IV, to 1535, when that other great survey the *Valor Ecclesiasticus* was drawn up.

During the middle ages Bath and Wells seems to have been well up in the hierarchy of bishoprics, more important than its two neighbours Exeter and Salisbury, but not in the first rank, which consisted of Canterbury, York, London, Durham, Winchester and Ely. Earlier most of the bishops at Wells had been content to live out their days in the diocese, and when they died they were usually buried there, but from the mid-fourteenth century there was a tendency to regard it as a mere stepping-stone in a career. Between 1363 and 1523 eight bishops out of thirteen came to it from minor sees, and six passed on after brief tenure to a more elevated position, three to Durham, one to Ely and one each to the archbishoprics of Canterbury and York.[1]

In these pre-Reformation days the status of the bishopric warranted its being held sometimes by a statesman of national importance. The outstanding figures are Robert Burnell (1275–92), the famous chancellor of Edward I; John Stafford (1425–43), keeper of the privy seal to Henry VI and lord high treasurer of England, who in 1432 was promoted lord chancellor while yet holding Bath and Wells; and Thomas Beckington (1443–65), private secretary to Henry VI.

Finally in this tradition of medieval church-statesmen there was Thomas Wolsey (1518–23), cardinal, papal legate and chancellor of England who held the see in *commendam* while archbishop of York. It would be idle to pretend that his connection with the see was anything but nominal and financial: he had farmed its revenues during the tenure of the previous notorious absentee bishop Adrian de Castello (1504–18). Wolsey's influence in the see was not withdrawn in 1523,

---

[1] Wolsey's transfer to Durham is included here but his tenure of York is ignored because it covered both episcopates.

however, for his place as bishop was taken by his nominee, his chaplain John Clerk (1523–41), and it was during this period, in the reign of Henry VIII, that the bishopric began its decline.

CHAPTER I

The Bishop's Estates: the Early Tudor Endowment

THE PALACE AT WELLS, THE LONDON AND NORTH SOMERSET PROPERTIES

A BISHOP in Tudor times had a double rôle: not only was ecclesiastical organization, the care and discipline of a diocese, his responsibility, but he was also the lord of vast estates, and the maintenance and management of these temporalities, which provided his income, was his concern. Today the Church Commissioners relieve him of estate administration in return for a fixed stipend, but in earlier times all the anxieties of the granting of leases, the collection of rents, the repair of buildings, walls and ditches, the care of forests, the litigation arising from disputed tenures, the control of markets and fairs, and the inefficiencies of stewards and bailiffs added to his distractions.

Allowing for regional differences of climate and topography which help to determine the farming practice of a district, the experience of the bishop of Bath and Wells was probably typical of the other bishops of his generation. His estates were not hereditary, but held in virtue of his office, yet he had his principal residence like any other territorial magnate. This residence was his palace at Wells, the heart not only of his ecclesiastical duties, but of his estate administration.

Wells was conveniently sited for this purpose on the southeastern slopes of the Mendip range, at the point where the hills' steep descent abruptly reaches the low-lying moors, and streams issue from the limestone block. The manor of Wells was the link between the episcopal properties scattered along the

northern and southern flanks of the Mendips, the outlying
manors in south-east Somerset, and those further out again in
the south-west of the county. Leland, who must have passed
through it in the time of Bishop John Clerk (1523–41), said: 'the
town of Wells is set in the roots of Mendip Hills, in a stony soil,
and full of springs, whereof it hath the name. The chiefest
spring is called Andrews wells, and riseth in a meadow plot
not far above the east end of the cathedral church.'[1]

The bishop's medieval, moated and fortified palace is to the
south of the cathedral and adjacent to it. Today it is substantially the same in structure and plan, at least as far as the ex-
terior is concerned, as when Bishop Clerk came to it in 1523.
The main entrance is by the great turreted gateway at the east
end of the market place, the Bishop's Eye, erected by Bishop
Beckington in 1453. This gateway and the room above now
form part of the diocesan registry, where many of the episcopal
records are kept, and the crowds which come through in high
summer are tourists. In Tudor times it was a livelier place all
the year round. Here every quarter day, or for the general audit
at Michaelmas, came the bailiffs and reeves of the bishop's
various manors, bringing the money rents in bags and the rents
paid in kind, such as corn, poultry and eggs. A black ox paid as
a heriot, or death duty, coming from an outlying manor, would
be driven across the drawbridge to augment the provisions of
the bishop's household. So too came loads of timber and wood to
heat the draughty rooms of the palace: in 1599 alone 409 loads
of timber were brought in. The kegs of wine which the bishop
had licence from the crown to import through Bristol were
trundled in by waggon: through the 1570's at least Bishop
Berkeley was bringing in wine at the annual rate of two tuns.[2]
Through the Bishop's Eye, too, came the country gentry and
yeoman farmers seeking leases, or the renewal of leases, jostling
with notaries burdened with parchment rolls, clerics seeking
ordination and justices of the peace coming to consult the
bishop. In addition to all his other duties the bishop sat on
the commission of peace and took an important part in
local government. When the council of the west was set up

---

[1] *Leland's Itinerary 1535–43*, ed. L. T. Smith (1907), II, 144.
[2] P.R.O. S.C.6/Add. 3545/84; S.R.O. DD/CC/31523.

in 1539 the bishop was a member and it sometimes met at Wells.[1]

The Bishop's Eye leads into an outer enclosure where there used to be a pond and where the citizens of Wells were accustomed to water their horses,[2] and beyond that runs an almost circular wall with an embattled parapet having loopholes and six bastions. The whole is surrounded by a deep moat crossed by a drawbridge leading to a portcullised gateway which is bridged by a stately gatehouse. All of this, the moat and the wall, and also the northern portion of the palace, which is built onto the outer wall, is of the fourteenth century, built by Bishop Ralph of Shrewsbury (1329–63). It is virtually unaltered today. The fortification encloses the palace itself, which is earlier in date.

The core of it and the glory of it all used to be the great hall, then intact and as Bishop Burnell had built it about 1280, but now a shell. Spacious and lofty, one hundred and twenty feet by seventy, it was lit by nine windows with pointed arches, and at each angle was an octagonal turret with a staircase giving onto the roof: 'in neither University or Inns of Court is there any Hall of a larger extent', wrote Nathaniel Chyles, the Restoration historian of the bishopric.[3] The hall was in fact the bishop's 'state room', large enough to accommodate an assembly of clerics, officials or tenants, and in size and magnificence it reflected his status. His private living quarters were originally confined to the single chamber block adjoining, which consisted of two chambers on the ground floor divided by a central passage and opening into the north end of the hall, and a great upper chamber above reached only by a private, semi-external stair which rose from the western end of the two-storey porch on the west wall of the block. This upper chamber was designed as a self-contained apartment, with a large fireplace, windows with seats and a garderobe in the south-west turret; here the bishop could retire from the ceremony of the hall and the bustle

[1] A. L. Rowse, *Tudor Cornwall*, p. 241.

[2] William Simes' map of Wells, 1735, shows this horse pond.

[3] Nathaniel Chyles, 'The History of the Cathedral Church of St Andrews in Wells' (*c.* 1680) II, 2, fo. 23. There are two extant copies of this manuscript history, one in Wells Cathedral Library and one among the Taunton Castle MSS, CH 22. Chyles was secretary to Bishop Peter Mews (1673–84).

of the courtyard. Nothing remains of the kitchen which is thought to have lain to the west of the chamber block and separated from it by an open court.[1] Bishop Burnell was also responsible for building the adjoining chapel, a fine double cube building fifty-two feet long and twenty-six feet broad.

Somewhere within the palace precincts, and supervised by the keeper of the palace, was the bishop's prison for criminous clerks, commonly called the Cowhouse. Its exact site is not easily determined: the local antiquary Buckle said it was a building of two storeys contained in one of the six bastions of the fortified wall.[2] The description in the grant of the keepership of the prison to Geoffrey Upton in 1546 seems to refute this. The prison was 'within the palace', which could mean merely that it was within the palace bounds, and Upton was to have 'two chambers above the prison, and another chamber in the New Work whose door is nearest the prison, with a small stable adjacent.' The New Work is outside the limits of the palace, on the north side of the market place. This suggests that the Cow-house was a part of the great, outer gateway, on the site of the present diocesan registry, but perhaps open at the back.[3]

To the south-west of the palace is the enormous bishop's barn, probably built in the first half of the fifteenth century; it is a hundred and ten feet by twenty-five and a half feet and has twelve buttresses along its sides. Here was collected the produce of the bishop's park and other demesne lands adjoining, the rents in kind and the heriots, death-duties usually in kind, from his tenants.

Besides being lord of the manor of Wells and of the hundred of Wells Forum, and enjoying certain rights within the liberty and town of Wells, the bishop also held a great accumulation of property bringing in a gross income of £1,642. 2. 8¼d. in 1509;[4] by the time the *Valor Ecclesiasticus*, Thomas Cromwell's great survey of church income, was drawn up in 1535 the gross sum from all these temporalities was £1,899. 4. 5¼d. (The

---

[1] P. A. Faulkner, 'Domestic Planning from the Twelfth to the Fourteenth Centuries', *The Archaeological Journal*, cxv, 174, 180–1.

[2] *Proc. Som. Arch. Soc.*, xxxiv, ii, 80.

[3] *Wells*, ii, 262–3. This was also the opinion of the late Mr A. T. Wicks of Wells.

[4] This reference is taken from an uncatalogued manuscript notebook in Wells Museum, fos. 8–9.

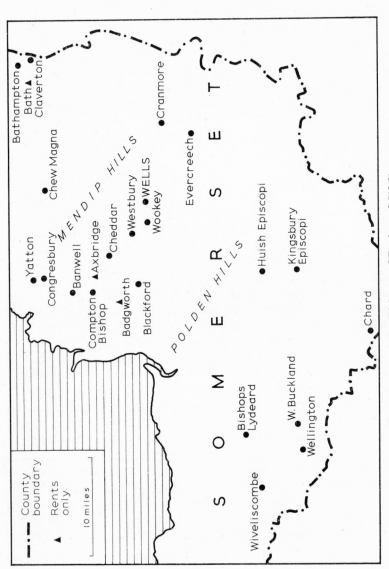

MAP 1. Manors of the Bishops of Bath and Wells 1535.

Not shown Gloucester (3), Hampshire (1), Compton Parva, Berks., and the London property.

bishop's income from spiritualities was assessed in the *Valor* at no more than £40.) The year 1535 was, in fact, the Great Divide as far as episcopal estates were concerned, for in that year Thomas Cromwell sent round his agents to collect information about the ecclesiastical estates in preparation for his wounding attack on them. Although the monasteries were to be the main target, the bishops also were forced by a mixture of persuasion and threats to part with some of their properties, and it is therefore instructive to sum up the total of the bishop of Bath and Wells' estates at that date. He then held twenty-six manors, of which twenty-one were in Somersetshire, three in Gloucestershire, one in Hampshire, and one in Berkshire. He owned also five townships, five hundreds, some small rents in Bath and Badgworth and a London house (*hospitium*).

Whereas in the Elizabethan and Stuart periods all but the most important properties were to be leased, in Henrician times only three were farmed out, the manor of Compton Parva in Berkshire, where distance would have rendered close supervision difficult, the palace at Bath and the manor of Blackford. All the other estates were kept in hand, the bailiffs and reeves collecting their rents. The bishop's steward in the earlier period —or rather the understeward, for the chief steward did little work—was a much busier man than his successors in office after 1559, when much of this property had been parted with.

There are no detailed accounts for the Henrician period, as there are after 1566, so that in trying to reconstruct the topography and condition of the estates in 1535 one has to draw mostly on the particulars for grants of the augmentation office for 1548 to 1553, and a much mutilated and partly incomplete account of 1527–9 now in Taunton Castle, occasionally using the accounts for 1566 onwards.

The grant of the London property to Bishop Harewell (1366–86) had provided a metropolitan residence, a very necessary appendage to the west country estates in an age when bishops often spent much time out of their dioceses on the king's business. Even if not statesmen, all bishops were lords of parliament and a London residence was a necessity to them. The Bath Inn, or Bath Place, or again Hampton Place, as it was later called, was in the parish of St Clement Danes without the

bar of the New Temple, and it is not to be confused with a
further piece of London property later acquired by the bishops
of Bath and Wells, the Minories at Aldgate. There was a
mansion or tenement annexed to the Bath Inn on the outer
side and also orchards and gardens and other tenements, two
of which were called the Cardinal's Hat and the Tabard.[1] This
London property was in the charge of a keeper, and in 1513
the office came to Jerome Vergil, brother of Polydore Vergil,
the historian who was then archdeacon of Wells. The keepership was to be held for life, but it could be exercised by a
deputy: in this case it almost certainly was. The wage was 2½d. a
day (£3. 16s. a year) with perquisites:

a robe of the suit of the gentlemen of the bishop's service against
Christmas, so often as the bishop or his successors gives livery of this
kind; and also a mess of food and drink, every day when the bishop
. . . [is] staying in the hospitium.

From 1539, when the Minories property came to the bishop, a
warden had to be provided for his house there. This post, with
the annual fee of 40s., went to John Moore, who with his wife
Elizabeth had a lease of some of the property.[2]

Apart from the London house and the palace at Wells, the
bishop owned eight mansion houses, often dignified by the
name of 'palace', at any one of which, except Bath which was
let out, he might pass a few days from time to time. The others
were at Wookey, Chew Magna, Claverton, Evercreech, Wiveliscombe, Banwell and Dogmersfield. The site of the palace at
Blackford, which has recently been excavated by Miss I. M.
Rendell of Sexey's School, Blackford and her helpers, was
probably abandoned before Tudor times, but its moated outline is still apparent. Banwell and Wiveliscombe were favourite
retreats to which the bishop could retire from the responsibilities and cathedral gossip at Wells without an unduly long
journey. Bishop Knight (1541–7) was at Wiveliscombe almost
continuously in the last year of his episcopate,[3] and after that
manor was lost to the bishopric, in Bishop Godwin's time (1584–
90), Banwell became the favourite. Bishop Godwin, a sick

[1] *Wells*, ii, 215, 227.   [2] Ibid., 232–3, 255–6.
[3] Ibid., 257–63.

man, scarcely left it and he built a fine new house for his eldest
son there.

To take the bishop's manors in geographical sequence going
westwards from Wells along the south flank of the Mendips,
adjacent to Wells was the manor of Wookey, then still largely
unenclosed waste land and swampy marsh.[1] The houses at
Wookey clustered around the church and the manor house,
separated from Knowle Hill by Wet Moor, and by common
fields and waste from the hamlets of Wookey Hole to the north-
east and Bleadney, Henton, Yarley and Worth clustering on a
promontory of high ground to the south. Wookey had three
common fields, Westfield, Northfield and Eastfield; Yarley
had a common field called Worth Field and arable fields on
the hill above called Goarway Field and Sheaf Field, and at
Wookey Hole there was Marley Mead. There were rights of
pasture for the bishop's tenants on the moors round about, and
in the hedges and closes surrounding the manor place and its
sixty-two tenements grew elms which provided timber and fuel
for the inhabitants.

The river Axe issuing from Wookey Hole flows through the
manor. From ancient times it had been diverted from its natural
bed, about a mile from the source, into an artificial channel on
higher ground to provide a mill-stream. The mill which it
drove belonged to the bishop and in 1553 it was let out for
£5. 13s. 4d. The stream also provided fishing rights which were
let out for 1s.[2] William of Worcester, visiting the neighbourhood
about 1470, had mentioned the varieties of fish caught by people
around Wells: trout, bullheads or miller's thumbs, loach, small
pike, perch or sticklebacks, crayfish, eels and flounders.

To the south-west of the church on a plot of ground about six

[1] The history of this manor, which was almost identical with the parish, has
been studied by the Rev. T. Scott Holmes, *The History of the Parish and Manor of
Wookey* (1886?), but he was not always accurate. He does not transcribe the
particulars of the grant to William Dunch in 1553 (P.R.O. E.318/1589) correctly.
He identifies a watermill in Wyke (p. 59) and the homage of Wyke (p. 66) with
Wookey, and builds up a false argument on this supposition, whereas accounts for
Wells manor show that they both relate to Wick (the moden Coxley Wick), which
makes much better sense. His evidence for saying that the area of the manor was
something over 1,200 acres (p. 68) is not apparent: the grant which he quotes
shows only that the cultivated land amounted to at least 230 acres.

[2] P.R.O. E.318/1589.

and a half acres in extent and surrounded on all sides by a moat, was the bishop's home, the manor-house. The site is now marked by Court Farm which incorporates what is left of the bishop's 'palace': the private chamber, the chapel and traces of the hall. Originally the building outlined a quadrangle about fifty feet square, and traces of a cloister have been found: it stood in the north-east corner of the moated enclosure. The water for the moat came from the mill-stream by an underground channel at the south-east corner. The moat ran close under the walls on the north side of the house, and the waters were kept clean by a sluice and underground channel which led out on the west to the original bed of the Axe. Within the moat and to the south-west were one or two fishponds.[1] It is doubtful whether the early Tudor bishops passed even a night in their Wookey home, although Bishop Clerk's brother Thomas lived there, probably as a tenant, and the next bishop, Knight, allowed him to stay there on lease. The last record of a bishop's being there is Bishop Beckington in 1446.[2]

Continuing westwards along the southern ridge of Mendip the next bishop's manor was that of Westbury, which adjoined Wookey. Less fruitful than Wookey to the bishop, it had nevertheless one important feature, Westbury Park. The keeper of the park and its deer was paid £2. 18s. 8d. a year, of which 6s. 8d. was for shoe-leather. He was also allowed to lease the grazing rights in the park, provided he left sufficient pasture for the bishop's game, and to take all trees that were windfalls.[3] When the ambitious Thomas Clerk, Bishop Clerk's brother, gained the keepership, which he had done at least by 1527, he was paid £3. 0. 10d., and by 1555 his fee had been advanced to £3. 6. 8d. There does not seem to have been that fixity of rents which there was at Wookey: the rents of both free and customary tenants amounted in 1552 to £39. 14. 8d., but they show no correlation with those of 1527, nor with those of the late Elizabethan period. Noticeable at Westbury is the large number of ploughing services and works which had been commuted into rents, 250 of them at 5d. each in 1552. The casual sources of incomes were like those of any other manor: heriots,

---

[1] Scott Holmes, *Wookey*, pp. 5, 9, 10, 23, 24.
[2] S.R.S., XLIX, I, 66.   [3] *Wells*, II, 160, 230.

fines, marriage licences and perquisites of the court. They amounted to only £2. 13. 4d. in 1552. Sales of wood from the park were a profitable item: in 1527 they brought in £7 9s. There was a dovecot sometimes let out for 6s. 8d. and a garden called the Court Orchard let to the reeve (*praepositus*) for 1s. 4d. in 1555. A peculiar feature was the payment of 'wynyard silver', amounting to 4s. 10d. in 1555, and it also appears in the Wookey accounts and at Wells, where the homage of Wick paid it at Hock-tide, varying in amount from 3d. to 2s. 1d.[1] This suggests that the bishop's tenants were cultivating vines on the sunny, south slopes of the Mendips where today the strawberry flourishes, and were paying him customary dues for doing so.

Proceeding still westwards along the southern slope of the Mendips and passing Stoke, from which the bishop derived a few odd rents, one reached the next episcopal manor, Cheddar. Cheddar Episcopi was one of four manors there. This was no place of swamp and marsh, but of wooded slope and towering cliff of grandeur unsurpassed in England, noisy too with the pounding of the mills fed by the subterranean streams which emerged from their hidden swallets to gush down the lower part of Cheddar Gorge. The bishop owned six mills there, five of them fulling-mills, and he paid an annual rent of 13s. 4d. to Lord Lisle for the upper mill. The stream also provided fishing rights which were let for 6s. in 1527, but only 1s. in 1548.[2] The bishop's woodland in Cheddar must have been quite extensive, for sales of wood in 1528 amounted to £22. 18. 10d., and there were two woodwards who were paid 10s. a year each. There were some free tenants at Cheddar, and a particular item of expense was 10s. a year for scouring and flooding the stream between Bulhurst and Collestonestrete. Cheddar was a valuable manor: the net income in 1528 was £89. 17. 2¼d. Recent excavations at Cheddar directed by Dr P. A. Rahtz have located the bishop's buildings, the site of which continued as the Manor Farm after the bishop ceased to have a direct interest.

A detour south from Cheddar would bring one to the next episcopal manor, Blackford, with its decaying, moated palace.

[1] P.R.O. S.C.6/P. & M./263.   [2] P.R.O. E.318/567.

The demesne land here was let out to William Coffin for £1,[1] but there were also fixed rents worth, in 1535, £40. 4. 3d.

From Blackford going northwards again one reached Badgworth. This manor, with that of Netherweare, had been held of the bishop since King John's time by fealty and one stork to be paid yearly by the family of de Hantone, or Hampton. Some time before 1542 it passed by an heiress to the Newton family, for in 1542 John Newton paid to the bishop £1 in lieu of a stork 'for the holding called Hamptons' and the Newtons kept it at least until 1598 when Sir Henry Newton was the holder.[2]

And so on to the manor of Compton Bishop tucked in an encircling fold of the Mendips below Wavering Down. The River Yeo flows from its source at Cheddar to the south of the village to join the River Axe beyond, and so the responsibility for keeping clear the watercourse fell to this manor at the point where the bounds of the manor of Cheddar ended, at Bulhurst, as the accounts for 1527 show:

Scouring and flooding water-course between Radclyff and Bulhurst and a water-course called Southmor Yeo—29s. 1d.

'Radclyff' was, of course, the Red Cliff, where there is an outcrop of red-sandstone on a particularly steep slope of the limestone Mendip range. It was sufficiently a landmark for Saxton to show it on his map of Somerset in 1575, and there was and is a bridge crossing the Yeo at this point. The manor was not one of the most valuable, being worth slightly under £50 annually, and there were here, as in other manors, sales of ploughing services, indicating arable cultivation on the lower slopes of the Mendips.

In the adjacent ancient borough of Axbridge the bishop also collected a few profits. In 1534 they included income from the fair worth 2s. 4d., and this was the last of his properties south of the Mendips.[3]

Across the Mendip ridge by Shute Shelve Hill and the Winscombe valley and descending the northern slope was the way to one of the most important episcopal properties, Banwell, that most favoured of the bishop's residences, second in im-

---

[1] T.C. MS, General Audit of the bishopric of Bath and Wells 1541–2, fo. 7r.
[2] Ibid.; Collinson, III, 565.   [3] P.R.O. S.C.6/Hen. VIII/3075.

portance only to Wells. The village hugs the side of the hill only just above the level of the marshes and moors, which, intersected by drains and ditches, stretch northwards and westwards uninterruptedly to the Bristol Channel. 'Banwell standeth not very wholesomely . . . the fens be almost at hand. Wood metely good about them,' was Leland's verdict. He does not mention the palace built there by Bishop Beckington, but now demolished, except the hall which in George I's time was converted into the house known as Banwell Court. The principal part of the palace was between the present house (or bishop's hall) and the church, to which there was communication by a stately gateway. The chapel of the palace at the east end of the hall was still complete with its pulpits and pews, and marriages were celebrated there, as late as 1730. But it was all there in Henry VIII's time, the handsome gateway, the porter's lodge, the extensive granaries, stables and other offices, and the orchard planted by Bishop Beckington nearly a century before.[1]

The Elizabethan accounts for Banwell are much fuller than the earlier ones and give some account of the demesne lands retained by the bishop for the provision of his household, although half of it was regularly let for £7. 18. 10d. (£7. 16. 2d. in 1527). There was a mill, as in 1527 let for the comparatively high rent of £15. 13. 4d.; there were also a meadow called the Lord's Meadow, a big garden known as the Court Orchard, three other gardens, some common pasture in Crosse Moor with tenements in Axbridge, and a park, which yielded together, £7 9s. a year.[2] The park, which lay to the east of the palace, was well stocked with deer, and in Bishop Clerk's time his complaints about poaching on these deer provoked a star chamber case. He alleged that late one June evening William St Loe, Robert Goodrich, and John Bademan of Knighton Sutton, with eighteen other evil and riotous persons, all armed, broke into the park and hunted there, killing four bucks and many other deer. Later, on an August evening, they broke in again and hunted the deer, and this time their bag was about twenty.[3]

---

[1] G. Bennett, 'The History of Banwell, Somerset' (1825), typescript, T.C. MS; R. W. Dunning, 'The Administration of the Diocese of Bath and Wells, 1401–91' (unpublished Ph.D. thesis, Bristol, 1963), pp. 233–4.

[2] P.R.O. S.C.6/Eliz./2008.   [3] P.R.O. St. Ch. 2/17/225.

Unlike all the other episcopal manors which had two, Banwell had five manorial officers: in addition to the reeve and hayward there were the beadle and the two wardens of the River Yeo who were responsible for keeping clear certain watercourses, or rhines as they are called locally. These rhines were fed by the River Yeo and formed part of the complicated drainage system of the lowlands on the north side of Mendip, a region always vulnerable to flooding by the sea breaking through from the Bristol Channel. The cost of scouring a stretch of rhine delimited by Ebdon's Bow, Uphill and Coldbridge was a recurrent item of expenditure in this manor, for the Yeo wardens were paid 13s. 10½d. a year. Of the other manorial officers the hayward got 11s. 1d. and the beadle 12s. 4½d., but the reeve's fee varied between 12s. and 17s. The making and mowing of hay and the carriage of wood, especially for the provision of the bishop's household, were other frequent costs in the manorial accounts. A typical item is one for 1599: 'Carriage of 40 cartloads of wood, posts, pales and rails to the mansion house at Banwell and the park there—20s.'[1] On the income side there were ploughing services and works sold for £29. 16. 5½d., and the Banwell reeve also collected rents in Axbridge and Worle.

And so northwards to Congresbury and Yatton. The former was a wealthy manor worth, in 1535, £123. 5. 7½d., and there must have been some woodland then, for sales of wood amounted to £4; Yatton was worth only £62. 2. 7d. Coming eastwards onto higher ground over hill and ridge one drops down into the valley of the Chew, the present site of a reservoir. Here, on the north side of the river Chew, was Chew Magna, or Bishop's Chew, the most considerable of the bishop's north Somerset manors. Chew yielded £129. 18. 5¾d. in 1535 and held the dignity of a borough: it had a market and was a busy clothing town, but it is doubtful whether the bishop drew any profits from its trade. Chew borough does not appear among the list of boroughs and hundreds owned by him in 1535, although he was clearly the lord of the hundred of Chew.[2] Chute (Chew Magna), said Leland, 'is a pretty clothing town, and hath a fair church. And at the south side of the church is a fair

---

[1] P.R.O. S.C.6/Add./3545/84.   [2] P.R.O. S.C.6/Hen. VIII/3075.

manor place of the Bishop of Bath.' Bishop Clerk, indeed, frequently resided in his palace there. It had the convenience of a bridge which crossed the church path to a door above the south window of the church. This door opened into a gallery over the chapel and the gallery was the bishop's pew.[1]

About twelve miles north, at Bath, there was another concentration of episcopal property, a small one, but it emphasized that the bishop was of Bath, not only of Wells. Apart from the palace, which was let out for £1, all that the bishop retained in property rights in the city of Bath was the fee farm, out of which he paid £5 annually to the Hospital of St John the Baptist there. The net profits handed over by the bishop's bailiff, Thomas Yasland, in 1535, were £8. 10. 2d. This sum, the fee farm of £8. 10. 2d., was that fixed as far back as the time of Edward III when the bishop had granted to the citizens the right to hold two weekly markets, on Wednesdays and Saturdays, for the sale of yarn, woollen cloth and other merchandise. These markets had flourished to the great profit of the citizens. Later, in 1567, when the bishop's rights in the city had passed to the Crown, the citizens resisted most vigorously the attempts of the inhabitants of Marshfield to set up a rival market when Bath was visited by plague and its market fell away.[2]

From Bath a toil up the slopes to the north-east of the city brought one to the manor of Bathampton, or Hampton, as it was called in the bishop's accounts. A small manor, this was never worth more than about £20, but it had a bailiff who was paid £1. 6. 8d., which was high as an episcopal bailiff's fee went, and a reeve, who was allowed a rent of 9s. in 1553. Despite its having these two keepers this distant manor was neglected. The demesne land was, of course, let out, and in 1553 certain cottages were totally decayed, as they had been for the last thirty years, so that the rent of 20s. due for them could not be accounted for.[3]

Now south along the slopes of the Avon valley to Claverton, where woods formed an important part of the manor. There were three woods belonging to the bishop, closes called Bishop's

---

[1] F. A. Wood, *Collections for the Parochial History of Chew Magna*, p. 225.
[2] P.R.O. S.C.6/Hen. VIII/3075, S.C.6/P. & M./257, Req.2/213/15.
[3] P.R.O. E.318/1560, S.C.6/P. & M./257.

Park, Short Wood and Hampton Cliff.[1] The *Valor Ecclesiasticus*
records sales of wood there worth 13s. 4d. Leland commented
on the bishop's park: 'this side Bath by south east I saw two
parks enclosed with a ruinous stone wall, now without deer.
One belonged to the bishop, another to the prior of Bath.'
This manor, Claverton, was another of the bishop's homes.
Bishop Ralph of Shrewsbury had built the original manor or
court-house, but at some distance in a field to the south stood a
later one used in Tudor and Stuart times.[2] The bailiff in charge
was again paid well, £1. 6. 8d. and in 1494 a keeper of the park
was appointed. The office went to Sir Amyas Paulet and
Edmund Myll jointly, but there is no further mention of this
keepership and it was probably a temporary concession.[3]

High on the rather barren, plateau-like upland country of
Mendip, bitterly exposed in winter, was the next episcopal
manor, nearly twenty miles away. This was the manor of
Cranmore, or East Cranmore, which had been raised into a
liberty by Henry I.[4] The manor had no free tenants and normally
did not produce more than £20 in profits, but in 1535 fines of
£12 brought the total to £35. 16. 0¾d.[5]

Southwards through Chesterblade one came to the last of the
Mendip range of episcopal manors, Evercreech, which contained yet another great park, Evercreech Park. It lay at the
south-west end of the parish bordering on Ditcheat and East
Pennard, and was an enclosure which had been divided up by
the time Collinson wrote his 'History' (1791) but which is
commemorated by the present Evercreech Park Farm. In the
centre was another palace, the court-house, built by the same
Bishop Ralph who had built the Claverton mansion in the early
fourteenth century.[6] Evercreech had been a frequent home of
medieval bishops,[7] but Bishop Clerk preferred other places and
in his time, on Leland's evidence, it was pulled down: 'a mile
by low pasture ground onto Evercreech village, where Clerk
last Bishop of Bath had a manor place, in whose time it was, as
a ruinous thing, clean in a manner taken down.' The keeper

---

[1] P.R.O. E.318/1535.   [2] Collinson, I, 146.   [3] *Wells*, II, 137.
[4] S. Lewis, *Topographical Dictionary of England*, 1,644.
[5] All figures for 1535 are taken from the *Valor Ecclesiasticus*, I, pp. 121 ff.
[6] Collinson, I, 414.   [7] e.g. S.R.S., XLIX, I, 9, 44, 67, 80.

of Evercreech Park was a regular member of the bishop's staff. In 1493 the post had been granted to Peter Gregory with a fee of £2; in 1500 Richard Runyon took his place with an increased wage, £2 1. 4d. Chyles gives the normal fee as £1. 14. 8d.[1]

Evercreech was one of the more valuable manors, worth about £50, but all the tenants were customary ones in 1535. A dispute about the customs of the manor of Evercreech came up in 1563, after the manor had passed out of the bishop's hands, which reflected the immemorial ways of copyhold tenure. At a court held at Evercreech in 1545 Bishop Clerk had granted to John Pointwyn, Isabel his wife and his two sons, Richard and William, by copy a small holding of customary land and one cottage for their lives. By 1563 many changes had taken place. John Pointwyn, the original tenant, had died, Isabel his widow had remarried without licence from the lord of the manor, thereby forfeiting her claim, and the son Richard claimed to be the rightful tenant. But John Haynes, who had the whole manor on farm, disputed the legality of Pointwyn's copy:

the custom of the manor of Evercreech is and time out of remembrance of man hath been that the customary lands of the manor are and be demisable for three lives at the most and not above and that if any demise be made of any of the customary lands of the manor in any one copy for any greater number of lives than three the grant so made is void.

The outcome of the case is not known, but Haynes implied that Evercreech followed the custom of the bishop's other manors in making grants for three lives only. This was indeed the rule, except for Wells, where copyholders could hold for five lives, including the principal, and only leaseholders were restricted to three.[2]

THE SOUTH SOMERSET ESTATES

The Polden Hills separated Evercreech and the other episcopal manors of north Somerset from those in the south: Huish Episcopi and Kingsbury Episcopi in the marshy lowlands, the manor and borough of Chard on the Devon-Dorset border,

---

[1] *Wells*, II, 130, 157; see below, p. 43.   [2] P.R.O. C3/145/9; see below, p. 32.

Wellington and West Buckland to the north of the Blackdown Hills, Bishops Lydeard on the southern slopes of the Quantocks, and finally that cherished home of so many bishops among rich, rolling, wooded country, Wiveliscombe.

Huish (Hewish) Episcopi was quite valuable, being worth £67. 16. 2¾d. in 1535 and nearly double, £107. 13. 8¼d., in 1555. There was a court-house there, but we have no record of the bishop's making it his residence. In fact all the adjuncts of episcopal residence were leased out. By 1555 the 163 acres of arable land which made up the demesnes had been divided into five lots and leased for £6. 4. 2d.; the dovecot was let out to John Higham for 5s., fishing rights in Huish Moor were leased to Thomas Gatyn for 1s. 8d. a year, and the wooded undergrowth in the lord's park was held by John Bourne for 6s. 8d. a year. The accounts reflect all the usual small stuff of manorial economy: in 1555 some rents were still paid in kind, such as the 55 cocks and hens which sold at 2d. each and brought in 9s. 2d., repairs to the pinfold cost 2s. 2d., while a cow taken as a heriot was worth £2. 13. 4d.[1]

Kingsbury Episcopi, sited on a slight ridge dominating the surrounding marshes with its fine Perpendicular church, was valuable, being worth £114. 2. 1½d. in 1535 and the bishop had a court-house there,[2] as he had also at Wellington on the site now marked by the Old Court House, Fore Street. At Chard the bishop held rights in town and manor and a survey of 1647 shows that there was then a manor house belonging to him with outhouses, stables, gardens and orchards occupying about three acres.[3] The bishop's income included the issues of a fair worth 1s. 10d. in 1535:[4] these were presumably the tolls of the beasts sold at the St James's Fair mentioned in 1647. The town of Wellington also provided the bishop with an income of £7. 7. 5d. in 1535 and the manor was a wealthy one, being worth £132. 4. 10½d. and having some free tenants, whereas West Buckland, which had originally been a part of the manor of Wellington, was much poorer, yielding only £54. 1. 11½d. in 1535, and the church on the high mound which dominates it was a chapel of Wellington.[5]

[1] P.R.O. S.C.6/P. & M./263.   [2] *Collinson*, II, 468.   [3] P.R.O. C54/4315.
[4] P.R.O. S.C.6/Hen. VIII/3075.   [5] Collinson, II, 468.

West Buckland had two mills, a water-mill called 'Aisshemyll' leased to John Combe for £2. 16. 8d., and a fulling-mill leased for only 5s. The demesne land, none of it arable, was all leased out for £14. 18. 9d., but ploughing services and works, sold for £4. 7. 10½d., indicate that there was some arable land in the manor. The manorial officers were allowed their perquisites: the reeve was acquitted a rent of 5s. 11d. and allowed one pasture called le Breche worth 10s., while the hayward was excused a rent of 6s. There were three *gardini* (gardens, or more probably in this part of Somersetshire, orchards) called Webhey, Colvershey and Balandshey.[1]

Wellington and West Buckland are on the south side of the vale of Taunton Deane: almost due north, on the southern foothills of the Quantocks, was another episcopal manor, Bishops Lydeard. One would expect to find here some evidence of trade originating from the grant of a charter to Bishop Robert Burnell by Edward I in 1291. This grant had given Bishops Lydeard the privilege of a Monday market and two annual fairs, on the feasts of the Nativity and of the Annunciation, each to run for six days, but it is doubtful whether the expected trade ever developed.[2] No income from markets and fairs appears in the early Tudor episcopal accounts, although Thomas Gerard was able, in 1633, to describe Lydeard as 'a slender market town'.[3]

The most significant feature of the economy of Bishops Lydeard was the annual sale of corn: from 1549 to 1551, 51 lb. at 8d. per lb. yielded £1. 14s. Since the demesne land was all leased out for £20. 18. 8d., and there were sales of ploughings and works amounting to £14. 10. 1d., it seems that no arable land was under the lord's own cultivation, and these sales of corn presumably come from corn rents. Water-mills, to deal with the corn, and fulling-mills—the number is not given— were leased for £11. 13s.[4]

The most westerly, and to some of the bishops the most important, of their manors, since it provided refuge from cathedral politics, was Wiveliscombe, or more properly the manors of Wiveliscombe and Fitzhead, lying under the Brendon

---

[1] Account of 1555. P.R.O. S.C.6/P. & M./263.   [2] *Wells*, I, 152.
[3] S.R.S., xv, 54.   [4] P.R.O. S.C.6/Ed. VI/420, E.318/2108.

Hills. Here at Wiveliscombe was another of their palaces, a manor-house built originally by Bishop Drokensford (1309–29), on the site of an earlier building, but added to by that great builder of episcopal homes, Bishop Ralph of Shrewsbury. All that now survives of the manor-house and the attached chapel where the bishops did so much of their business are the remains of the outer gateway.[1] This gateway with its arch was probably the main entrance to the palace, which fronted south and had a large park before it extending down into the valley to the east. Between the north wall and the road was a large courtyard, formerly called the Palace Green. As late as the 1830's the kitchen was in existence and the north wall stood at a good height, with Gothic windows at intervals through its whole length. Water from a spring at the foot of Bend-knee Hill at Hartswell was supplied to the palace through leaden pipes. The supervision of the palace rested with a keeper paid £1.6.8d. a year. At the east end of the Palace Green stood the tithe barn, forming at one period a portion of the main house. In a field later known as Pond Close there was the usual stewpond for carp, ensuring the bishop's supply of fresh fish, and there were gardens. The Rotten Row adjoining, formerly the Routine Row, marked the passage of religious processions to and from the residence.[2]

The demesne land, of which the fields later known as High Parks formed a portion, consisted of 271 acres, let out in 1551, with the garden of the manor-house, for £10. 10. 4d. There were three water-mills, one of them called the New Mill, also leased out. One mill was driven by water deflected from the same spring which supplied the bishop's household. As at Bishops Lydeard, there were corn rents, measured in quarters, coming from tenants in both Wiveliscombe and the hamlet of Fitzhead. The village was well-wooded and one at least of these woods, Cottcombe Wood, with its limestone quarries and its hundreds of great oaks, elms and ashes, belonged to the bishop.[3]

The bishop drew rents from the township of Wiveliscombe as well as from the manor. Thirty-one of these came from burgesses

---

[1] F. A. Hancock, *Wifela's Combe*, pp. 73–5.
[2] *Proc. Som. Arch. Soc.*, XXIX, i, 15 ff.   [3] See below, pp. 149–50.

holding burgage tenements for which, in theory, they paid 1s. a year each, and 7s. in rent came from fourteen shops next to the Shambles, although when the account for 1555 was balanced the shopkeepers had not paid up.

The process of assarting, that is, reclaiming from the waste, was still going on in Wiveliscombe: in 1555 a new rent of 6d. was collected from Christopher Prowse for a piece of waste land twenty-four feet long and twenty feet wide near Ryecross. Cows were still being taken as heriots and driven to Wells to the bishop's household, presumably for consumption.[1]

MANORS OUTSIDE SOMERSET

Outside Somerset the bishops held a few manors in Gloucestershire, Berkshire and Hampshire, and of these Dogmersfield in Hampshire was probably the most valuable to them, providing a convenient 'half-way' halting place on their journeys from the west country to London. Even so, although there are several references to the bishops' being there at earlier times, it was probably little used under the Tudors.[2] Generally the manor and park were left to the care of a keeper, who was paid £3. 1. 4d. according to Chyles;[3] in 1547, when Sir John Wallop was keeper, his fee was near that mark, £3. 0. 10d. The under-stewardship, worth 13s. 4d., had perhaps become a family monopoly, for in 1535 Michael Kidwelly held the post and in 1547 Peter Kidwelly. Even the demesne lands, which were surely those designated as 'le farme growndes', were leased out: in 1531 one Edith Draper held them of Bishop Clerk for twenty years at £7 a year.[4]

The site of the palace, surrounded by various buildings, orchards, gardens and ponds, topped a slight mound which gave excellent command of the surrounding countryside, but now a more modern residence there houses an order of religious teaching brothers. When I visited it in 1953 all that appeared to remain of the bishop's palace was a brick-walled rectangular enclosure which was being pulled down to make space for a tennis court. The bricks in the walls were of the

[1] P.R.O. S.C.6/P. & M./263.
[3] See below, p. 43.
[2] *Wells*, II, 576, 596, 694.
[4] P.R.O. E.318/2107.

old, narrow type, and the caretaker informed me that it had
been hoped to use them again, but they had proved to be too
ancient and brittle. At least once in Tudor times this brick-
walled palace of the bishops had been a scene of activity and
excitement: that was in the time of Bishop Oliver King (1496–
1503), when he received Catharine of Aragon there on her
arrival in England in 1501. He was there by at least 25 August,[1]
doubtless making preparations, and on 4 November the Spanish
Princess arrived there, accompanied by her retinue and escorted
on her journey from Plymouth to London by the Earl of Surrey
and the Duchess of Norfolk. The king, Henry VII, was already waiting to receive her in the chamber adjoining the
great hall, and half an hour later her bridegroom, Prince
Arthur, rode into the courtyard.[2] The royal visit was a singular
honour for the bishop of Bath and Wells. There is no record
of its being repeated by a Tudor.

Of the bishop's Berkshire manor, Compton Parva, which lies
south-east of Wantage, little is known: its identification as a
Berkshire manor is given in a grant of 1494.[3] It was let out to
farm at least as early as 1509 at a rent which remained consistently at £2. 13. 4d. throughout the entire period under
review, that is to 1647, except in 1538 when it jumped to
£52. 2. 0½d., possibly to include a fine for the renewal of a lease.[4]
From Elizabethan times onwards it was held by a family called
Smith.

The Gloucestershire manors, Pucklechurch, Westerleigh and
Wyke (the modern Wick), formed a group at the southern end
of the Cotswolds, north-west of Bath. All three are in the
hundred of Pucklechurch, which also belonged to the bishop,
and the livings of Westerleigh and Wick are united to the
vicarage of Pucklechurch. Westerleigh did not have a church
until the fourteenth century, so quite clearly Pucklechurch was
the original settlement and manor from which the other two
had been carved.[5] The bishop kept a reeve in each place, and
the one at the manor of Pucklechurch was allowed an acquitted

---

[1] S.R.S., LIV, 58–62.   [2] G. Mattingly, *Catharine of Aragon*, pp. 35–6.
[3] *Wells*, II, 136.
[4] P.R.O. S.C.6/Hen. VIII/3076; S.R.O. DD/CC/13324, Account for 1538 and
fo. 363 ff.
[5] Lewis, *Topographical Dictionary*, IV, 461, 499.

rent of 20s., the highest of any allowed to such an official, perhaps because his post was regarded as one of special trust in view of the distance from Wells; by contrast, the reeve of Pucklechurch hundred was paid but 8s. 8d.[1] The dean and chapter of Wells also had a part of Pucklechurch as a separate manor, but its chief feature, the park, came within the bishop's manor.[2] The park, which was 'very good mead and pasture', was stocked with deer; it was cared for by a keeper and had never been let out but was kept in hand for the bishop's own enjoyment. It was valued at £6. 13. 4d. in 1550 when in the care of the Crown.[3] The keepership of the park was one of two granted to Sir Amyas Paulet, who was the bishop's high steward, together with Edmund Myll in 1494.[4] Such a post would, of course, be an additional sinecure to Sir Amyas: the care of the deer on the spot was the business of the reeve.

Particulars of Westerleigh in 1552 show some free tenants paying rents of £2. 13. 10d., although the *Valor Ecclesiasticus* shows none, and in 1552 the demesnes were all let out by indenture to various tenants for rents totalling £13 8s. A house called Church House was let for 8d., and rents in cocks and services were valued at 5s.[5]

Pucklechurch was only one of the five hundreds over which the bishop had the lordship: that of Winterstoke, covering the whole of the western flank of the Mendips, from Priddy to the Bristol Channel, was the most considerable.[6] The *Valor Ecclesiasticus* shows it attached to the manor of Banwell, but it was rightfully appendant to the manor of Cheddar.[7] The hundred of Wells Forum was adjacent to it and included Wells, Priddy, Westbury and Wookey, and it had an outlier, West Cranmore and Evercreech. The hundred of Chew, much smaller in extent and centred on Chew Magna, lay to the north. The hundred of Kingsbury was divided into five segments and embraced all the bishop's manors in the south of the county.

This review of the bishop's estates reveals certain significant facts. In the manors flanking the Mendip Hills and giving on to

[1] P.R.O. E.318/1687.
[2] *Wells*, II, 50, 54.
[3] P.R.O. E.318/1687, E.318/1889.
[4] *Wells*, II, 137.
[5] P.R.O. E.318/1889.
[6] Collinson, I, frontispiece.
[7] See below, p. 109.

the Somerset Levels the drainage arrangements were a particular feature of manorial economy and several fulling-mills attest the importance of cloth manufacture among the bishop's tenants. Sales of wood in many manors suggest a landscape still well-wooded, and corn rents in the west Somerset manors show the greater importance of arable farming there. Payments of vineyard silver point to viniculture on the sunny slopes around Westbury and Wick, near Wells.

To the modern mind perhaps the most remarkable fact about the bishop's estates is the number of 'palaces' watched over by keepers for bishops who rarely came. Bishop Oliver King (1496–1503) in particular seems to have performed most of the functions required of him as bishop of Bath and Wells in his Bath Inn in London, 'his accustomed residence'; he sometimes visited his palace at Bath and that at Chew Magna, but seldom Banwell and probably never Evercreech or Wiveliscombe.[1] Two other notorious absentees were Bishop Adrian de Castello (1504–18), who is reputed to have farmed the temporalities,[2] and Bishop Thomas Wolsey (1518–23); and Bishop John Clerk (1523–41) favoured Chew on the rare occasions when he resorted to his diocese. Not only were there empty palaces, but also well-stocked deer parks where the deer had nothing to fear save from poachers.

WELLS: MANOR AND TOWNSHIP

Even Wells, the heart of the diocese, where the bishop held control over palace, manor and township, seems to have been neglected until the time of the Marian Bishop Bourne. The manor of Wells was of large extent, but it did not compare with the enormous Norman manor of Wells. During the five hundred years following Edward the Confessor's grant of it to the bishop in 1034, various properties had been separated from it to form other manors, most of them on the lower slopes of the Mendips, leaving to the bishop the upper, barren plateau of this ridge and the marshy lowlands of the Somerset levels, where a few islands of firm ground protruded above the level of the surrounding

---

[1] S.R.S., LIV, 9–84.   [2] Phelps, II, 11, 119.

swamps.[1] Although many of the bishop's tenants had obligations for scouring the watercourses as a condition of tenure, it
may be doubted whether these drainage arrangements were
always very effective, and the evidence of Saxton's map of
Somerset in 1575 shows that adjoining the manor on the south-
west was the extensive quagmire of the undrained Meare
Pool.

Any description of the manor must be tentative, but one can
draw some rough bounds. The manor extended as far south as
Hartlake Bridge, which presumably had some importance as a
local landmark since it too is shown on Saxton's map of 1575.
Godney Moor and Knowle Moor were the south-west bounds
where the bishop's tenants shared rights of common with those
of the next manor. (They also shared with them Ashmoor and
Haymoor, not shown on the modern map.) To the west the
bishop's own manors of Westbury and Wookey adjoined, and to
the north-west, although part of Priddy was held separately,
the bishop still owned wide tracts of these bleak hummocks
and drew ever-increasing royalties in kind from the Priddy lead
mineries. Here, to the north, the bishop's manor encroached on
the ancient Forest of Mendip, and Stock Hill seems to have
been his northernmost limit. To the north-east Whitnell
(represented by the modern Whitnell Farm and Whitnell
Corner) and Hawdon (Haydons Farm?) came within the manor.
There were tenants in West Horrington, Chilcote, Dulcote and
Worminster, and Queen's Sedgemoor or Little Sedgemoor,
where again the bishop's tenants shared common rights with
others, was the limit to the south. The episcopal tenants seem
to have enjoyed Crannel Moor and Pill Moor to themselves.
By 1566 fifty acres of North Moor were enclosed meadow let
to ten tenants. The important hamlets were West Horrington
in the north, and Wick, Coxley and Polsham in the south. In
Saxon times there had been an episcopal palace at Polsham,
and there were several holdings in Polsham Meads and Gar-
slade. The bishop owned mills, described as water-mills, at

[1] The ensuing account of the manor of Wells is composed from Phelps, II, 22–7,
184, 189; S.R.O. DD/CC/12357, fos. 1 and 51 ff. (1647 Survey), DD/CC/31523;
and an 'Agreement of the Manor of Wells, 1564' in the Wells Museum Notebook,
fo. 314 ff. mentioned above.

Burcot and Keward (there are still mills there), and four other mills in Wells called the Out Mills and the In Mills.

Comparison of the account for the manor of Wells for 1527–9 with that of 1566 shows absolutely no change in the income from rents within the manor, although this was a period of price-rise. In 1529 there were seven free tenants holding by military service, and although this number had been increased to twelve in 1566 this was presumably by sub-division, perhaps on inheritance, for the total rents involved, £4. 3. 9d., stayed constant. There were also nine free tenants holding by socage, that is, in return solely for a money rent, whose rents totalled 18s. 10d., while the rents of the customary tenants came to £35. 9. 1d. The total income from these three groups of tenants was £40. 11. 8. The other rents, from leased land, which totalled £74. 17. 9d., were made up as follows: leases of overland or demesne land, £14. 2. 5d.; leases of pasture, £15. 10. 4d.; leases of meadow, £45. 5. 0d. The fact that this total was nearly double that derived from the more ancient rents of assise, or fixed rents, reflects the profitability of leases to the bishop.

All six of the mills were also leased out for £28. Casual sources of income included fines, licences to marry, heriots, rents in kind paid in cocks, hens and geese, perquisites of the manorial court, and sales of wood from the lord's park. The homage of Wick paid vineyard silver at Hock-tide, varying in amount from 3d. to 2s. 1d. In 1528 the bishop's income was also augmented by the royalties in lead which he drew from the Priddy Mineries and which, based on a rate of 200 lb. of lead-ore at 1s. 8d. per 100 lb., amounted to 3s. 4d. This was a very small sum compared with the yield a century later when it soared to 17 tons at a gross value of £182. 6. 11d. in 1634.[1]

Something is known of the customs of the manor of Wells. Copyhold tenements were held for five lives and no grant or surrender could be made without the consent of every reversioner. Leaseholds were granted for three lives. The manor court was held four times a year, and courts leet twice a year. At every Michaelmas court leet the homage of Coxley presented three customary tenants to the lord's steward from whom he

[1] S.R.O. DD/CC/13324, fo. 367.

chose the reeve for the coming year, and three more from whom he chose the hayward. The reeve was to have an oak out of the lord's park and the rent of his own copyhold as remuneration for his duties, and the hayward was to receive 7s. 11d. The reeve was to seize all strays and give owners the chance to redeem them when they had been 'prized' by three or four of the tenants. After the lapse of a year and a day strayed animals which were still in ward became the property of the reeve, but he had to pay a due for them to the lord of the manor. Although the bishop, in this capacity, could claim so much under these varied headings, he also had his responsibilities: it fell to him to keep the bridges at Crannel Moor, Coxley and Wick in repair.

Not only was the bishop lord of the manor of Wells and of the hundred of Wells Forum, but he also enjoyed certain rights within the liberty and town of Wells: these included some rents, the perquisites of the court, and, most important of all, the income from fairs and markets. The economic grip of the bishop on the city was of long standing, but none the less resented for that. Not until the time of Elizabeth I, by letters patent of 1589, did the city achieve a degree of emancipation.[1] The fairs at Wells were among the oldest in the country and three of them, those of the Invention of the Holy Cross (3 May), St Calixtus (14 October) and St Andrew (30 November), can be traced back to within a century of the Norman Conquest. They were, of course, the offspring of the great festivals of the church, when men gathered to pray in the cathedral and stayed to barter in the adjoining market place. By 1201 the bishop had granted a fourth fair, that of the morrow of St John Baptist (25 June). King John's charter of 1202 to the city allowed the introduction of a fifth fair, the Translation of St Andrew (7 May), and this one, from which the bishop drew no tolls, still functions, as does the fair of 30 November.

In the middle ages the bishops had waged constant battle with the townsfolk in their efforts to get stalls and booths removed from the cathedral precincts to 'the broad places of the town', and in 1334 a commission appointed to inquire into the matter awarded the bishop £3,000 damages. As a result of this

[1] S.R.S., XLVI, 14.

trouble Bishop Ralph of Shrewsbury even persuaded Edward III to cancel the city's charter for a while.[1]

In Elizabethan times, under the weak Bishop Godwin, who gave his consent in 1588 to the city's obtaining not only a renewal of their ancient liberties but also a new grant of other liberties, the citizens tried to introduce two new fairs.[2] One was to be held on the Monday following the Feast of the Ascension, which would generally be about mid-May, and the other on 21 June. A grant to this effect, allowing each fair to last three days, was obtained by letters patent from Elizabeth I on 23 July 1589. At the meeting of the common council on 24 November it was decided that the first day of each of these fairs should be a wholesale one and that the second and third should be devoted to retail sales; the council expected sales of wool, yarn and other merchandise and also of horses, beasts and cattle.[3] This action of the common council may well have been one of low cunning; the dates they chose avoided those fixed for the bishop's fairs, although one of these fell in early May and another, St John Baptist's fair, began the day after a new one ended. If the burgesses could establish two independent fairs they might both avoid the episcopal tolls and kill two of the hated old fairs. They apparently failed. When the parliamentary surveys were drawn up in 1647 the bishop was still enjoying the profits of four fairs.[4] As the May, June, October and November fairs, they were observed in Wells at least until the eighteenth century.

Figures of the bishop's income in tolls from the fairs in the Tudor period are very imperfect, but they show that there was a decline in trade after the mid-century and a gradual recovery in the 1570's but never again to the level of Henry VIII's time. In 1535 the total income from the fairs was £5. 17. 3d., but by 1556 it had dropped to £3. 1. 2d. and in 1566 to £1. 2. 9d. That was the lowest point: there was then a gradual recovery until 1570 when it reached another peak of £4. 1. 4d. Thereafter it remained more steady. These figures should not be assumed to be a fair index of the movement of trade in Wells in Tudor times: it is far more likely that the decline in profits in

[1] N. F. Hulbert, 'A Survey of Somerset Fairs', *Proc. Som. Arch. Soc.*, LXXXII, 112 ff.
[2] S.R.S., XLVI, 122.   [3] C.W. Act Book 1553–1623, fo. 184.
[4] Wells Museum Notebook, fo. 285.

mid-century reflects the disintegration of episcopal affairs. Only when they became more stable, after 1559, did the profits rise again. Of the four fairs, the late autumn ones, those of St Calixtus and St Andrew, were always far more important than the early summer ones, those of the Invention of the Holy Cross and St John the Baptist. For some unknown reason the takings of the Holy Cross fair increased about five-fold in 1570 and 1571 to 19s. and 16s., and then dropped again to their normal level, 3s. 8d.[1]

Two other fairs, of less importance, came within the bishop's jurisdiction over the hundred of Wells Forum, Priddy Fair and Binegar Fair. They are thought both to have been Wells fairs originally, but to have moved out, to Priddy in 1348 and to Binegar where the fair was established by 1534, in both cases on account of plague.[2] Binegar Fair was held on the Wednesday and Thursday of Whitsun week for the sale of horses, cattle and sheep. It has been said that the bishops derived a fee of 10s. from the fair, but this was certainly not true of the sixteenth century; the income fluctuated from year to year, but it was usually slightly above 5s. Priddy, at least by Elizabethan times, yielded only half that amount. Both fairs survive: that at Priddy, in the heart of the Mendip uplands, is held as a sheep fair on 21 August.[3]

Time out of mind the bishop had also had control of a common market held weekly in Wells throughout the year on Wednesdays and Saturdays for the buying and selling of grain and other kinds of provisions. The bishop had right of toll on all grain, which covered wheat, barley, malt, beans, dredge and any other kind of corn, but there is no evidence of his taking toll on goods other than grain.[4] He was entitled to demand one pint for every bushel set or pitched in the market *with intent to sell*, that is on all grain entering the market, whether sold or not. A proportionate amount, one sixty-fourth, could be taken on smaller quantities. These grain tolls were, at least from 1535, farmed out by the bishop to his bailiff of the town, who also

---

[1] See Appendix A.   [2] P.R.O. S.C.6/Hen. VIII/3076.
[3] Phelps infers that the tolls of Priddy Fair were *always* paid to the corporation of Wells, but this was not so.
[4] P.R.O. C3/262/7.

acted as the clerk of the market, for 6s. 8d. a year.[1] By 1593 the bailiff was paying 10s. a year for the farm, and in 1597 Bishop Still was trying to arrange a composition fee with Leonard Crosse, the bailiff, of £3 for the markets and fairs. Unfortunately, later accounts do not separate out the income from the town in such a way that one can tell whether or not this arrangement went through. Exemptions from this grain toll in Wells market was, by ancient privilege, allowed to all persons dwelling within the town of Glastonbury and the twelve hides of Glaston.[2]

The farming of the tolls gave every incentive to the bailiff to be assiduous in their collection, and in 1541 the zeal of the bailiff, Thomas Clerk, who was Bishop Clerk's brother, raised the anger of the burgesses. They complained in common council that 'the privileges and freedom and liberties which hath been granted by kings and confirmed by bishops cannot be used and enjoyed according to their charters' because of the wrongs and injuries done to them by the bailiff. They alleged that they could not be free in markets and fairs without paying a certain sum yearly to the bailiff and that no burgess could bring grain to the market without paying toll 'which is contrary to the liberties of the said town, for the town of Wells is a free borough for all burgesses to buy and sell without paying any manner of toll or custom'. This claim was valid: according to the testimony of the homage of Coxley in 1647, customary tenants of the manor of Wells were free of the markets and fairs.[3] The other specific complaints in 1541 were that bakers, brewers, fishmongers, butchers, innkeepers and ale-vendors could not pursue their trades without the payment of yearly tolls to the bishop's bailiff, and that farmers of the bishop's new mills also had to make payment. The townsmen also alleged that they were harshly fined in the bishop's court, that is, the three-weeks court.[4]

Trouble flared up again in Bishop Barlow's time, and on 17 June 1552 the common council approved ordinances for the

---

[1] P.R.O. S.C.6/Hen. VIII/3075, C2 Eliz./C.14/4.
[2] P.R.O. S.C.6/Eliz./2008, C2 Eliz./C.14/4, C3/262/7.
[3] S.R.O. DD/CC/12357, fo. 51 ff.
[4] C.W. Act Book, 1450–1553, fo. 416.

regulation of the market which had been agreed by the bishop and Thomas Clerk, who was still his bailiff, on one side, and the mayor and representative burgesses on the other. No doubt the ordinances were merely a restatement of custom. The market bell was to be rung every market day at ten o'clock, and no one was to open any bag or sell any grain before that bell or after one o'clock on pain of forfeiture. The buyer was to be present in person. No butchers or fishmongers were to sell their goods after one o'clock and no baker was to buy grain before eleven o'clock. Millwards were entirely prohibited from buying grain, doubtless to protect the domestic consumer.[1]

The bishop's privileges also brought him the profits of four jurisdictions. For the manor of Wells he held his court baron relating to free and customary tenants, and the income from it was returned under the heading 'perquisites of the court' for that manor. Fines of land and heriots usually formed a substantial part of it. Twice a year, at Hocktide and Michaelmas, the hundred court for Wells Forum was kept by the steward of all the bishop's estates in the Guild Hall at Wells. He was assisted by his subordinate, the bailiff of Wells Forum, who rendered accounts for this court and for the Priddy and Binegar fairs.[2] The hundred of Wells Forum comprised a core formed by the liberty of St Andrews and the In Parish and Out Parish of St Cuthbert, Wells, and beyond these a surrounding area which included several neighbouring villages and hamlets; its exact limits are, however, impossible to determine, at least for the sixteenth century. The Guild Hall where the hundred courts were held must not be confused with the present Town Hall in the market square: it is at the western end of Chamberlain Street.

The bishop's third source of income in his seigneurial capacity derived from the township or *burgus* of Wells, and arose from the jurisdiction of the three-weeks court. There were usually sixteen of these courts held in the course of a year. Most of the bishop's accounts do not separate out the income from the various courts: only those for the Elizabethan period show some of the detail of the machinery. The issues for the

[1] Ibid., fos. 553-4.
[2] Chyles MS, v, i, fo. 44; S.R.O. DD/CC/31523 and other references.

three-weeks court were accounted for by the bailiff of Wells Forum, who, acting also as clerk of the market, drew a munificent fee, £14. 6. 8d., for his joint offices, but by Bishop Still's time (1593–1608) the bailiff of Wells *burgus* had taken over the profits of the court, a more appropriate arrangement.[1] Part of a roll of this court for 1597 illustrates the type of offence for which the citizens were presented. Richard Bord and some other fishmongers were fined 3d. each for breaking the assise, probably by giving short weight. James Morris, a miller, was fined 3s. 4d. for taking one pound and a half out of a peck of wheat, which was an excessive toll; Geoffrey Bright and others had to pay 3s. 4d. each for letting their mastiff dogs loose in the streets; Paul Methwyn's failure to scour the watercourse before his ground in Tucker Street cost him 6s. 8d.[2]

Finally, there were the rights which the bishop enjoyed under the franchise of Wells Liberty. By the testimony of Robert Powell, who was the bailiff of the liberty in 1620, these included, among other privileges,

the return of all writs and processes whatsoever within the city or borough of Wells and the hundred of Wells Forum free and exempted from the intermeddling of the sheriff of the county for the time being or any of his bailiffs,

by grant of Edward IV.[3] But it was more than that: Edward IV made the grant by letters patent to Bishop Thomas Beckington, which must have been between 1461 and 1465. The terms were that Beckington and his successors were to have all those fines, issues and amercements known as the Green Wax within their lands and fees, and also from those of the priory of Bath, the dean and chapter of Wells and the canons and vicars of the Cathedral Church at Wells.[4] The extent of this liberty was undiminished in the early Tudor period, but after the dissolution of Bath Priory and the depletion of the episcopal estates in the mid-century, the area of the bishop's franchise was much restricted.

The collection of the Green Wax was the function of the

[1] S.R.O. DD/CC/31523; P.R.O. S.C.6/Add./3545/84.
[2] Chyles, v, 1, fos. 41–3.　　　　[3] P.R.O. St. Ch. 8/Jas.1/241/17.
[4] S.R.O. DD/CC/13324, fo. 252.

bailiff of the liberty. In the words of Leonard Crosse, who was the bailiff in 1597 and got into trouble with Bishop Still because he failed to render proper accounts:

The bailiff of the liberty hath always from a time when the memory of man runneth not to the contrary, been used to receive, collect and gather the green wax, viz. the fines, issues and amercements happening to fall within the liberty.[1]

The best description of what the Green Wax profits involved is that in the oft-quoted account prepared for Bishop Adrian Castello in 1510: fines from outlaws and escapees, the goods and cattle of felons and fugitives, shipping duties and wrecks of the sea, reliefs and sales of wardship, issues from minors' estates held by the lord, and issues from the courts of king's bench and exchequer, and from the royal assizes.[2] John Brugge, who was the bailiff in the time of Bishop Clerk (1523–41), had also levied fines for bloodshed and affrays. He was very active, indeed over-zealous; 'by colour of his office' he had extorted various sums of money and great quantities of goods from the bishop's tenants, wrongfully calling these escheats, and he refused to restore them, 'to the great slander of the bishop'. He had taken goods to the value of 40 marks (£26. 13. 4d.) from Thomas Adams, chaplain, wrongfully suspected of felony, and he had seized sheep and cattle from William Hobbes and William Prigges in the bishop's far-off manor of Pucklechurch in Gloucestershire.[3]

In Henrician times the value of the liberty was small: there was no income from it in 1510,[4] in the *Valor Ecclesiasticus* it was rated at £2. 9. 0½d., in 1539 it was worth £1. 2. 9d., in 1542 again nothing, and in 1550 £2. 9. 0½d.[5] These amounts seem surprisingly low. Bailiff John Brugge claimed that the bailiff's office had been worth £44 or £45 to the bishop's predecessors.[6] Perhaps he was including the income from the *burgus* of Wells, but even so the accounts do not bear out his figure. In the Elizabethan period, when the area covered by the bishop's

[1] P.R.O. C2 Eliz./C.14/4.
[2] Chyles, III, I, fo. 30; S.R.O. DD/CC/13324, fo. 252.
[3] P.R.O. St. Ch. 2/17/225.   [4] Chyles, III, I, fo. 31.
[5] P.R.O. S.C.6/Hen. VIII/3076, E.318/1412; T.C. MS, Audit 1541–2, fo. 8r.
[6] P.R.O. St. Ch. 2/17/225.

liberty had shrunk enormously, the income from the liberty was not shown separately, but the accounts for 1566–78, which fall in Bishop Berkeley's period, are seldom complete. Later, in Bishop Still's era the amount rose phenomenally, evidence of the bishop's skill as an administrator: an account for 1596 gives arrears for three years of 'fines, issues, amercements and forfeitures from the Queen's court', in other words, the Green Wax: 1593 £106. 6. 1d., 1594 £158. 18. 3d., 1595 £285. 5. 6d. When in 1597 the bishop took his bailiff Leonard Crosse to chancery for failing to account for the profits he alleged that Crosse was collecting the Green Wax at the rate of £300 a year.[1] This was probably correct. By 1634 the proceeds had dropped considerably, for the Green Wax was farmed to the Crosse family for only £40 a year, and for 1635–40 the bishop had to acquiesce in the acceptance of only £30.[2] By 1647 the Green Wax was valued at only £10, but this small sum doubtless reflected the political disruption of the times.

The Crosse family managed to acquire a monopoly of the three offices of bailiff of the city, clerk of the market and bailiff of the liberty, as the grant of these by Bishop Montague in 1616 'to John Crosse and his assigns for the life of William Crosse of Wells, gent., Leonard Crosse of Tottenham, Wilts. gent., John Hewlett of New Sarum Wilts. gent.' plainly shows. Crosse was to have the right to distrain on the appurtenances of the manor of Wells if his annual salary of £14. 6. 8d. was left unpaid for a year, and he was to render an annual account.[3]

THE BISHOP'S OFFICERS

The establishment for the administration of the bishop's temporalities was quite distinct from that which, headed by the chancellor, took care of his ecclesiastical jurisdiction: it was comparable to that of any owner of large estates. Consequently in this age of ambitious and opportunist gentry there was much competition among local families for posts in the management of the episcopal properties. As in the estates of monastic houses,

---

[1] P.R.O. S.C.6/Eliz./2008, C2 Eliz./C.14/4.
[2] Wells Museum Notebook, fo. 284.
[3] Transcripts of Documents in Wells Museum, II, 86.

where local gentlemen held key positions as stewards, surveyors, auditors and the like, and were ready to use the knowledge and influence so gained to convert service into ownership when the dissolution came, so it was in episcopal estates, at least in those of Bath and Wells.[1] The bishop could not afford to ignore the local gentry: its patronage and support had to be bought to counteract the influence of those who were advocating the abolition of bishops and the confiscation of their estates. Grants of office were one way of accommodating local men, and there is ample evidence that they were also given rights of presentations to livings. Whereas in the fifteenth century one at least of the bishop's most important offices, that of receiver-general, had been the preserve of clerics, by the middle of the sixteenth it was held by laymen.[2]

The local gentry did not, however, acquire a monopoly of episcopal administration. Inevitably each new bishop arriving in the diocese brought with him his friends and clients and, after the Reformation when the bishops like other clergy were allowed to marry, his sons and sons-in-law. The bishop's relatives in particular were in a precarious position because his estates were an adjunct of his office and could not be bequeathed to them on his demise as the estates of a temporal lord could be used to endow his family. Consequently relatives battened on the estates during his life time and competed with the gentry for posts which provided local influence and personal wealth. Nepotism was rife, and not only in the diocese of Bath and Wells. Numerous were the grants made to his relatives by Bishop Taylor of Lincoln (1552–4) and his successor Bishop Watson (1557–9).[3] Yet for officials of local origin, whose claims did not depend so much as those of relatives on the patronage of particular bishops, there was more certain tenure in serving a bishop than a lord, for episcopal estates were not subject to crises arising from lack of heirs or attainders. The bishopric might be vacant, but as an institution it was immortal. Only a revolution like that of 1646 could abolish it completely

---

[1] G. Baskerville, *English Monks and the Suppression of the Monasteries*, ch. ii.
[2] *Wells*, II, 243, 246, 252; R. W. Dunning, op. cit., p. 238.
[3] *Chapter Acts of Lincoln 1547–59*, ed. R. E. G. Cole (Linc. Rec. Soc., xv), pp. 157, 160, 163, 167.

and involve also the loss of many lucrative offices. No wonder
there was competition to serve the bishop.

Nor was it difficult for the bishop's officers to consolidate their
local power and influence. Several bishops of the Tudor and
Early Stuart periods played a passive part in the control of their
estates, either through absence or physical incapacity. Bishop
Clerk (1523–41) was much employed on embassies to Rome and
France by Wolsey and on state affairs by Thomas Cromwell,
so that he could have seen little of his diocese. His spiritual
duties there were performed by three suffragan bishops, and
his brother, Thomas Clerk, had charge of the episcopal
estates. Bishop Godwin (1584–90) was a semi-invalid, so that
his officers had abundant licence and took it, and Bishop Laud
(1626–8) never even visited his diocese.[1] Only three bishops,
Berkeley (1560–84), Still (1593–1608) and Peirs (1632–70),
seem to have made any real attempt to direct the administration of the estates personally, although Bishop Berkeley was
another of those bishops who were handicapped by ill-health.

Yet although the temporal side of his affairs was separated
from the spiritual, and although the episcopal estates were a
distinct entity from the capitular ones, all the important acts
of the bishop, such as the grant of leases or the appointment of
officers, were subject to the approval of the dean and chapter
of Wells and, until 1542–3, of the prior of Bath.[2] This
check was intended as a safety device to prevent an unworthy or
foolish bishop from committing the episcopal endowment to a
policy which might prove injurious to himself, or, worse still, to
his successors. Normally confirmation by the dean and chapter
was automatic: it usually followed within a period of days. But
sometimes the ultimate sanction of the dean and chapter proved
to be very real.

Chyles gives a list of the bishop's officers and retinue 'which
formerly he had'. Although undated it must apply to the pre-
1539 establishment, for it includes the officials at Dogmersfield,
which the bishop lost in that year. The list is of interest because
it gives the size of the normal administration with the salary
attached to each post:

[1] H. R. Trevor Roper, *Archbishop Laud*, p. 92.
[2] *V.C.H. Somerset*, II, 35.

High steward	£13.	6.	8d.
Under-steward	£3.	6.	8d.
Surveyor-general	£6.	13.	4d.
Receiver-general	£10.	o.	od.
Auditor	£6.	13.	4d.
Keeper of Wells Palace	£13.	6.	8d.
Keeper of Wells Park	£1.	6.	8d.
Porter and keeper of Wells Prison	£2.	o.	od.
Store bailiff	£3.	6.	8d.
Keeper of Banwell Park	£3.	6.	8d.
Keeper of Banwell House	£3.	6.	8d.
Bailiff of Wells Burgus	£4.	o.	od.

These posts were those which were to endure throughout the period from 1535 to 1643, but before the upheavals of the mid-sixteenth century robbed the bishopric of much of its temporal endowment there were others important enough to be added to the list:

Keeper of Westbury Park	£2.	18.	8d.
Woodward of Cheddar	£1.	6.	8d.
Bailiff of Claverton	£1.	o.	od.
Keeper of Evercreech Park	£1.	14.	8d.
Keeper of Dogmersfield	£3.	1.	4d.
Under-steward of Dogmersfield		13s.	4d.
Bailiff of Chew Hundred	£1.	o.	od.
Bailiff of Winterstoke Hundred	£2.	o.	od.

Although they are omitted from Chyles's list, there was a keeper of the bishop's mansion house at Wiveliscombe who was paid £1. 6. 8d., one of the London house, and another at Puckle-church.[1] Besides park keepers and bailiffs there were presumably also keepers of the mansion houses at Evercreech and Chew. Another omission from Chyles's list is the bailiff of the bishop's liberty, who was also the clerk of the market at Wells.

Such evidence as exists indicates that on the whole the salaries and wages of the bishop's officers were not advanced during the period, although it was one of rising prices. No doubt, however, this remuneration should be regarded as

[1] P.R.O. S.C.6/P. & M./263, E.318/1412; *Wells*, II, 232–3, 255, 256.

purely nominal, for there were both official perquisites and unofficial rewards which gave these posts a value far beyond their meagre stipends. The under-steward, William Godwyn, in 1553, besides drawing his fee of £3. 6. 8d., was allowed four yards of the best woollen cloth worth £1. 6. 8d., two loads of wood worth 2s. and two loads of hay at 10s. This brought the total value of his office to £5. 5. 4d., apart from fees which he pocketed as steward of the various manorial courts.[1] The bailiff of the store at Wells had the use of a stable rent free, for which an allowance of 5s. was made in the annual accounts. When Geoffrey Upton was bailiff of the store in 1553 he also drew three yards of woollen cloth worth £1, two waggonloads of hay worth 10s., and two loads of wood worth 2s.; if these were the normal adjuncts of the office, they brought its total emoluments up to £5. 3. 8d.[2]

The key position of keeper of the palace, usually held with the keepership of the prison called the Cowhouse, was one of the most lucrative. When they were granted to that same Geoffrey Upton in 1546 the terms were given in detail. Besides a salary of £13. 6. 8d. he was to have as accommodation, the equivalent of modern service quarters, two chambers above the prison and another chamber in the New Work, the one with the door nearest the prison. He was also given the use of a small stable, four loads of firewood from the park, two loads of hay and three yards of the best cloth of the bishop's livery. But he was to find sureties in £300 to indemnify the bishop against the king lest he should let any prisoners escape.[3]

In addition to these officers there was the reeve of each manor who was an integral part of the administration. In some of the outlying manors, such as Wiveliscombe or Pucklechurch, remote from the control of the steward at Wells, they must have been petty lords. A reeve usually had an assistant, the hayward, and they were remunerated by having their rents acquitted. In 1555, when the estates had already been much reduced, the total allowance in exempted rents for reeves and haywards on the episcopal estates was £5. 2. 7½d.[4] Additional

[1] P.R.O. E.318/1412.
[2] P.R.O. S.C.6/Hen. VIII/3076, S.C.6/P. & M./263, S.C.6/Eliz./2008.
[3] *Wells*, II, 262–3.   [4] P.R.O. S.C.6/P. & M./263.

reeves were appointed in the two manors where there were responsibilities of a special nature. The manor of Wells was served by two lead-reeves who were responsible for the collection of the 'lot lead', the tithe of the produce of the lead mines on Mendip, which was the perquisite of the bishop as the lord of the manor of Wells. They were responsible to the bishop's steward. The manor of Banwell had three special reeves known as the Yeo wardens, who were responsible for keeping clear certain water-courses; it also had an additional officer, a beadle, which no other manor had, and a keeper for the bishop's swans there.[1]

Altogether the wages bill for administering the episcopal estates on the eve of the cataclysm, that is about 1535, was approximately £100, or $8\frac{1}{2}$ per cent of total income, but this did not include expenses, such as the cost of travel for the bishop's officers, provisions for those holding manorial courts, parchment and ink for the clerks who kept the records, or the attorneys' fees which were regularly paid. During a vacancy in the see, in 1582–3, when the revenues were being paid to the far-off exchequer in London, the expenses of 'the auditor, receiver, surveyor, steward, understeward, and other officers of the bishops with their servants and horses being at Wells for the audit' came to £27. 3. 4d.[2]

The salaries and wages paid to all these officers by the bishop were probably normal for the period. Comparison with those of the staff of the bishop of Lincoln reveals that some were higher, some lower. The auditor at Wells was paid £6. 13. 4d., at Lincoln £5; the surveyor at Wells received £6. 13. 4d., but the Lincoln surveyor had double that amount, £13. 6. 8d. The keeper of the bishop's palace and prison at Wells was treated more favourably than the keeper of the palace and prison at Buckden. The former earned £13. 6. 8d., the latter £7, both with certain well defined perquisites.[3]

The bishops were in a difficult position in making estate appointments: whether they appointed from the local gentry or from their own relatives and friends, the occupant of an office was usually appointed for life, and sometimes with the right to

---

[1] Ibid.   [2] P.R.O. S.C.6/Eliz./2011.
[3] *Lincoln Chapter Acts 1547–59*, pp. 64, 148, 160, 163.

assign it to another, and he often outlived the bishop who preferred him and so remained to be an embarrassment to his successor. There he stayed, immovable in his post, armed with the letters patent of his appointment signed by the former bishop, until he died. Sometimes a local family acquired a long monopoly of an office. An extreme case is that of the most important office of all, that of chief steward, which was held by the Paulet family of Hinton St George for the entire period under review. The post was obviously honorary, given to the Paulets in order to gain the goodwill of this leading county family and retained by them by force of tradition and influence, for there is no evidence that they ever took any active part in the administration of the estates. Indeed, how could they? They were national figures, occupied with the governance of Jersey, the safe keeping of Mary Queen of Scots and other commissions of state, so that the effective supervision of the bishop's estates was done by the under-steward, who was in a key position. It is curious that a family of such pronounced puritan leanings as the Paulets should have retained the post of chief steward in episcopal estates which the puritans yearned to confiscate. In the event when the testing time came they declared for the royalist side and suffered sorely in the king's cause.[1]

The interest of the Paulet family in the cathedral estates can be traced back to the beginning of the fifteenth century. The accounts of the dean and chapter for 1401 show a fee of £1 being paid to William Paulet and in 1408 it is described as annual. At the end of the fifteenth century the relationship between the cathedral and the Paulets was formalized, but it was to the bishop, and not to the chapter, that Paulet was accredited. In 1493 the chapter confirmed the bishop's action in appointing Sir Amyas Paulet as his steward for life with a pension of 20 marks.[2] This £13. 6. 8d. was the fee attached to the office at least until 1598, but by the early Stuart period it had been reduced to £11. 6. 8d.[3] Sir Amyas was presumably steward when Bishop Clerk began his episcopate in 1523, but by 1535, when the *Valor Ecclesiasticus* was drawn up, his son Hugh

---

[1] S. W. Bates Harbin, *Members of Parliament for Somerset*, pp. 125, 127, 136–7.
[2] *Wells*, II, 35, 41, 61, 129.   [3] S.R.O. DD/CC/13324, fo. 357.

had succeeded to the office. He is there described as Hugh Paulet Esq., as his father, who died in 1538, was still alive. Sir Hugh retained the office, now designated as that of chief steward, through all the troubles of the episcopates of Bishops Knight, Barlow and Bourne, during which time the episcopal estates were so depleted that an honorary steward was certainly superfluous. He still held office under the Elizabethan Bishop Berkeley, and in 1572, then an old man, Sir Hugh made provision for an approaching end by procuring from the bishop a grant of the office for himself jointly with Amyas Paulet, his son and heir. Chief stewards they were to be 'of all the hundreds, lordships, manors, lands and tenements in Somerset and elsewhere in the realm of England belonging to the bishopric', and their fee was to be the usual 20 marks, now deducted from their annual rent for Chard manor which they had acquired on lease from Bishop Barlow. The next year Sir Hugh died.[1]

While the old Bishop Berkeley was still alive—he was then eighty—the Paulets again took pains to secure the chief stewardship. The office was confirmed to Sir Amyas Paulet and his son Anthony in 1581 on the same terms as the grant of 1572, with the addition of a grant to them of the prebend of Ilton.[2] Bishop Berkeley died seven months later and Sir Amyas was chief steward, at least nominally, during the ensuing vacancy which ended with Bishop Godwin's appointment in 1584.[3] Although presumably retaining the office, he was away in 1585 on a commission to the Low Countries and he then became a privy councillor and the keeper of Mary Queen of Scots at Tutbury and later at Fotheringay.[4] His heir, Sir Anthony Paulet, was acting as chief steward in the following decade, in 1590, and again, in accordance with the usual Paulet practice of having the office confirmed in the family during the lifetime of the holder, in 1598 the chapter approved Bishop Still's grant of it to Sir Anthony and his son John. They acted none too soon, for Sir Anthony died in 1600. His son John had as

---

[1] Bates Harbin, p. 127; *Wells*, II, 202.
[2] Wells Cath. Chapter Acts, Bk. H, 1571–99, fo. 16.
[3] P.R.O. S.C.6/Eliz./2013, Rentals and Surveys, Roll 951.
[4] Bates Harbin, p. 127.

distinguished a career as his grandfather, Sir Amyas, and was made a baronet in 1627. That same year the office of high steward was renewed in his family, to himself and his heir John.[1]

Before that grant expired, however, the civil war broke out and episcopal estates were swept away. Lord Paulet was one of the royal commissioners for the negotiations with the Scots at Ripon, and at the outbreak of the civil war it was thought by some that he would take the Parliamentarian side. But he declared for the king and suffered imprisonment and fines in his sovereign's cause. He was still, presumably, the chief steward of the episcopal estates when they were confiscated in 1646, for he did not die until 1649. The Paulet family had kept that office for just a century and a half and their monopoly was renewed at the Restoration, in 1662.[2] No other post in the episcopal establishment remained the exclusive perquisite of any one family, but then no other family of the rank of the powerful Paulets was concerned with the estates. Patronage and protection are the key to their pre-eminence.

To trace the history of all the offices in similar detail would provide tedious reading, but by way of comparison another, the auditorship, may be dealt with, both because its history is so different from that of the chief stewardship and because it ranked next in seniority. There was a general audit of the episcopal estates once a year at Michaelmas when all the bailiffs and reeves brought their accounts to the auditor, and from 1494 this auditor was Thomas Hobson, appointed for life.[3] He probably died about 1513, for in that year Thomas Twesell was appointed in his place. He was allowed to perform the duties of auditor himself or through a deputy, and he received a fee of £6. 13. 4d. with an additional emolument of 13s. 4d. for writing up the account and of £1. 6. 8d. for expenses when he had to make the long four-day journey to London, presumably to report to the bishop when he was staying in the capital. In 1538 his appointment was joined with that of Richard Mody: they were now both auditors of the bishop for life or the longest liver at the usual salary of £6. 13. 4d. Their appointment still

[1] *Wells*, II, 336, 387; Bates Harbin, p. 136.
[2] Bates Harbin, p. 137; *Wells*, II, 432.   [3] *Wells*, II, 137.

held good when Bishop Knight succeeded Bishop Clerk in 1541.[1]

Nothing further can be traced of the office of auditor until the first half of the episcopate of Bishop Berkeley in Elizabethan times. Then the office was held by John Rawlins. Not only was he responsible for the revenues of the episcopal estates, but Bishop Berkeley 'reposed very great and especial trust' in him and made him also collector of all the tenths and subsidies due to the crown from the diocese of Bath and Wells. The bishop had cause to regret the appointment, for Rawlins got into arrears for 'divers and sundry great sums of money (notwithstanding he is well known to be a very perfect keeper of a book of account if he list)'. Such was the confusion into which Rawlins had allowed the finances to lapse that no one could understand the truth of the situation and the bishop failed to persuade him to balance his accounts. At last some of the 'men of worship' in Somerset urged him to make an account to a certain alderman of the city of London. This was done in 1563 and Rawlins handed £1,000 over to the bishop. Yet he was still indebted for about £480 and later, through the testimonies and acquittances produced by persons within the diocese, other sums which he had received were traced. When gentle ways and persuasion had failed, the bishop was forced to take the case to chancery.[2] By 1566 Rawlins had been replaced by Thomas Rosewell,[3] but his debt of £480 to the bishop remained, for when the bishop on his deathbed on 31 October 1581 had his will read over, the clause he had inserted in making it in 1567 was allowed to stand:

that where John Rawlins is not able to answer his accounts by any lawful discharge as plainly appear before Mr. Alderman Hayward appointed indifferently between the said Rawlins and me by the sum of £480 and nothing to show for his discharge, yet on considering the great oaths he hath taken upon salvation and damnation [I will] that hereafter he be not molested by such as shall have to do for me if he will be quiet . . . I will that whereas Gabriel Newman laid out into the Exchequer fifty pounds yet not answered at the

---

[1] Ibid., p. 232; P.R.O. S.C.6/Hen. VIII/3076; T.C. MS, Audit 1541–2, fo. 9d.
[2] P.R.O. S.C.6/Add./3545/83, C3/9/32.
[3] S.R.O. DD/CC/31523.

commandment of the said Rawlins that if he cannot get it of Rawlins, that then he shall be allowed so much of mine executrix as shall answer the said fifty pounds.[1]

Just seven months before the bishop died a new and significant appointment was made to the post of auditor. It went to Edward, Robert and Francis Berkeley, three of the sons of Sir Maurice Berkeley of Bruton in Somerset, at the usual yearly fee of £6. 13. 4d., but with an additional £2. 13. 4d. instead of the previous 13s. 4d.[2] Although the descent of Bishop Berkeley is not sure, he claimed to be one of the great Gloucestershire Berkeleys of whom Sir Maurice was a younger son. As one of the leading Somersetshire gentry, and as a kinsman, Sir Maurice had a double claim on the patronage of the bishop. In 1583 the three Berkeley sons were considering deputing their office of auditor to Hugh Sexey, a Bruton man later auditor to the queen, for there is an uncompleted draft of such an agreement; they apparently decided in favour of Sexey who, in 1595, was performing this office.[3]

This Berkeley monopoly established by Bishop Berkeley lasted well. Edward, Francis and Robert were the second, third and fourth sons of Sir Maurice, and they were still holding the office during the vacancy following Bishop Berkeley's death in 1581, but Robert must have outlived his brothers because he alone was auditor when the next bishop, Godwin, died in 1590.[4] He was still in office when Bishop Still took over in 1593, drawing his original fee of £9. 6. 8d.,[5] but the history of the auditorship is then quite obscured until 1634. A rental of that date, probably drawn up to guide Bishop Peirs in taking over the bishopric, shows Richard Hicks to be the auditor for life, still at the old fee of £6. 13. 4d. and the allowance of £2. 13. 4d. as in the Berkeley days.[6] Hicks had been appointed by 'Bishop William', presumably Laud (1626–8). He was certainly acting as auditor in 1635, but in the following year he was displaced by one who seems to have been a particular

[1] P.C.C. 43 Darcy.
[2] *Wells*, II, 303; Wells Cath. Chapter Acts, Bk. H, fo. 16.
[3] *D.N.B.*; P.R.O. S.C.6/Add./3545/83, C2 Eliz./C.14/4.
[4] Bates Harbin, p. 118; P.R.O. S.C.6/Eliz./2011, 2012 and 2013.
[5] P.R.O. S.C.6/Add./3545/84.   [6] S.R.O. DD/CC/13324, fos. 243, 355.

favourite of Bishop Peirs, Arthur Mattock. Mattock became auditor in 1636 and Hicks then had to be content with the more onerous job of steward, at the lower fee of £5. 6. 8d., which would seem to have been a clear breach of his original grant by patent for life. In 1640 Arthur Mattock was appointed receiver-general, a post which he may have combined with that of auditor.[1]

The descent of these senior offices, the chief stewardship and the auditorship, has been traced in detail to illustrate the general principle of tenure for life by grant of letters patent and of renewal of the original grant to perpetuate a family monopoly. The actions of one bishop tied the hands of his successors, for they, willy nilly, inherited the existing officers. Yet sometimes the dynastic claim was broken, and here all too often nepotism found its opportunity.

[1] Ibid., accounts for 1635, 1636; *Wells*, II, 425.

CHAPTER II

Decline Begins

URING the years 1518–23 the bishopric of Bath and Wells was a step in the career of the lord chancellor, Thomas Wolsey. He used his brief tenure of it to enrich his natural son, Thomas Winter, whom he made, as a school-boy, dean of Wells.

When Wolsey relinquished the diocese for the greater wealth of Durham, it became the reward of his chaplain, Dr John Clerk. It was during Clerk's episcopate that a steady diminution of the temporalities of the bishopric began which reached its climax in the time of Bishop Barlow (1547–53). The critical years were from 1535 to 1539 after which no bishop could feel secure of his ancient endowment, since the government was none too sympathetic to the economic problems of the episcopacy. Not until the time of Charles I was a stand made to conserve the remaining resources of the bishops.

The new bishop, Dr John Clerk, was one of the great scholars of his day, a civil lawyer and one of the early members of Doctors' Commons. He took his place, in the opinion of Erasmus, with More, Linacre, Colet, Tunstall and others in bringing credit to the court of Henry VIII. He was the government's expert on Italian affairs. Originally graduating from Cambridge, he then moved to Bologna where he became associated with Richard Pace, the musician and humanist, who was also a scholar there, and there he took his doctor's degree. He and Pace began their careers together in the entourage of Cardinal Bainbridge, after whose 'murder' at Rome in 1514 they had returned to England and had accepted the patronage of Wolsey.

Wolsey was quick to realize Clerk's value as an agent in foreign affairs, for by 1516 he was promoted dean of the Chapel Royal.[1] By joining Wolsey's entourage Clerk became acquainted with Thomas Cromwell: this was an association which was to have momentous results for the west country diocese when Clerk took it over.

Clerk was now almost continuously employed on the king's business, usually abroad, being supported meanwhile by several small livings in England, and then by the archdeaconry of Colchester (1520) and the deanery of Windsor (1521). His first big assignment came in the spring of 1521 when he was sent as ambassador to Pope Leo X to whom, in October, he presented Henry VIII's book against Luther, *Assertio Septem Sacramentorum*. Clerk himself wrote the preface of this book. Inevitable promotion followed his return: in October 1522 he became master of the rolls, but not for long, as in the next year Wolsey resigned the bishopric of Bath and Wells and Clerk took his place. Service to the state was the accustomed road to a bishopric then, especially for one trained in the civil law.

The temporalities of the bishopric of Bath and Wells were handed over to Clerk in May 1523, but it was not to be expected that one who had proved so able in foreign affairs would be allowed to rest in the semi-retirement of one of the lesser dioceses, especially since his old colleague Richard Pace was now the king's secretary. For the next six years Clerk was almost continuously engaged abroad. First he was again off to Rome, which he entered on 3 June, and he was consecrated as bishop there in December. After two and a half years he left in November 1525, but not for Wells: he was too useful as a diplomat. The next year he went abroad again, as ambassador to France, and then in 1527 he had another spell in Rome. That was apparently his last visit to the city where he had sojourned so long enjoying the company of like-minded scholars. Reginald Pole knew him as one of the 'divers worshipful men of England' who, with Dr Wotton and Dr Bennet, was among the brethren of the Hospital of St Thomas there; Pole particularly mentioned Clerk as one of its benefactors.[2] In August 1528 Clerk was once more *en route*

---

[1] L. Baldwin Smith, *Tudor Prelates and Politics 1536–58*, pp. 42, 44, 53, 72, 73n.

[2] *L. & P. Hen. VIII*, xv, 337.

for England, to return to a country where clerical opinion was divided over the attempt of Henry VIII to gain papal sanction for the annulment of his marriage to Catharine of Aragon. Clerk's travelling companion was none other than Cardinal Lorenzo Campeggio, the absentee bishop of Salisbury, commissioned by the Pope with Wolsey to hear the divorce case in London.

THOMAS CLERK, BROTHER OF THE BISHOP

During all these years there is no reference to the bishop's being in his diocese, and it is doubtful if he had even entered it. His register runs from 1523, but its first reference to his being in Somerset is on 10 September 1530, when he was in Wells.[1] In the bishop's absence his spiritual duties were performed by suffragan bishops, but the care of his temporalities was probably left to his brother, Thomas Clerk, an ambitious man of business. Thomas was certainly acting as his surveyor-general as early as 1525 when the bishop was in Rome, and in subsequent years he built up a predominating position for himself in his brother's episcopal estates.[2] This arrangement was probably to their mutual advantage: Thomas Clerk was an experienced man, and, like his brother, one of Richard Pace's circle. He had served the king's affairs many times with Pace, 'his old master', as he said, in Switzerland, Rome and other places.[3] He was with Pace in Padua in 1519 and his standing in government circles is indicated by the fact that he had responsibility for Wolsey's son, Thomas Winter, whilst the boy was in Italy.

The bishop and his brother were almost certainly the sons of Clement Clerk, of Much Livermere in Suffolk, whose will, proved in 1502, mentioned a son Thomas and his several brothers who were monks; Thomas Clerk in his will was to leave 3s. 4d. to the church of Much Livermere.[4] Thomas married a girl called Anthona (or Anthoni) who outlived him and was remarried to one John Drew.[5] Thomas and Anthona had four

---

[1] S.R.S., LV, 80.

[2] P.R.O. Misc. Surveys 4/257/83, fos. 189–204.

[3] P.R.O. S.P.1/142. By courtesy of The History of Parliament Trust I have been able to draw on their detailed biography of Thomas Clerk.

[4] Scott Holmes, *Wookey*, pp. 145–7.   [5] P.R.O. C3/32/5.

children, Thomas, Henry, Ann and Alice.[1] The bishop allowed
Thomas Clerk to make the episcopal palace at Wookey his
home and the fact that he was there as early as 1524 is another
reason for thinking that he took over the management of the
bishop's affairs from the outset.[2] He was always described as
'Thomas Clerk of Wookey'.[3]

Thomas Clerk became a pluralist in episcopal administration. By 1539 he had acquired four offices: he was receiver of
all the spiritual tenths of the diocese in the county of Somerset,
receiver-general and also surveyor of the bishop's temporalities,
and keeper of the house and park at Dogmersfield with an
allowance of seven yards of cloth worth £2 and rights of pasture
worth four marks yearly. His total income from these posts was
£108. 13. 4d., and by 1552 he had added another £17. 6. 8d.
to it by becoming the bailiff of the town and liberty of Wells
and the keeper of Westbury Park.[4] He also acquired an annuity
of 13s. 4d. secured on the manor of Wookey for himself and his
wife for life, but this annuity seems to have been discontinued
when the manor went to the Crown, which in turn sold it to
William Dunch in 1553.[5] It would thus be safe to say that for
the greater part of Clerk's episcopate his brother drew an income
of at least £109. 6. 8d. from the bishop's estates. The terms on
which he lived at Wookey Palace are unknown: the hidden
perquisites attached to his position may well have been worth
more than his total salary.

There were other kinds of pickings for Thomas. In 1534
the bishop gave him and Thomas Horner of Mells jointly the
next presentation to the parish church of Mells when vacant,
and in 1539 he and his daughter Alice gained the reversion of a
close in Wells, called the West Garden, with the adjacent garden
place, and of lands in Westbury, Congresbury, Wellington and
Wyke-by-Pucklechurch, for eighty years, at a rent of £6. 7s. 4d.[6]
Although this intended long lease was the kind of mortgage on
the future which later bishops so much deprecated, it may never

---

[1] Wills of Bishop Clerk and Thomas Clerk, S.R.S., xxi, 61, 159. Scott Holmes
says that there was another daughter called Antholin who married John Newton.
[2] Scott Holmes, p. 15.
[3] e.g. H.M.C. 10th Report, Parts 3–4, Appendix p. 227.
[4] P.R.O. S.C.6/Hen. VIII/3076, S.P.1/142, E.318/1412.
[5] P.R.O. E.318/1589.   [6] *Wells*, ii, 243, 251.

have been effective, for within ten years all these manors, except Westbury, had been permanently alienated from the bishopric.

A grant of more reality was that which Bishop Clerk gave his brother of a lease for sixty-three years of three closes of land under Wells Tor and within the bishop's park at Wells. This was the lease which Thomas promised to relinquish in return for a lease of the manor and mansion of Wookey, a bargain which he struck with Bishop Knight in 1544.[1] The ownership of Wookey soon passed out of episcopal hands into those of the Crown, but Thomas Clerk was apparently allowed to retain the tenancy of the manor house, for he died there in 1555. It is doubtful, however, whether Thomas Clerk surrendered those three closes in Wells for which Bishop Knight bargained. An account for 1555 shows exactly how much of the episcopal estates had come into Thomas Clerk's hands and suggests that he had retained the closes. He held three closes of pasture, one of about sixteen acres lying in Torfurlong rented at 16s., one called the Camerhey next the bishop's palace at 10s., and one next to the Camerhey called 'le pestelle' which John Pestell formerly held at 3s. 4d.; he also held eight acres of the presumably open pasture in Torfurlong worth 8s., a fourth part of the West Park worth 9s. 2d., and two closes of meadow, one called Waterlese worth 40s. a year, for which he paid only 26s. 8d., and one called Chauntersmede at the same rent.[2] The closes given by name were a part of the demesne lands of the manor of Wells, but Thomas Clerk had other holdings there: a twelve-acre share of thirty-eight acres out in the moors had been granted to him and his wife Anthona in 1535. This rent had not been paid when the account was made up in 1555, presumably because of Thomas's death that year. Clerk also had an interest in the manor of Westbury: besides being keeper of the park there, he had a lease of meadow land, from which pasture for the bishop's deer was reserved, for £5. 6. 8d.

More significant still is the monopoly which Thomas Clerk acquired of the mills in Wells, that manor of many streams. With the exception of one water-mill and one fulling-mill held by Walter Paynter, Thomas Clerk had them all for a total rent

---

[1] Scott Holmes, p. 57.   [2] P.R.O. S.C.6/P. & M./263.

of £28. He held the water-mills at Burcot and at Wick, for which he paid a rent of 40s. each, and the four mills known as the Out Mills and the In Mills at a rent of £6 each.

Clerk's attempt to corner the milling trade at Wells brought him into dispute with Thomas Body, the owner of Dinder mill, one mile from Wells. Body alleged that for the last eighty years it had been customary for the inhabitants of Wells to bring their barley, rye and oats to be ground at Dinder. He, the miller, had sometimes sent his servants into Wells to fetch the grain, but now John Godwyn, the constable of Wells, acting on the orders of Thomas Clerk, had tried to prevent Body's servants carrying grain from Dinder and had caused Body to be fined in the bishop's court, hoping that by this oppression Body would relinquish his right and title in Dinder mill.[1]

The privileged position and undue influence of Thomas Clerk were bound to raise resentment, particularly within Wells. Some of the local feeling against him is reflected in the case brought by Patrick Whyte in which he charged Clerk with having deprived him of the office of registrar to the bishop 'without any good ground, right, title or interest, but only of his extort power . . . and by reason of such office and authority as he then had by his brother late bishop of Bath'. Whyte alleged that Thomas Clerk had warned several persons that if they refused to obey him he would not accept them as friends of his brother, the bishop, and that he had incited others to stir up slander against Whyte. Clerk's defence was that Whyte had published a false will and mislaid official records, and that he was generally unsuitable for his post. Verdict was presumably found in Clerk's favour, for he was allowed to depart at liberty.[2]

Thomas Clerk was a man of such standing that he could communicate direct with Thomas Cromwell, the king's chief minister. On one occasion he petitioned him for the manor of Combe which was worth £18 a year. He made this a special request because Bath Monastery, to which the manor had belonged, was indebted to him for £61. 14. 2¾d., and it had been paying him an annuity of £2. 13. 4d.[3] Clerk was also

---

[1] P.R.O. C1/File 1103/70.   [2] P.R.O. Req. I/X/258.
[3] P.R.O. S.P.I/142.

commissioned by Cromwell to act with Thomas Bamfelde in hearing a case of seditious words against William Cruche at Laverton, and reported the completion of this task to Cromwell from Bath in February 1540. But one must not assume that Thomas Clerk's position depended solely on the patronage of either Thomas Cromwell or of the bishop. After Cromwell's execution in July 1540, and the bishop's death in the following January, he continued to cut a figure in local affairs. Between 1526 and 1534 he was frequently on the commission of peace and again in 1543 and he was on a commission to collect a benevolence; in November 1545 he was on the escheator's roll;[1] and from 1547 for six years he represented Wells in parliament.[2] He may have been the Thomas Clerk who was concerned with the provisioning of Boulogne in 1545 and who was granted some unspecified office at the recommendation of Mr Secretary Paget in October 1546.[3]

All this time Thomas Clerk was building up his personal estate, apart from pickings from the episcopal endowment. In January 1542 Sir John St Loe mortgaged the manor of Locking to him; in October Clerk bought it outright, and in 1545 he rounded off this purchase by acquiring the rectory and the advowson of Locking. His will mentions lands in Blackford and Kingston Seymour as well.[4]

And there Thomas Clerk stayed all through the episcopates of Bishops Knight and Barlow, a man of consequence supported by estates and offices. He died during the episcopate of Bishop Bourne, to whom by his will made in 1554 he left a ewer of silver. There were small bequests to the churches of Wookey, Locking, Kingston Seymour and Great Livermere; to friends, including Dr Edgeworth, who had a pot of silver with a cover; to his servants, including William Gervys who had his mill and ground at Keward; and to his family, including his son-in-law, Hamond Claxton, to whom he left his barber's basin and his ewer of silver. (This may have been a kinsman of Master Claxton who was the almoner and chaplain of Bishop Clerk.[5])

[1] *L. & P. Hen. VIII*, xv, 61, xx (i), 317, 326, xx (ii), 447.
[2] Scott Holmes, p. 145.   [3] *L. & P. Hen. VIII*, xxi (ii), 89.
[4] Ibid., xvii, 28, 563, xx, 229; S.R.S., xxi, 159–60.
[5] *L. & P. Hen. VIII*, x, 253.

Thomas Clerk was, appropriately, buried in Wookey Church in an altar tomb which is still there and which carries the inscription: 'Here lyeth the body of Thomas Clarke, Esquyer, and Anthona his wyf; which Thomas departed to God the 2 daye of March 1555, of whose soules Jesu have mercye.'

BISHOP CLERK AND THE REFORMATION

To revert to the career of Bishop Clerk, he was a conservative in religion who sympathized with Queen Catharine, so that after his return to England with Campeggio in 1528 he came into conflict with Henry's policies and with his old acquaintance, Thomas Cromwell. As a result he was one of the fifteen divines who, in the summer of 1530, were charged with offences under the statute of *praemunire* before the king's bench. He was the only bishop to protest against the submission of the clergy in May 1532, but was soon sobered into acquiescence, for having deserted Queen Catharine, he joined in pronouncing the decree against her at the court held by Archbishop Cranmer at Dunstable in May. The fact that he originally opposed 'the King's Great Matter' may account for the hold which Cromwell later seemed to exercise over him.[1]

At last, on 1 July 1533, he was in Banwell and now he had apparently come belatedly to tend his diocese, for during the rest of that year and from 1534 to 1537 he was intermittently at both Wells and Banwell.[2] By the autumn of 1534 he could, in fact, ill afford to neglect his diocesan interests. Encouraged by the progress of the Reformation, religious reformers and opportunist nobles alike were openly discussing proposals to confiscate church wealth. The question was, how far should the confiscation go? Should monastic wealth alone be touched or should the bishops, deans and chapters also be mulcted? One opinion was that a compromise should be struck about the bishops. They should be allowed to retain a sufficiency to support their position, but their surplus wealth above an

---

[1] *Burnet's History of the Reformation of the Church of England*, ed. Pocock 1, pp. 217, 219; A. G. Dickens, *Thomas Cromwell and the English Reformation*, pp. 46, 166.

[2] S.R.S., LV, 69; *Wells*, II, 243, 245; *L. & P. Hen. VIII*, x, 253; P.R.O. Req. 2/16/46.

agreed figure should be taken over by the state. Such a scheme, which Professor Stone assigns to the autumn of 1534, suggested that the archbishop of Canterbury should be allowed to retain 2,000 marks, the archbishop of York £1,000 and every other bishop 1,000 marks.[1]

Another paper dated October 1534, which Dr Elton attributes to the hand of Sir Thomas Wriothesley, that notorious bishop-hater, suggests an even lower figure for the primate, £1,000, and specifically recommends 1,000 marks for the bishop of Bath.[2] The Imperial ambassador Chapuys reported these rumours to the Emperor Charles V on 28 November and said that only fear of rebellion made the king desist from whole-sale confiscation:

the King, who . . . was intending to take back into his hands all Church property . . . is for the present satisfied to leave the church-men in possession of their property, provided they will contribute to him a yearly rent of £30,000, and grant him the first fruits of all benefices. . . . Since the king was determined to bleed the church-men, he has done much better to do it thus than to take all their goods, to avoid the murmur and hatred, not only of the clergy but of the people, especially of those who have endowed churches, or of their successors; moreover, it would have been necessary, to stop the mouths of many people, to give the greater part of those goods to gentlemen and others.[3]

In the event only the smaller monasteries were touched in 1536 and the bishops were spared, but the controversy about them went on. A paper which Professor Stone assigns to 1536–7 took up the secularization of church lands again. This document is in the form of a petition of both houses for the con-fiscation of the surplus wealth of the larger monasteries and bishops, and Dr Elton suggests that it is the work of a religious fanatic, Thomas Gibson, who was a protégé of Latimer. It may indeed have emanated from that group of religious re-formers who in the next decade acquired the name of Common-

---

[1] The proposal to confiscate episcopal wealth is discussed, with full reference to the contemporary documents cited, in a series of articles in *Bull. Inst. H.R.*: L. Stone, 'The Political Programme of Thomas Cromwell', (xxiv, 1 ff) G. R. Elton, 'Parliamentary Drafts, 1529–40', (xxv, 117 ff) and 'A Further Note on Parliamentary Drafts in the Reign of Henry VIII', (xxvii, 198 ff).

[2] 'Parliamentary Drafts', p. 129 n.   [3] *L. & P. Hen. VIII*, vii, 551–2.

wealth men. Had this petition gone through as a bill it would have put a ceiling of 1,000 marks on the income of the arch-bishops and bishops, on the grounds that 'enormities of religion' had arisen from excessive wealth and that the sum named was sufficient for hospitality. (One of the grounds on which the bishops always countered the charge of their being unduly wealthy was that their position carried with it many obligations of hospitality.) The confiscated surplus wealth, urged this reformer, should be devoted to the defence of the realm and he suggested a pattern which looked back to ancient Rome. The greater part of the proceeds was to support a perm-anent army of horsemen and footmen arranged in units of a hundred under the command of a captain and a petty-captain. The commander-in-chief was to bear the title of lord admiral of the centeners. The sum of £1,000 was to be expended on the repair of castles and fortifications and a further £1,000 was to be devoted to the repair of the highways. A new department, the court of centeners, or the *curia centenariorum*, was to be set up to administer the sequestrated wealth, and this court was to be at Coventry for the relief of that city, which was decayed, and because it was the centre of the realm. Officers called the provost and the lord admiral of the centeners were to be directors of the court, which was to have an establishment of a treasurer, receivers and auditors.[1] This particular scheme was not adopted, but as late as June 1539 similar plans were being debated. The English Reformation might have to be defended by a military force and the wealth of the bishops could be used to finance it.

Bishop Clerk was no fool: he undoubtedly saw the drift of future policy. It is significant that in December 1535 he granted Cromwell an annuity of £20 secured on the manor of Puckle-church. Accounts for 1537-9 show that it was paid.[2] Thus began an attempt at propitiation, a granting away of this and that, mostly presentations to livings, to laymen in high places. The tempo of this movement increased with the passing months in an attempt to buy protection and security, for the bishops

[1] B.M. Cotton MS Cleo. E. vi. fos. 214-20. A transcript is given by L. Stone, loc. cit.

[2] *Wells*, II, 245; P.R.O. S.C.6/Hen. VIII/3076; *L. & P. Hen. VIII*, XIV (ii), 273.

were now, after the break from Rome, the political dependants of the Crown.

Cromwell patently used the uncertainty of the times to exact concessions from his old acquaintance, now in the bishopric of Bath and Wells. The bishop's anxieties are reflected in a series of letters from him to Cromwell, beginning on 13 September 1537: their servile tone, as between contemporaries who had been equals in the entourage of Wolsey, is nauseating. The first was written from Banwell as a reply to Cromwell's demand for a vacant prebend for one of his nominees. Clerk put aside his own candidate and sent the prescribed collation, with a blank for the name to be inserted, straight to Cromwell. Then followed a fawning supplication for Cromwell's continued favour:

Most humbly beseeching your good Lordship that the king's majesty may upon some opportunity (as ye shall best occasion) know how prone and well willing I am to follow and accomplish his grace's pleasure, whereby my trust is that I may better assure myself of his highness his grace and favour towards me, which I take God to record I do esteem more than all the treasures of the world . . . And therefore my singular good Lord in my heart here even upon my bare knees lifting up my hands *etiam cum lachrimis* in my most humble manner and as earnestly as I can I beseech your good Lordship to continue still my good Lord and to be no less faithful and earnest minister for me herein to his majesty now and in time coming than you have been in time past, especially at my last being at London as I then found by experience—so much to my comfort that I shall never be able to deserve it.[1]

The Fitzjames family, who were of both local and national importance, and lived at Redlynch in the south-east of Somerset, were others whose favour the bishop sought. The head of the family, Sir John Fitzjames, who was chief justice of the king's bench, was in 1536 given the next presentation to the prebend of Whitchurch. James Fitzjames was the chancellor of the cathedral, and in 1538 Nicholas Fitzjames was given the wardenship of the bishop's park at Evercreech.[2]

In the summer of 1537 Clerk was one of the bishops engaged on 'The Bishops' Book', or (to give it its proper name) 'The Institution of a Christian Man', which marked a return to

---

[1] P.R.O. S.P.1/124, fo. 104.   [2] *Wells*, II, 246, 250.

traditional doctrine,[1] but back in Banwell in the autumn the policy of propritiating the influential with scraps of patronage went on. Sir Thomas Wriothesley and William Petre, two of Cromwell's subordinates, were given the next presentation to the prebend of Litton when vacant.[2] At the same time a crisis developed through the death of Richard Wollman, the dean. On 23 September the bishop gave the chapter his formal consent to elect a new dean, but Cromwell intervened swiftly. By 26 September the bishop heard that it was the king's pleasure that Cromwell should be the new dean, and he wrote from Banwell expressing satisfaction at the king's choice and declaring that it would be profitable for the cathedral to have such a protector. But the giving was not all one-sided: the bishop slipped in a request that a servant of his should have the keepership of Cromwell's park at Wedmore. The canons residentiary also expressed their gratification at the appointment. The king was highly pleased: he sent a most gracious letter of thanks to the chapter on 1 October.[3]

The deal was a Munich, as the bishop and chapter soon found. Shortly afterwards Clerk received a message and letters from Cromwell through his brother, Thomas Clerk, and finally on 4 October from the king himself, all demanding the advowson of the archdeaconry of Wells for the king upon the next vacancy. The next day the bishop wrote to both the king and Cromwell from Banwell. He replied that he had already promised the office to one of his chaplains, but, perceiving from the king's and Cromwell's letters how earnestly they desired the appointment for the Crown, he had put aside his former promise. He hoped it would please the king 'to furnish your cathedral church of Wells with no worse an archdeacon than you have already furnished it with a dean'. He protested that he was 'the gladdest creature living' in acquiescing in the king's will in this matter. He sent Cromwell the actual grant of the office made out for the king at the next vacancy, and thanked him for the gift of a book (unfortunately not mentioned by name) and approved its solemn and sincere doctrine. He assured Cromwell that there was much honour spoken of him

---

[1] Smith, *Tudor Prelates*, p. 194. [2] *Wells*, II, 247.
[3] *L. & P. Hen. VIII*, XII (ii), 247, 274, 283; *Wells*, II, 247.

in the shire, both publicly and privately, and that he had many friends and servants there of all sorts.[1]

Certainly Cromwell's patronage was not undervalued at Wells. Very soon, on 21 October, the subdean and chapter were writing to him begging his aid in various controversies in which they were involved and requesting an audience with him for their representative, Dr Edgeworth, 'knowing right well that your Lordship may do us more good with your word or your writing than large expenses by us to be made retaining learned counsel towards the law'. Presumably Cromwell gave them attention: the chapter accounts for that year include 'fee to the noble man Thomas Cromwell—£4'.[2]

Deserting Banwell, the bishop spent much of the next year, 1538, at Chew. He was there in the spring and again in December, and it was from there on 25 February that he granted Cromwell, Wriothesley and another the next presentation to the prebend of Dultingcote when vacant.[3] Then his feckless nephew, Stokes, occupied much of his attention. On the evening of 15 March 1538 the bishop, at Chew, received letters from Cromwell bidding him send his nephew up to London. Stokes, who had arrived at Chew the previous day and had then left for Wookey to visit his other uncle, Thomas Clerk, had to be sent for hurriedly. He arrived back on the morning of the 16th and was dispatched to wait upon Cromwell with all speed. Clerk begged Cromwell to be a good lord to the boy 'for he is but a simple, rude, unbroken scholar without audacity'. On 8 April, when Thomas Clerk went up to London with the money due for the king's tenth, the bishop took the opportunity to write to Cromwell 'to put you in remembrance that such poor service as I can do you is and shall be always at your commandment'. He also thanked Cromwell 'for your goodness lately showed in the dispatch of my nephew Stokes as for other your manifold goodness towards me'.[4]

Stokes had been a student at Oxford and then at Paris, and the 'dispatch' of which the bishop spoke was apparently to Louvain, for he is next heard of consorting with the students

[1] Wells, ii, 247; P.R.O. S.P.1/125, fos. 131–3.
[2] P.R.O. S.P.1/125, fo. 266; Wells, ii, 249.
[3] Wells, ii, 248.   [4] P.R.O. S.P.1/130, fo. 61, S.P.1/131, fo. 62.

there and associated with one who was described as 'that arrant traitor Phelyps'. Edward Carne, who was in Brussels with Wriothesley, wrote at length to Cromwell about this matter on 7 February 1539. Phelyps, after being committed to custody, had negligently been allowed to escape. 'The bold coming of Phelyps to Stokes' lodging and the diversity of Stokes' sayings makes me suspect that Phelyps and the English students at Louvain are all of the same sort,' concluded Carne ominously. Two days later Wriothesley himself wrote from Brussels to Cromwell about the students at Louvain suggesting that restrictions should be placed on Englishmen going there.[1] The significance of all this as far as the bishop was concerned was that Stokes was obviously in disfavour with authority at home and he was always described as 'Stokes the bishop of Bath's nephew'. This was an embarrassment indeed for a bishop at such a juncture.

There is yet another indication that Bishop Clerk was not always secure in the favour of the king. In 1537 he had written to Cromwell, 'I beseech your favourable report to the king's highness, whom to have thus displeased I am the most sorriest man living.' No wonder that the concessions to Cromwell from the diocese of Bath and Wells continued. In December 1538 the bishop granted him the next presentation to the office of provost.[2] Other *douceurs* to Cromwell's entourage were made in 1539, a year of extreme menace to the economic position of the clergy. The Church of England, the new church which was being shaped by Henry VIII and Cromwell, was nearer to impoverishment in 1539 than at any time until the holocaust of 1646. The Elizabethan puritans were not the first to suggest mulcting the bishops.

Cromwell's agent, Dr William Petre, was given an annuity of 40s. for life by the dean and chapter on 10 January 1539, but this did not prevent his investigating the cathedral wealth with Dr John Tregonwell, another of Cromwell's men, a few weeks later and confiscating some of it. An agitated subdean and chapter wrote to Cromwell about it on 6 March hoping for some redress. Tregonwell and his colleague Petre, they alleged,

---

[1] P.R.O. S.P.1/143, fo. 54.
[2] *L. & P. Hen. VIII*, xii (ii), 490; *Wells*, ii, 250.

had recently visited them to confiscate jewels and plate for the king. The chapter sent an inventory of the riches of which they had been deprived and asked Cromwell to intercede with the king to see if any of these costly things might yet remain to the honour of God and the necessary use of the church.[1] The pace quickened. On 31 May John Roke, who may have been related to Anthony Roke, Cromwell's servant, was one of three given the next presentation of the prebend of Timbers-combe, and on 22 June Edward Seymour, Earl of Hertford, whose future interest in the bishopric was to be so fatal, picked up the next presentation to the prebend of Compton Bishop. Eight days later Cromwell himself was given another sacrifice: a small property in the parish of St Bartholomew the Less, London.[2]

The crisis month for the bishops may well have been June 1539. Parliament had met in April and the dissolution of the larger monasteries had been put in hand, many of them by 'voluntary' surrender. What was to be the future of the bishop-rics? Drastic schemes were still being pressed by some. Among the State Papers there is a draft memorandum addressed to the king which has been dated 2 June 1539. The anonymous writer says that, thinking it the duty of every subject to assist the king's efforts for the advancement of true religion, he has drawn up a bill for the further reformation of the church, which is still suffering from sore disease engendered by great possessions and superfluous riches. 'The naughty tree is not mortified by lopping of the bows: but only by the cruel plucking up of the roots.' The confiscation of church wealth must proceed further. The king should assign to bishops such lands as are necessary for their reasonable support and use the surplus to endow newly instituted bishops or for other means. The lands of all cathedral churches, collegiate places, free chapels and chantries should also be at the king's pleasure. The author advocates another of those all-embracing Cromwellian inquiries as to the lands held and the fees exacted by archdeacons, commissaries and other bishops' officers. This proposal to trim episcopal wealth is

[1] *Wells*, II, 250; *L. & P. Hen. VIII*, XIV (i), 178.
[2] G. R. Elton, *The Tudor Revolution in Government*, pp. 136, 336; *Wells*, II, 250–1.

endorsed 'A bill drawn and not put up for the parliament house.'[1]

These radical proposals to nationalize church wealth were not put through and one would like to know what considerations stayed the king and what debates took place about the proposal. Professor Stone's view is that Cromwell and Henry disagreed over the issue of the bishops. Cromwell would have preferred a policy of gradualness in the demolition of the monasteries, but he would more readily have attacked the bishops. Henry, theologically more conservative, was anxious not only to preserve the episcopacy but to augment it: hence his plan for the creation of thirteen new bishoprics, of which six were actually established. Moreover, Henry realized the value of the bishops as propagandists and considered the support of the catholic ones absolutely essential during the national crisis created by the Franco-Imperial invasion threat. This would seem a credible interpretation of the situation.[2]

TERRITORIAL CHANGES BEGIN

But one such act of parliament confiscating episcopal wealth did go through, one that was solely concerned with the bishopric of Bath and Wells. Passed on 27 June 1539, it is entitled 'An Act for the Assurance of Bath Place to the Earl of Southampton.'[3] The beneficiary, William Fitzwilliam, Earl of Southampton, was lord high admiral, and the bishop's town house, the Bath Inn, which was sacrificed to him, was in the fashionable part of the capital in the Strand, where the Earl of Hertford and other nobles were settling. The preamble to the act explains that when the king repaired to his palace at Westminster he needed to have his nobles and counsellors near him, and they in turn needed an adjacent residence, which the Earl of Southampton at present lacked. But a town house was also a necessity for the bishop, and so by way of

---

[1] *L. & P. Hen. VIII*, xiv (i), 489 and P.R.O. S.P.1/152, fos. 11–13. See Appendix B for the text.

[2] Stone, loc. cit. p. 8.

[3] 31 Hen. VIII c. 25; *L. & P. Hen. VIII*, xiv (i), 524; P.R.O. S.P.1/151, fos. 78d–79.

exchange the bishop was to have the site and premises of the dissolved monastery of our Blessed Lady of the Order of St Clare, commonly called the Minoresses. This property, more often known as the Minories, lay without Aldgate and had been surrendered by the last abbess Elizabeth Salvadge on 30 November 1538.[1]

The bishop acquired with the Minories some of its other small properties in London, three tenements with gardens and one without in adjacent parishes, and three shops in Fish Street; he was to have the whole in perpetuity for an annual rent of £4. 6. 4d. Although the Bath Inn which he had relinquished was worth £11 more than the Minories, a clause in the act which effected this exchange provided that the bishop was to continue to pay his former amount of tenths to the king without any deduction or allowance; thus the bargain was in every way detrimental to the bishop's interests.

So the London home of the bishops passed out of their hands. We learn from John Hussey, writing to Lord Lisle on 15 August 1539, that Southampton had already taken possession: 'My lord Admiral has left his new house here, late the bishop of Bath's, for Byfleet.'[2] One wonders what were the feelings of Bishop Clerk in parting with this residence, for Southampton was well known to him; they had been on an embassy to France together in 1526. Subsequently Bath Place, or Bath Inn as it was called, acquired the name Hampton Place, presumably while it was held by the Earl of Southampton, but it soon passed to Thomas Seymour, then to the Crown on his attainder, and in November 1549 to Henry, Earl of Arundel. The name Bath Place became attached to the Minories so long as the bishops held it, but when it ceased to be their property the old name of the Minories was resumed.[3]

The next property to go was that convenient half-way house between London and the west country, the manor of Dogmersfield. Among Cromwell's memoranda for September 1539 is the significant item: 'My lord of Bath's answer for the manor of Dogmersfield.' There is no doubt what that answer was: Dog-

---

[1] E. M. Tomlinson, *History of the Minories*, p. 76.

[2] *L. & P. Hen. VIII*, XIV (ii), 15.

[3] *D.N.B.*; *C.P.R. 1548–49*, p. 245; Tomlinson, *Minories*, p. 86.

mersfield was not listed among the bishop's properties when his accounts for 1539 were drawn up, and in December 1540 it was being handled by the court of augmentations. It did not remain in Crown hands for long: in July 1547 Edward VI granted it to Thomas Wriothesley, the new Earl of Southampton.[1] In October 1539 Cromwell was still making a note 'to diminish some of the bishoprics', but the immediate crisis for Bath and Wells had ended. Nothing more was taken in Bishop Clerk's time. In November he was back at Chew, and when Christmas Eve came round Thomas Clerk was once more despatched to London with 'a poor remembrance' for the king and a letter to Cromwell offering, in spite of all, the bishop's 'true heart and service'.[2]

Down there in the shire the small routines of life continued: the bishop was on the commission for gaol delivery and on the commission of peace. He was also a member of the ephemeral council of the west set up in 1539, but unlike his colleague, the bishop of Exeter, who had to give continual attendance, Clerk could make the journey to Tavistock, where the council was based, at his pleasure.[3]

In March 1540 the bishop was in Wells, and some time during that summer he unwittingly took farewell of it for all time, for on 12 July Henry VIII's marriage to Anne of Cleves was annulled and the aged diplomat was called out of his semi-retirement to go to the Duke of Cleves to explain this away. He and others of the conservative faction had already been placed on the council and Cromwell's fall was imminent. He was probably out of the kingdom when Cromwell, to whom he was so beholden and yet who had used him so shamelessly, was beheaded, on 28 July.[4]

On returning from his embassy the bishop fell sick at Dunkirk and in the presence of his two chaplains, Richard Clerkeson and George Dogyon, drew up his will on 27 September 1540. He asked to be buried in the principal church in Calais and left money for distribution to the poor there. He also asked for obits

[1] P.R.O. S.P.1/153, S.C.6/Hen. VIII/3076, E.318/776; *L. & P. Hen. VIII*, XIV, 714.
[2] *Wells*, II, 251; P.R.O. S.P.1/155, fo. 172.
[3] *L. & P. Hen. VIII*, XIII (i), 133, 565, XIV (i), 360.
[4] *Wells*, II, 252; *D.N.B.*; Dickens, *Cromwell*, p. 168.

to be said at Wells, Chew and Banwell, and left alms for the
poor in those places. Subservient to the governing hierarchy
to the last, he left £100 to the king; two gilted standing pots to
the new lord privy seal, the Earl of Southampton; a bell of
silver to John, Lord Russell, who was president of the council
of the west; and various other remembrances to other nobles.
His servants and chaplains were well cared for and the residue
was left to his brother, Thomas Clerk, who also had his gown
of satin, and to his mother for the preferment of Alice, Annie
and Thomas, his brother's children, and Alice the wife of
Thomas Semarke.[1]

The bishop lived to reach England, at least the Minories, his
new London home. He was there on 3 December using the two
chambers and garden which had been reserved for his private
use. Some of the rest of the premises had been leased away in
June. Ralph Pilkington, a citizen and haberdasher of London,
had a forty years' lease of the friars' hall, the parlour, buttery,
and four chambers called the friars' chambers and a garden,
all for a rent of £1. 7. 8d. In the lower quarters lived Alice,
widow of Thomas Lupsett, citizen and goldsmith of London.
She leased two low chambers and a kitchen near the church
within the precinct of the bishop's palace.[2]

As the bishop lay there dying, poisoned it was rumoured, he
knew that his king was not ungrateful for this last service from
his old envoy. On 27 September Clerk had been granted certain
properties which were a useful addition to his manor of Wells.
These were the house and site of the dissolved hospital of St
John, Wells, with the church, steeple, churchyard and demesne
lands, and its other scattered possessions. These included the
rectory and advowson of the vicarage of Evercreech and
messuages in Wells and Wookey. He was also given Malberry
Wood, the wood near Keward Mill and three woods at Beryall
in Wells. The rent was to be £7. 15. 0½d. free of many charges
and also of first fruits and tenths.[3] The end came for the bishop
on 3 January 1541. He was buried in the Minories, and it was
probably when the interior of that church was remodelled in

---

[1] S.R.S., xxi, 61.
[2] *Wells*, ii, 252–3.
[3] *D.N.B.*; *L. & P. Hen. VIII*, xvi, 55.

1568 that his monument was removed to St Botolph's nearby. The inscription on it was still there in 1631.[1]

The bishop's will was proved by his brother, Thomas Clerk, on 17 January 1541. Among the bequests to his servants the bishop ordered mourning clothes 'to all my household servants and chaplains a livery of black cloth, to the chaplains five yards and the other five yards'. This gave rise to a dispute between Thomas Clerk and Thomas Dey. Dey had been a chaplain and also clerk of the kitchen to the bishop, and he claimed his five broad yards of black cloth at 6s. 8d. a yard. Dey also claimed from Thomas Clerk, as the bishop's executor, the sum of £5 which Dey had spent out of his own purse on the bishop's behalf, and £5. 8s. for the board wages for thirteen months and two weeks at the rate of 2s. a week for his meat and drink which the bishop owed to him when he died. Thomas Clerk also personally owed Dey £10, the first fruits of the benefice of Yeovilton which he had had as the gift of the bishop. Clerk had retained this £10 instead of paying it over to the king's use.[2]

BISHOP KNIGHT

On 8 February Dean FitzWilliam and the chapter were petitioning the king for licence to elect a new bishop. The monarch had another of his diplomats to hand ripe for reward, William Knight, archdeacon of Richmond. By 27 May it was all settled and the temporalities had been handed over to Knight. He was consecrated on Sunday 29 May 1541 by Nicholas Heath, bishop of Rochester, assisted by two suffragan bishops, in the chapel of his new London home in the Minories.[3] A product of Winchester and of New College Oxford, where he was a fellow, Knight was destined for a diplomatic career from the outset. He was a canon lawyer of no great intellectual brilliance, although associated with learned and cultured disciples of the New Learning, and a personal friend of Sir Thomas More. He

[1] S. H. Cassan, *The Lives of the Bishops of Bath and Wells*, p. 444, repeats the story that there was doubt about the place of Clerk's burial; but see Tomlinson, *Minories*, pp. 97–8.

[2] S.R.S., XXI, 61; P.R.O. C1/File 1117/13–14.

[3] *Wells*, II, 253; Cassan, *Bishops of Bath and Wells*, p. 451 n.

has been described as 'a loyal and able Tudor workhorse', and
'a skilled and hard-working civil servant', and the fact that he
was out-paced by many of his generation and had to wait for
substantial reward until he was sixty-five speaks for itself. He
was a known adversary of the Reformation, but rarely expressed an opinion except on administrative and diplomatic
affairs.[1]

Knight had gone to court in 1495 and become secretary to
Henry VII, and in the next reign he was frequently employed on
embassies abroad, to Spain in 1512 and to the Low Countries in
1514. With the Emperor Maximilian he found so much favour
that he received great gifts from him and the grant of a special
coat of arms, but when, between 1516 and 1520, he was several
times sent to the Emperor Charles V while still only chaplain
to the king and dean of the collegiate church of Newark,
Charles protested that to send an ambassador of such humble
status was an insult to his imperial dignity.[2] He was present at
the Field of Cloth of Gold as one of Henry's chaplains and from
1526 to 1528 he was the king's secretary, taking the place of
Richard Pace. But this post did not keep him at home; although
he complained in 1527 that he had grown old and weary and
that his sight was failing, Henry sent him to Rome to promote
the divorce business, a mission on which, by reason of Spanish
hostility, he was nearly murdered. More years of plodding
diplomatic activity followed, and although he collected some
minor ecclesiastical preferment, he was still only archdeacon of
Chester when the more able diplomat, John Clerk, became
bishop of Bath and Wells in 1523. When Knight in turn took
over the bishopric in 1541 he resigned the posts of prebendary
of Westminster and archdeacon of Richmond, which he had
held since 1529.

Bishop Knight stayed in the Minories at least until 12 July
1541 and then he went to his diocese. He was at Chew in August
and September. He clearly intended to make little use of his
London property, and by 1544 he seems to have abandoned
any intention of residing there again: no doubt he was by now
too old and weak to undertake the journey. Accordingly he

---

[1] Smith, *Tudor Prelates*, pp. 44, 57; Elton, *Tudor Government*, p. 56.
[2] Cassan, p. 450; Smith, p. 83.

arranged to be relieved of the responsibility of the premises. In February 1542 some more of the buildings within the precincts were leased to Ralph Pilkington, who was already established there, and whose previous lease was extended to eighty-nine years.[1] Troubled no doubt by the fact that some of the buildings were 'old, deformed and ugly', the bishop came to an agreement about them in May 1543 with one John Moore, his servant. Moore was given a lease of the ground on which these buildings stood. It was called 'the lawndrie' and was forty feet by thirty-six feet. To the west it was bounded by a path which led to an old gate by a well, to the east by the wall of the church, on the north by the side of the monastery, and on the south by the buttery. John Moore was to repair and rebuild the old buildings to make a mansion house at his own cost. He was also to have a garden place, and the whole of this was leased to him for sixty years at 5s. a year. The next year, in March, the bishop appointed John Moore and his wife Elizabeth to the wardenship of the house reserved as his own residence, for a fee of £2.[2] Bishop Knight had been in the Minories from January to April of 1543, but that was probably his last visit there.[3]

Evercreech was another episcopal home now quite abandoned, and Bishop Knight let out to Raff Hannam, a yeoman of Evercreech, the site of the manor-house which Bishop Clerk had pulled down and the demesne lands attached.[4] His chief residence, the palace at Wells, was likewise neglected by Knight, as by several other Tudor bishops, although he was there at least in July 1543. Wiveliscombe was clearly his favourite and most permanent home. He was there in the summer and autumn of 1541, and all through the winter months, September 1543 to March 1544, although he occasionally left in the summer months to visit Chew and Banwell. After such a visit in July 1544 to Chew and in August to Banwell he was back in Wiveliscombe by 14 September for the winter and it is doubtful if he ever left it again. During the next three years, in this modest mansion of which the most striking feature was perhaps the great chamber with its hang-

[1] S.R.S., LV, 91; *Wells*, II, 254.　　　　　[2] *Wells*, II, 255–6.
[3] S.R.S., LV, 99, 100, 102.　　　　　　　[4] Ibid., XXI, 172.

ings of red and green say, he led an apparently retired and
rustic life.[1]

These years were not, however, without their anxieties. The
drive to deplete the bishoprics continued, unofficially and in
piecemeal fashion, as did the efforts of the bishop to placate laymen of standing and so to buy a reprieve. Nor must we imagine
that this condition was peculiar to the diocese of Bath and
Wells. During the 1540's numerous letters were being sent to
bishops and to deans and chapters commanding them to part
with manors, outright or on lease, to the Crown or to its
favourites; sometimes they were given impropriate parsonages
in return. The bishop of Exeter was heavily involved, and
similar demands were made of the bishops of Winchester,
Coventry and Lichfield, and St Davids.[2] Whether the ultimate
result of these exchanges of land between Crown and bishops
was greatly to the bishops' disadvantage only detailed studies
of individual dioceses would show. Cranmer's 'great exchange'
of the Canterbury lands was partly a geographical and administrative simplification, but it also resulted from pressure from
Crown and court, and by 1546 Cranmer was the worse off by
about £300.[3] His colleague of York was also involved in
exchanges of land.[4]

Bishop Knight was very generous, we might almost say rash,
in granting away presentations of livings. One gets the impression that he could not withstand the pressure of those who
sought to seize ecclesiastical wealth. The local gentry were large
beneficiaries of this generosity, especially Cuthbert Walker,
who had a share in eight grants, and William Hillacre. Thomas
Clerk, the late bishop's brother, shared in the next presentation
to the prebend of Combe VII by grant of September 1544. But
it is the grants of the rights of presentation to livings made to
great personages which are significant. They began with one
to the lord chancellor, Thomas, Lord Audley, in July 1544
and went on to include John, Lord Russell, Dr John Tregonwell
and Thomas Howard, Duke of Norfolk. When Thomas, Lord

---

[1] Ibid., LV, 91, 97, 99, 103, 104, 108–17, XXI, 97.
[2] *L. & P. Hen. VIII*, xx (ii), 444, xxi (i), 143, 728, xxi (ii), 327, 405.
[3] F. R. H. Du Boulay, 'Archbishop Cranmer and the Canterbury Temporalities',
E.H.R., LXVII, 19 ff.   [4] *L. & P. Hen. VIII*, xxi (ii), 152.

Wriothesley became lord chancellor in May 1544 the bishop had to find *douceurs* for him, and they included an annuity for life of £20 from September 1545.[1]

Nothing could make clearer the tenor of the times than the peremptory letter which Edward Seymour, Earl of Hertford, wrote to Knight in 1545 because the bishop had apparently tried to deprive Hertford's nominee to the prebend of Ilminster of the perquisites of the appointment, a garden, a stable and a priest's chamber in La Mountroy in Wells:

> I have thought it good [wrote Hertford] to will and require you at the contemplation hereof [his letter] to permit and suffer him to enter thereunto and to enjoy the same, as of right he ought to do, rather than otherwise to move any matter that might turn you to displeasure.[2]

The grants of rights of presentations may have been a sign of weakness on the part of the bishops, but they did not diminish the bishop's personal wealth. Other means were employed to do that. In the summer of 1544 Chancellor Wriothesley was devising extraordinary means of taxation to support the war against France. On 14 July, three days before he crossed to Calais, Henry himself wrote round to the bishops asking them for a 'loan'.[3] Only 'upon information of the bishop of Bath's great substance', the king asked him for a specially large loan of £3,000, and the better to persuade Bishop Knight, the letter was sent in the charge of Sir Thomas Arundell, who delivered it to him a week later. The bishop, then on one of his rare visits to Wells, denied to Arundell that he had any such store of wealth, but he confessed to having £1,000 in angels and £200 or £300 more in ready money, and he promised to 'show himself a good and frank subject'. The council were satisfied that he would pay up. What was their surprise, then, when the bishop's messenger, his receiver Thomas Clerk, appeared in London with only 1,000 marks in plate and money, of which but £200 was in money. Clerk also brought a letter from the bishop in which he begged the king to accept this sum as his 'free and poor gift'. The bishop protested that he

---

[1] *Wells*, II, 255–9, 260–2. [2] Ibid., p. 260.
[3] J. D. Mackie, *The Earlier Tudors*, p. 409.

would have given as much as the king demanded if only he possessed it. His gentleman bearer would give a true account of his substance, supported by his books of record, if only the king would give him audience.

But the king was in France and the council took a poor view of Thomas Clerk as an accredited representative; although he was a man of substance he was also a knave who had broken the laws of the realm by passing the seas without licence. They sent him back to the bishop to express their dissatisfaction 'hoping that his master would thereupon stretch a point and, at this need, break his hoard, though it were much against his appetite'. Thomas Clerk reappeared in London with but 500 marks more, and the council and the queen, Catherine Parr, were inclined to take a harsh view of the bishop, 'as we think that he proceeds very unkindly', and they considered holding Thomas Clerk in London until the king's pleasure could be known. They drafted a letter to Paget asking for instructions, but it was not sent. Perhaps the council realized that they were being too high-handed with Clerk, who enjoyed Paget's favours.[1]

The bishop paid up. When the accounts of the court of augmentations were made up at Michaelmas, in the list of aids given by the clergy the bishop of Bath and Wells was put down for £1,333. 6. 8d., of which £333. 6. 8d. had yet to be paid. This was correct. The bishop had already paid £1,000, but no other bishop was being asked for so much. The second highest demand was from the bishop of Lincoln who had to find £1,000. The archbishop of York and the bishop of Durham had to find £500 each, the bishop of London £300 and others smaller amounts. Since the bishopric of Bath and Wells was not one of the senior or wealthy bishoprics, but was in the middle of the range, it seems that undue demands were made upon it.[2]

Nor did this end the bishop's humiliations. In June 1545, 'moved by special arguments and considerations', he granted

---

[1] Bishop Knight in his letter of 28 July to the king says: 'The gentleman bearer hereof is my receiver.' This must have been Thomas Clerk, who held the office for life. P.R.O. S.P.1/190; *Wells*, II, 278.

[2] *L. & P. Hen. VIII*, XIX (ii), 114, 171; P.R.O. S.P.1/190.

another of his outlying manors, Wyke in the south of Gloucestershire, to the king. That grant marked the end of the depredations of the reign of Henry VIII. At the values of 1538, the total
losses of the possessions of the bishopric had been £118. 13. 5d.,
made up of the Bath Inn, London, valued at £38, and the
manors of Dogmersfield and Wyke, valued at £25. 14. 0½d. and
£54. 19. 4½d. respectively.[1] Against this the bishop had gained
(at 1542 values the nearest available to those of 1538) the
Minories in London, worth £26. 18. od. and the Hospital of St
John at Wells, worth £45. 5. 2d., a total of £72. 3. 2d. He was
thus on balance £46. 10. 3d. worse off.[2]

So Bishop Knight passed away, some say in London, some at
Wiveliscombe, on 29 September 1547.[3] Since he was at Wiveliscombe at least as late as 2 June and seems to have been there
continuously for several years before that, it is unlikely that he
ventured to London in his closing months. His will was drawn
up on 12 August, but it does not say where. The first parliament of Edward VI's reign did not assemble until 4 November, so that cannot have been the reason for his being in
London, if he was, on 29 September. It is more probable that
the £100 left in his will 'for the charges of my burial, bringing
down of my corpse and making of my tomb' refers to the
journey from Wiveliscombe to Wells, since he specifically asked
to be buried in Wells Cathedral. Tradition has it that the stone
pulpit near Hugh Sugar's chantry in the nave of Wells Cathedral
was the work of Bishop Knight, since it has his arms on it, and
that he was buried near it.[4]

Another tangible memorial of his connection with Wells was
the market cross in the market place standing on fourteen pillars
of stone and leaded on the top. Round the stonework just above
the arches in capital letters were the words: 'Ad honorem Dei
omnipotentis [et] commodum pauperum mercatorum Welliae
frequentantium, impensis Gulielmi Knight Episcopi et Ricardi
Wooleman hujus ecclesiae Cathedralis olim Decani, hic locus

---

[1] *Wells*, II, 260; *L. & P.*, xx (i), 483; S.R.O. DD/CC/13324.
[2] T.C. MS, Audit 1541–2.
[3] Cassan, *Bath and Wells*, pp. 451, 453; Phelps, II, 122.
[4] S.R.S., xxi, 97–8; *Murray's Handbook for Somersetshire* (1899), p. 59; R. H.
Malden, *The Story of Wells Cathedral*, p. 41.

erectus est. Laus Deo, Pax Vivis Requies Defunctis. Ann. Dom. 1542.'[1] Dean Wollman died in 1537, and there is no direct mention of a legacy to build a market cross in his will, but it was to Bishop Knight, then Doctor William Knight, the king's secretary, that he left the residue of his estate after all other bequests.[2] Bishop Knight may well have devoted these proceeds to the erection of the cross. In his own will the bishop directed that all the profits arising from the standings within the cross (it was presumably what we should think of as a market-house open on the ground floor rather than a market cross) at the time of the two fairs of St Calixtus and St Andrew were to be spent by the dean and chapter for the benefit of the choristers. Cuthbert Walker, that monopolizer of presentations, was to be the trustee of the funds, and he was left £20 and a standing cup for his pains.

In another form of charity the bishop left money to the poor in most of the places with which he had been associated, including his Somerset manors of Wells, Wiveliscombe, Banwell, Cheddar, Wellington, Chard, Chew, Congresbury Bishops Lydeard, Kingsbury, and Huish, and the Gloucestershire manor of Pucklechurch. Apart from all the usual bequests of featherbeds and small sums of money to friends and servants, the most notable features of his will are the gifts to Lord Russell, now the lord privy seal, who was bequeathed some hangings and a ring of gold with a turquoise and who was to be the overseer of the will, and to John Tregonwell, who was to be an executor, and who received a bowl with a pounced foot and £40.[3]

But no gifts could deflect the purpose of those out to despoil the bishoprics. The new reign and the new bishop were to be equally disastrous to the bishopric of Bath and Wells.

---

[1] To the glory of Almighty God [and] for the benefit of poor merchants doing business in Wells, this place was erected through the munificence of Bishop William Knight and Richard Wollman formerly dean of this cathedral church. Praise to God, Peace to the living, Repose to the departed. In the year of our Lord. 1542.' Wells Museum Notebook, fo. 13.

[2] S.R.S., XXI, 4–6.   [3] Ibid., pp. 97–8.

CHAPTER III

Bishops' Families

T HE next bishop, William Barlow, differed from his predecessors in two important ways: he was the first bishop of
distinctly Protestant leanings and the first married bishop
to come to Wells.

Of all the religious changes probably none had such long-
term or profound effects on the administration of the temporalities as giving the bishops permission to marry. The temporalities
which came to a bishop on his appointment were not his
personal property to dispose of at his own will; they were held
as it were in trust, as the endowment of his office, to be passed
on intact to his successor. For that reason all grants or leases of
property, or grants of offices, had to be sanctioned by the dean
and chapter. All that belonged to the bishop for his personal
expenditure was the net income from the estates for the duration of his episcopate.

The marriage of bishops also set them the problem of their
making material provision for their children, and for their
wives during widowhood. If a bishop could effect any personal
saving out of his income there was nothing to prevent him from
investing it in goods or lands and passing it on to his children,
either during his lifetime or as a legacy at his death. Some
bishops managed to amass a personal fortune, notably Bishop
Still (1593–1608), but this saving demanded the most scrupu-
lous supervision of income and expenditure. The task was all
the more difficult for the bishops because the new economic
burdens of marriage coincided with rising prices and, as far
as the bishopric of Bath and Wells was concerned, from the

1550's with a great diminution of the endowment. Yet a bishop was expected to maintain the part of a noble lord and to meet the traditional demands of hospitality and charity, and his sons were expected to live like gentlemen. At the bishop's death the episcopal palace at Wells and the favourite mansion houses at Banwell and Wiveliscombe would be closed to his children as homes. Their remedy was to get a continuing stake in the episcopal fortune, if possible by leases and offices.

The letters patent for the appointment of Bishop Barlow were issued on 3 February 1548, the see having been vacant since 29 September 1547. The revenues were meanwhile in the king's hands, and the dean and chapter were unable to meet their obligation of collecting £180 due upon the bishopric for the first fruits and tenths, and they later asked to be acquitted of this amount. It was normal procedure for the temporalities of a void see to come into the king's hands. He had the custody of them, with the profits accruing, so long as the vacancy lasted. When the new bishop had been consecrated he could of right demand restitution of the temporalities, which he then held in freehold as long as he remained bishop of the diocese. If he died or resigned, or was translated to another bishopric, the temporalities once more reverted to the king.

Although profits and privileges arising from a vacant see were entirely at the king's command, he could, of his own good will, assign these to another. Such grants were called grants of custody and might be retrospective or prospective. Retrospective grants were made when the king wished to hand over to the new bishop profits which had accrued during the vacancy. These grants seem to have been rare in Tudor times, although Cranmer had one. Prospective grants of profits and rights were made to a bishop elect where there might be some delay in consecration. Such grants were temporary and were automatically terminated on the bishop's investiture, from which time he could claim the freehold of the temporalities.

This consideration of the circumstances in which a bishop received his temporalities is relevant to the accession of Barlow when he became bishop of Bath and Wells. His ecclesiastical career was already notorious before he came to Wells in the spring of 1548. He originated from a well-connected family owning considerable property in Essex and Hertfordshire. His father, John Barlow, had four sons altogether; three of them entered the church, and the fourth, Roger Barlow, was a Bristol merchant who had ventured to Spain and Portugal and associated with Robert and Nicholas Thorne and Sebastian Cabot. There was one sister, Elizabeth, who became lady-in-waiting to Margaret Tudor when she went to Scotland to marry James IV, and herself became Lady Elphinstone.[1]

Of the three ecclesiastical brothers, Thomas was for some time a country parson, but when his brother William became bishop of St Davids he and the third brother Roger joined in the purchase of church lands in Slebech and Haverfordwest in that diocese. Roger settled down there as a country squire and in 1549 became vice-admiral of the Pembroke coast; as late as 1554, long after their brother, the bishop, had left the diocese, Roger and Thomas were holding prebends there. More important than either of these two brothers was John Barlow. Chaplain to Sir Thomas Boleyn between 1525 and 1528, he was well known as Anne Boleyn's servant and was much employed in promoting the king's divorce. He was known to be a reformer and he eventually became dean of Worcester.

William Barlow, the later bishop, began his clerical career in East Anglia with a succession of priories. He was a canon of Bicknacre which was dissolved in 1509 through lack of numbers, then prior of Tiptree where there was but one canon in addition to himself; from 1525 to 1528 he was prior of Bromehill, and when that house was dissolved in 1528 he received a pension of 40s. There is a gap in his story from 1528 to 1534, but he may have been the king's chaplain, of that name who was given the living of Wotton in Lincolnshire in 1528 and who was frequently engaged on diplomatic work. Employment in the king's service and the Barlows' connexion with the Boleyn family would explain his subsequent preferment.

One of the remarkable things about William Barlow was his

---

[1] E. G. Rupp, *The English Protestant Tradition*, ch. iv; Glanmor Williams, 'The Protestant Experiment in the Diocese of St Davids', *Bulletin of Celtic Studies*, xv, III. The following account of Bishop Barlow is taken from these sources which supersede the account in *D.N.B.*, which, as Professor Rupp says, conflates the careers of two or three, possibly four, Barlows.

ability to ride a crisis; he was to do so several times, and if in
Mary's reign exile could not be avoided he lived to enjoy
reinstatement as a bishop in Elizabeth I's reign. Yet he had all
the characteristics likely to lead to personal failure; he was
overbearing, greedy, tactless, impetuous, unprincipled, and
over-ambitious for the advancement of his family. Added to
all this, he was frequently accused of heretical views, and yet it
may well have been the sincerity of his Protestantism and
his desire to spread Renaissance learning that carried him
through.[1]

Advancement came for him in 1534 when he was made prior
of Haverfordwest in Pembrokeshire, almost certainly by the
patronage of Anne Boleyn, who had been created Marquess of
Pembroke in 1532. This position gave him control of three
pulpits in the town of Haverfordwest, and these he used to give
anti-papal sermons which raised against him the enmity of
both the secular clergy and the Black Friars there. The bishop
of St Davids, Richard Rawlins, even complained about him to
the council, but Barlow was too securely in the favour of Cromwell and Anne Boleyn to be unseated. In 1535 he was promoted
prior of Bisham in Berkshire and later that year he was sent on
an embassy to James V of Scotland in an attempt to induce him
to abandon Rome. It was while he was in Scotland, in January
1536, that he was promoted bishop of St Asaph, but before he
could assume his duties there he was translated to the bishopric
of St Davids.

The fact that he was a travelling ambassador while receiving
two promotions in quick succession perhaps gave rise to some
dislocation of normal procedure. That, and the pressures of
clerical work which led to some hiatus in the records, is the
explanation given by Dr Claude Jenkins of the mystery of
Barlow's consecration. A whole literature has arisen on this
subject by reason of the fact that Barlow took a leading part in
the consecration of Archbishop Parker in 1559. Perhaps the
most telling of Dr Jenkins' arguments in favour of Barlow's
consecration is that he was 'taken and reputed to be a bishop

---

[1] Professor Rupp doubts whether he was the William Barlow who signed the
letter recanting heretical views. See T. Wright, *Letters Relative to the Suppression of the
Monasteries*, p. 6.

in the full sense at all times by them (the chapter at St Davids) as by his brother bishops'.[1]

By the autumn of 1536 Barlow was back in the diocese of St Davids where previously he had been so unpopular a prior, and he did nothing to diminish that unpopularity. He was soon involved in disputes with the cathedral chapter over his proposals to move the see from St Davids to Carmarthen (which would have been a more convenient administrative capital) and his attempts to enlarge his authority. Barlow survived the death of Anne Boleyn, and he managed to keep his position after the fall of his patron, Cromwell, possibly because he had by then undermined the resistance of the chapter at St Davids by grants of benefices and advowsons to his kinsmen. The old story that he stripped the lead off the roof of the palace at St Davids to provide dowries for his daughters cannot be true, for it is unlikely that any of his children was born before he left Wales; but he may have been responsible for letting the building fall into decay, since he wished to make Carmarthen the cathedral city, and he himself lived there.

Another criticism of Barlow is that he alienated the manor of Lamphey, one of the richest possessions of the see, in return for very inadequate compensation, the advowson of the rectory and vicarage of Carew. In this there was nothing unusual, for the securalization of church lands was going on everywhere; what is remarkable is that the manor should have gone to an old antagonist, Richard Devereux. The Devereux were moving to the left in religion, and the Lamphey transaction may represent a compromise between the Barlow and Devereux families, especially since tradition has it that Richard Devereux's son Walter, later the Earl of Essex, was Barlow's godson and eventually received the manor.[2]

THE BARLOW FAMILY

Barlow himself was certainly reformist in religion. Early in the reign of Edward VI he preached before the king against

[1] C. Jenkins, 'Bishop Barlow's Consecration and Archbishop Parker's Register', *Journal of Theological Studies* (1922), reprinted by The Church Historical Society (1935), which is an effective reply to A. S. Barnes, *Bishop Barlow and the Anglican Orders*, pp. 69–71.　　　　[2] Glanmor Williams, op. cit., pp. 222–3.

images and although he thereby offended Gardiner, the leader of the conservative bishops, his views were acceptable to those in authority, especially Cranmer. He also enjoyed the patronage of the Protector Somerset, and his promotion to Bath and Wells followed. He may have married just before he moved to Wells, probably after convocation sanctioned clerical marriage in December 1547, for the letters patent for his translation to Wells were issued after that, on 3 February 1548.[1] Parliament legalized the marriage of priests early in 1549, and a supplementary act legitimizing priests' children followed in 1552. Five of the next ten bishops of Bath and Wells were to be married men, and three had large families. Clerical marriage was at first, however, far from secure. In 1553 Mary I repealed the Edwardian acts, and Elizabeth I did not re-enact them; she left clerical marriage to be regulated, somewhat unsatisfactorily, by the injuctions of 1559, which grudgingly allowed the marriage of the clergy. In the case of bishops, marriage was to be subject to the approval of the metropolitan of the province and such commissioners as the queen should appoint. Not until 1604 was Edward's act allowing clerical marriage made lasting.[2] Bishop Barlow was certainly married by 1550. His wife was a former nun, Agatha Welsborne, the daughter of Humfrey Welsborne, and she bore him two sons, William and John, and five daughters, Anne, Elizabeth, Antonia, Margaret and Frances. Some of these children must have been born at Wells.[3]

While the Barlow nursery was being formed the father was undergoing a most trying experience. He inherited sizable endowments with his new bishopric, but at different stages he was made to relinquish nearly all of them until only three manors remained for the support of the episcopal family. At one point, in December 1550, the bishop's own palace at Wells was annexed by the Duke of Somerset, and the bishop was compensated with the deanery to which he and his family presumably moved.[4] After the fall of Somerset the bishop re-

---

[1] *D.N.B.*, J. Ridley, *Thomas Cranmer*, p. 310; *Wells*, II, 266.

[2] H. Gee and W. J. Hardy, *Documents Illustrative of English Church History*, pp. 366–8, 378, 431–2.

[3] P.R.O. S.P.10/10/19 and 20.

[4] *See* ch. iv for details of these territorial changes.

ceived back his palace and property in Wells and a fraction of his confiscated estates. But because of the sick condition of the young king by the early months of 1553 Barlow must have known that his tenure of Wells was limited. A bishop who had been accused of heresy even in the reign of Henry VIII had little hope of a future under Catholic Mary, and the death of Edward VI on 6 July and the failure of the Duke of Northumberland's plot to ensure a Protestant succession were disastrous for him. There was no place in England now for a married bishop with a family. How could he provide for them all?

No doubt it was in desperation that on 3 September 1553 the bishop made over one of the episcopal estates to his son William, who was still an infant. It was a lease for eighty years of one of the rectories he had received in the reshuffle of property in Somerset's time, the parsonage of St John the Baptist at Glastonbury with three appurtenant chapels; the lease was a reversionary one to take effect when that held by Sir Maurice Berkeley expired, and the rent payable to the bishop was £40. 13. 4d. William Barlow, the son, in turn assigned the lease to his brother John. Confirmed by the dean and chapter, the arrangement seems to have held good despite the exile of the Barlow family in Mary's reign.

In 1568, when the Barlows were back in England, now at Chichester, this 'insurance policy' of Bishop Barlow paid a dividend. On 10 April John Barlow assigned his interest in the lease to Thomas Huchins and John Dawes for a fine of £280. The half interest thus acquired by Thomas Huchins he made over to his mother, Dorothy, who afterwards married Gregory Morgan, but in the course of quarrels over the property between Morgan and John Dawes the rent reserved by John Barlow fell into arrears and he resumed possession. It was finally agreed that the former lease should be surrendered and a new quadripartite deed was drawn up by which John Barlow assigned to John Dawes, John Young and a newcomer, William Hatch, the remainder of the eighty-year lease originally granted by Bishop Barlow to his son William; by this deal John Barlow netted another £180 by way of a fine, while the lessees were discharged of any further rent, except that of £40. 13. 4d. due to the bishop. The Barlows had thus made

£460 in thirty years out of this property, apart from any rent which they had drawn.[1]

The drafting of this lease to his son was one of the last acts of William Barlow as bishop of Bath and Wells, although he may have made other dispositions of property to his family's advantage. On 15 September 1553 he was committed to the Tower and by 4 October he had resigned, no doubt in anticipation of the parliament which met the next day and which repealed the acts of 1549 and 1552 on clerical marriage and offspring.[2]

So fearful was Barlow of the new régime that in April 1554 he apparently tried to flee the realm, aided by one William Mariner of Bristol and in the company of John Taylor, alias Cardmaker, vicar of St Bride's, Fleet Street and chancellor of Wells. The trio were apprehended by Sir John Arundell of Lanherne in Cornwall, and their helpful seaman, William Mariner, was sent to the Marshalsea prison; Sir John was thanked by the privy council for his diligence and instructed to take bonds for £200 each from Barlow and Taylor for their immediate appearance before the council. Barlow was released on 10 May. In November he made an equally unsuccessful attempt to get abroad with Cardmaker, and this time he ended up in the Fleet. On 22 January 1555 he procured his release from prison by recanting his 'heretical' views before Gardiner, the chancellor, and he then fled to Emden in East Friesland where there was a Protestant settlement. He became a member of the Duchess of Suffolk's household at Weinheim, presumably as her chaplain, and in 1557, still in the Duchess's service, he went into Poland where John à Lasco offered them asylum.[3]

On the accession of Elizabeth I, the daughter of his old patroness, Barlow returned from exile and, appointed one of the queen's chaplains, was sent, not back to Wells where he would have been ill received, but to the bishopric of Chichester. There he died on 13 August 1568 and was buried in the cathedral, where his tomb is still to be seen. As he lay dying,

---

[1] P.R.O. C2/Eliz./E.1/63.

[2] *Wells*, II, 276; C. H. Garrett, *The Marian Exiles 1553–59*, p. 80.

[3] Dasent, *Acts of the Privy Council 1554–56*, pp. 13, 20; W. Hunt, *The Somerset Diocese, Bath and Wells*, pp. 177–8; *D.N.B.*; Garrett, *Exiles*, p. 80.

some confusion arose about his will. Five days before his death Edward Foster, his receiver, asked whether he had made one. Barlow replied that he had and he sent his wife, Agatha, with Foster to search for it in the coffer in his study. They were unable to find it, and when Foster and 'Mr Barlow', the physician (possibly John Barlow, the second son), asked the bishop if he intended Mrs Barlow to be the sole executrix of all his goods and lands, he answered 'Yea, yea'. On 22 September 1568 probate was granted to his widow, but what property was left by one who had been four times bishop and an exile in Poland the will does not say.[1]

Yet his family weathered the storms of ecclesiastical change. The truth is that this new social group, the bishops' families, tended to become close-knit, perhaps in self-defence against their obvious legal insecurity. In the palmier days of the Elizabethan restoration all five of Bishop Barlow's daughters married bishops, and it is interesting to trace some of the ties which were to bind together a group based on Chichester and Salisbury. Margaret, the eldest daughter, married William Overton a canon of Chichester, who became treasurer of the cathedral the year before her father died, and in 1579 bishop of Coventry and Lichfield. She died before her husband, who married again and was buried with his two wives at Eccleshall in Staffordshire. In addition to his Chichester connexion Overton was from 1570 a canon of Salisbury, where he perhaps met Tobias Matthew who two years later became a prebendary of Salisbury and, briefly in 1583, precentor there. Matthew had been educated at Wells, and it may have been either a childhood friendship with the Barlow girls or this Salisbury connexion which led him to Frances Barlow, another of the bishop's daughters, who was by then the widow of Matthew Parker, second son of the archbishop. Archiepiscopal households were obviously indicated for Frances, 'a prudent and provident matron', as in 1606 Tobias Matthew became archbishop of York. He died in 1628 and before her death the next year his widow gave his library of over 3,000 volumes to York Cathedral.

In 1561 or 1562 another daughter, Elizabeth Barlow, married William Day, younger brother of George Day, her father's

[1] *C.P.R. 1558–60*, p. 452; P.C.C. 17 Babington.

predecessor in the see of Chichester. William Day may well have been living in Chichester when the Barlow family arrived, but in 1560 he became a fellow, and the next year provost, of Eton. His vice-provost there from about 1570 was William Wickham, who became his brother-in-law by marrying Antonia Barlow. In 1584 Wickham became bishop of Lincoln and in 1595 of Winchester, but he survived this promotion less than three months and on his death William Day, after thirty-four years at Eton, succeeded him as bishop of Winchester. Day, in turn, soon died, in September 1596. Both Elizabeth and Antonia outlived their husbands; Antonia was buried in 1598 at Alconbury in Huntingdonshire. The fifth daughter, Anne, also married into the Salisbury circle. Her first husband was Augustin Bradbridge (or Brodbridge), who held a prebend there, and her second Herbert Westfaling, bishop of Hereford (1585–1602); she died in 1597. There were at least eleven children of these various marriages.

When that remarkable old lady Agatha Barlow, the mother of these five daughters and of two sons, died at the age of about ninety on 13 June 1595 in her son's house at Easton in Hampshire, her daughter Frances had a mural tablet to her memory erected on the south side of the chancel of St Mary's church, where it is still to be seen. She was, we read, 'a woman godly, wise and discreet from her youth, most faithful to her husband both in prosperity and adversity and a companion with him in banishment for the gospel sake; most kind and loving unto all her children and dearly beloved of them all for her ability of a liberal mind and pitiful unto the poor'.[1]

The son who lived at Easton was the eldest, William Barlow, who became rector there in 1577 and held the living until his death in 1625. He too was of the Salisbury circle, being arch-deacon there, and a man of some scientific reputation who inherited his uncle Roger's interest in navigation. When he brought out his book *The Navigator's Supply* in 1597, the introductory verses contained this couplet:

> This booke was written by a bishop's sonne,
> And by affinitie to many bishops kinne.

---

[1] *Easton and its Church*, anonymous local guide (1952), pp. 7–8. All the preceding family relationships have been taken from *D.N.B.*

The book's dedication to Robert, Earl of Essex, suggests that the Barlows had retained the goodwill of the Devereux family from their Pembrokeshire days.[1] Of John Barlow, the second son, there is no mention beyond his negotiations over the Glastonbury rectory in 1568.

BISHOP BOURNE AND HIS BROTHER RICHARD

At Wells, after Barlow's disappearance, the next bishop was of course a Catholic, but although untrammelled by wife and children he had other kin to satisfy. During the winter of 1553–4 the bishopric was left vacant, but early in the new year the machinery was put in motion for the election. The dean and chapter put forward their plea for permission to elect on 25 January, but the choice, of course, lay with the queen, and she had one marked out for preferment. Dr Gilbert Bourne was the nephew of her principal secretary of state, Sir John Bourne, and he had already attracted some publicity as a Catholic protagonist. A Worcestershire man, Gilbert was the son of Philip Bourne. He went up to Oxford in 1524 and by 1531 had become a fellow of All Souls. It was appropriate that he should become in 1541 one of the prebendaries of the king's new foundation of Worcester. In 1545 he became a prebendary of St Pauls and in 1547 proctor for the clergy of the diocese of London. He must have complied sufficiently with the Protestant régime of Edward VI's reign, for in 1549 he was appointed rector of High Ongar in Essex and archdeacon of Bedford. Emboldened perhaps by the accession of Mary in 1553, he preached a sermon at Paul's Cross on 13 August justifying the conduct of Bishop Bonner of London, whose chaplain he had been. This sermon provoked a minor riot and a dagger was thrown at Bourne. Such zeal had its reward; on 28 March 1554 Gilbert Bourne was elected bishop of Bath and Wells, on 1 April he was consecrated with five others, and on 20 April he received the temporalities of his see.[2]

---

[1] *Easton and its Church*; *D.N.B.* which says however that he was born at St Davids, which is doubtful since Convocation did not sanction clerical marriage until December 1547.

[2] *Wells*, II, 277; *D.N.B.*; Hunt, *Bath and Wells*, p. 178; *C.P.R. 1553–54*, p. 6.

The new bishop did not immediately move down to his diocese, but by 30 April he had taken possession of his London residence, now the Minories, and he was there until at least 20 May. There is no record of his being in the palace at Wells until July 1555; later he was frequently in Wells, and in October 1556 he was at Wiveliscombe and in January and February 1557 at Banwell. His visits to London doubtless coincided with meetings of parliament.[1]

It is said that of all his homes Bishop Bourne 'made his most abiding' at Wiveliscombe, and it was certainly there, in West Somerset, that the Bourne influence was chiefly felt. The bishop was followed down to his diocese by Richard Bourne his brother, a citizen and draper of London, who seems to have been to him what Thomas Clerk had been to Bishop John Clerk. Richard Bourne married Sylvester Tybolde and they had six sons: Gilbert (d. 1595); John (d. 1622), who became a doctor of divinity, a canon residentiary of Wells and treasurer of the cathedral; William; Roger (d. 1624), who settled in Wells; Thomas, who when his father's will was made was 'detained' in a foreign country, but who died, presumably in England, in 1595; and Jasper, described as 'of London gent', who lived at Stanmore in Middlesex.[2]

The Bourne family made Wiveliscombe their home. Richard Bourne acquired a lease of the mansion house there, which in the bishop's absence was being kept by one John Huchins. Under the next bishop, Berkeley, they stayed on in Wiveliscombe, but not in the mansion. They built a house called Bourne House, one room of which was embellished with an elaborate ceiling of Elizabethan character. This house, immediately north of the church and now called Bournes, still stands.[3]

The Bournes also built up their position by the acquisition of episcopal offices. The aged Thomas Clerk, still alive at Wookey, blocked the way to their advancement, but on 20 October 1554, 'expectant on the death of Thomas Clerk', the

[1] S.R.S., LV, 120-56.

[2] Hancock, *Wifela's Combe*, p. 237; F. Brown, *Abstracts of Somersetshire Wills* v, 76–9.

[3] P.R.O. S.C.6/P. & M./263; Hancock, p. 237; N. Pevsner, *The Buildings of England. South and West Somerset*, p. 351.

bishop granted the office of the surveyor of his manors to his uncle Sir John Bourne, the principal secretary, and to Sir John's son Anthony, for their lives. On the same day the bishop gave the reversion of the office of receiver-general to his brother Richard and Richard's son Gilbert.[1] They had not long to wait for the fulfilment of their hopes; Thomas Clerk died on 2 March 1555. By the time of Bishop Berkeley, both the surveyorship and the posts of receiver-general and bailiff of Wells had come to Richard Bourne and his son for three lives with, according to Berkeley, 'great and unreasonable fees'. There were other perquisites, such as that of 12 June 1559 when Richard Bourne and Richard Snow, who was one of the diocesan registrars, received from the bishop the next presentation to the prebends of Whitchurch and Whitelackington. The office of somner, which was not one of estate personnel, was also in Richard Bourne's patronage and was now more costly to the bishop: in Bishop Berkeley's words it was 'even heretofore without any charge to the bishop now given out by Bourne at the bishop's charge with meat, drink and livery'.[2]

Not all the evidence of what the Bournes received from their kinsman the bishop survives, but some of the story came out when the Marian bishop was replaced by the Protestant Berkeley. On 7 March 1560 Berkeley wrote to Sir William Cecil, the queen's principal secretary, alleging that Bishop Bourne, who was by then a prisoner in the Tower, knowing that his deprivation was certain, had since the parliament of 1559 schemed to dissipate and spoil the bishopric in order to derive the maximum profit from it. In this he had been assisted by his brother, Richard Bourne, and by Humphrey Colles, 'a man learned in the common laws of this realm', who, though a justice of the peace, was a party to all the conveyances of the spoil.

As an insurance against the future Bishop Bourne had indeed tried to effect a last-minute switch to his brother and nephews of three important episcopal manors, Banwell, Westbury and Wiveliscombe, which he leased to them for twenty-one years. Banwell was held by the Bournes on specially favourable rent-free terms,

---

[1] *Wells*, II, 278.   [2] Ibid., 278, 281; P.R.O. S.P.12/16/27 (ii).

the bishop receiving no manner of profit . . . and yet bound by the
said lease to pay all tenths, subsidies, fees of woodkeepers and other
allowances, notwithstanding the woods there and elsewhere being so
leased out without impeachment of waste are so spoiled as pity it is to
see.

True, Richard Bourne paid a rent of £47 for Westbury, but he
held it 'with all the chief woods that should serve the bishop for
his house . . . to the utter destruction of the same manor considering the spoil made.' Finally Wiveliscombe, the plum, was
held for a rent of £73 12s. The result of these leases was that
only one home remained for Bishop Berkeley, the palace at
Wells. This lack of an alternative residence was a special complaint. As the result of territorial losses in Barlow's time the
episcopal palaces of Bath, Chew Magna, Evercreech and
Wookey had by now been irrevocably lost, but nominally there
remained three, Wells, Banwell and Wiveliscombe. Bishop
Bourne had gone, but his brother Richard lorded it still in
two of the bishop's homes to the humiliation of the new bishop.
In Berkeley's own words:

where there were of late days three mansion houses for the bishop
to repair unto there is now but only one which is not very wholesome
to dwell in because it standeth low and in a cold air, now worse than
ever it was because such wood as was for the maintenance of the
house and the help of the whole township is now let out to Richard
Bourne, citizen of London, and likewise two of the houses whereof
one of them called Wiveliscombe is most necessary for the bishop as
well for the wholesomeness as also for edifying the people there being
distant from Wells about thirty miles.

Poor Bishop Berkeley! One can sympathize with his disliking
'the cold airs' arising from the moat around the palace and the
many springs at Wells. Banwell on its gentle slope up from the
Somerset levels within reach of the salt breezes of the Bristol
Channel, or wooded Wiveliscombe sheltered by the hills of
West Somerset, was very desirable by comparison. Bishop
Godwin, his successor, fought to save them both.

The queen did not intervene and the leases were allowed to
run, and since the manor of Banwell is entirely omitted from the
accounts we can assume that it was, as alleged, let to Richard

Bourne rent free for twenty-one years. The crux of the matter was that for a period the already depleted bishopric was robbed of the full benefit of four of its manors. Supposing that these grants of Bishop Bourne had, as Berkeley maintained, been made in 1559, they would have expired sometime in 1580. There is evidence in favour of this supposition; on 15 June 1579 Richard Bourne brought a case against one of his Wiveliscombe tenants and his bill of complaint contained the statement that his 'term and estate in the manor is shortly to expire and determine'.[1]

Berkeley's charge that the Bournes were monopolizing three of the episcopal offices was also substantially true. Right up to 25 March 1584, when the temporalities were handed over to Bishop Godwin, Richard Bourne was still acting as receiver-general at £10 a year and as bailiff of the liberties with a fee of £14. 6. 8d. But the third office, that of surveyor, was at some time during Berkeley's episcopate taken from the Bournes and awarded to Arthur Hopton.[2] The doughty Richard Bourne lived on till 1593,[3] but he did not retain his offices all that time. Where Bishop Berkeley had failed Bishop Godwin succeeded; at some time between 1584 and 1590 Bourne was ousted to make way for favourites of the new bishop. None the less, the appointments of Bishop Bourne had affected the administration of the episcopal estates for four decades.

Equally far-reaching in its effect was the lease of the manor of Wiveliscombe, which was a cause of trouble both to Bishop Berkeley and to the Wiveliscombe tenants: it resulted in several chancery cases. What Richard Bourne held, according to Berkeley's own statement, was not the whole manor but the demesne lands of about 300 or 400 acres of land, meadow and pastture.[4] Such a limited grant would not, presumably, carry with it any manorial rights or control over the tenants of the manor. The normal working of the manorial court under the bishop's direct control is reflected in the Court Book of the manor of Wiveliscombe, which undoubtedly refers to this episcopate, for the entries are annotated by Berkeley himself.[5] Although only

[1] P.R.O. S.C.6/Eliz./2012, C3/204/17.   [2] P.R.O. S.C.6/Eliz./2012.
[3] Hancock; *Wifela's Combe*, p. 238; Brown, *Wills*, v, 76.
[4] P.R.O. C3/205/21.   [5] T.C. MS, P.R./37; Hancock, pp. 92 ff.

two of the entries are dated, they bear dates which are about the time of the expiry of the Bourne lease, namely 8 August and 15 December 1580, and they are the fourth and third entries respectively before the end. If, as is probable, the book is in roughly chronological order, the earlier entries of the surrenders and grants of property run concurrently with the Bourne lease.

Quite soon after the grant of the Bourne lease John Yonge of Wiveliscombe was disputing this family's pretensions: the holding of $190\frac{1}{2}$ acres of demesne lands was in question. Yonge's case rested on the grant of this land to John Mere in 1535. Mere had died about 1550 and his widow Alice then married Richard Wyer, but the original tenancy held good for the lives of Alice and her first husband's son, also called John Mere. About 1555 Richard Wyer and Alice had sub-let to John Yonge for twenty-one years or the lives of Alice and her son John Mere, whichever was the shorter, although Alice and her family remained as the under-tenants of Yonge. This harmonious arrangement was shattered by the arrival of the Bournes. Let Yonge tell the story:

Now of late Gilbert Bourne, John Bourne and William Bourne being the sons of Richard Bourne of London, draper, brother of Gilbert Bourne late Bishop of Bath and Wells, being of very tender years and age by the greedy and covetous practice of Richard Bourne their father and by colour of a supposed lease of the premises lately to them made by the said Gilbert late bishop of Bath by the procurement of their father hath wrongfully entered into the same premises meaning thereof to expel and put out the complainant and avoid wholly the lease.

Yonge added that the Bournes had commenced an action, to be heard at the next assizes, against Richard Wyer and his family for trespass in the lord's pond-yard, his garden and close, and for fishing in certain ponds. The document giving the Bournes' defence is too mutilated to be very helpful, but it shows that they excused themselves by virtue of an abortive lease made to Sir Edward Rogers by Bishop Bourne and by the lease made to Richard Bourne himself. It appears that Alice Wyer (Mere) or her son capitulated to Bourne, for when the final case came up against him in 1580 his defence was that John Mere the son held by survivor and had transferred his estate and interest in part of the Wiveliscombe demesne lands, now said to be about 209 acres, to Bourne.[1]

Richard Bourne's attempt to exploit his Wiveliscombe grant brought him into conflict with other local inhabitants. In 1566 four of them, headed by Robert Wynter, brought action against him. Their complaint concerned the leasing of demesne lands to copyholders. They asserted that in addition to the ancient customary and copyhold tenements in the manor of Wiveliscombe and Fitzhead, there were certain lands in Fitzhead, once demesne lands, which for the last 140 years had been leased out by copy to the existing copyholders of the manor, who paid rents and duties for them to the lord of the manor. Then came Richard Bourne with his lease 'for divers years yet enduring' and made forcible entry on certain of these lands, namely five closes called Waterslode Mead, Fullwell, Ridgeway, the Parish Close Mead and the Barton, and sued the complainants for trespass. Richard Bourne averred in reply that they could not prove their title to these lands, nor the extent of them. Moreover, the five closes had been let only at the will of the lord for rent corn, and he was no longer prepared to extend this benefit 'for that the complainants do abuse the same benignity as well by detaining the rent corn and other things in that behalf'.[2]

Bourne's domination of Wiveliscombe was again demonstrated when a further case came up in 1570. Audrey Wager, a widow of Sevenoaks in Kent, claimed that he was preventing her from taking lawful possession of a fardel of land in Cornford and other lands in Wiveliscombe of which she had purchased the reversion on 2 October 1551, eight years before Bourne acquired an interest in Wiveliscombe. The previous tenant had died in August 1569 and the Widow Wager's two attorneys, Peter Bishop and John Huchins, yeomen of Wiveliscombe, should have taken possession on her behalf. Although she had several times travelled to Somerset 'at great cost and charge' to request them to do so, they refused. Peter Bishop's defence was that he dared not undertake the action unless he were given an indemnity against an unlawful act, such was the intimidating influence of Richard Bourne, who denied that Bishop was an

---

[1] P.R.O. C3/201/28, C3/205/31. See below, p. 127.
[2] P.R.O. C3/189/31.

attorney in the matter and forbade him to enter or take possession.[1]

The next dispute concerning Richard Bourne came into court
in 1579 when his lease was running out and he was obviously
trying to exploit the remainder of it. The grant of reversions of
copyhold tenements was in question. Bourne admitted that
local opinion held that the lord of the manor of Wiveliscombe
could not grant the reversion of a customary or copyhold tenement without the assent of the tenant in possession, and unless
that tenant first surrendered his estate and interest in it to the
lord. The action was brought by Bourne against William
Pownsbury of Wiveliscombe, who held a customary tenement of
thirty acres for life. Bourne alleged that Pownsbury had forfeited his tenure through various transgressions of the custom
of the manor. At a manor court held about a year before,
Bourne had asked his steward to investigate the matter. Pownsbury with some of his friends then pleaded with Bourne who,
being moved because Pownsbury was an old man, agreed to
forgo the forfeiture, on Pownsbury's faithful promise that he
would surrender his copyhold tenement whenever Bourne
required it. He was then to have a new estate for life with other
persons nominated by Bourne. Since then Bourne had several
times asked Pownsbury to surrender his lease according to his
promise but without effect. Bourne's complaint that since his
own lease would shortly expire it was a great hindrance to be
unable to make a further grant reveals what was at stake: as
Pownsbury said, Bourne hoped by molesting him to force him
to surrender his estate so that Bourne could receive the fine for a
renewed tenure of copyhold.[2]

If, as is probable, the leases made by Bishop Bourne were due
to expire in 1580, the ageing Bishop Berkeley must have hoped
to outlive them. But that did not prevent his fighting Richard
Bourne to the end. As late as 8 May 1580 he brought a case
against Bourne in which he declared that the indenture by
which his predecessor granted Richard Bourne the lease 'if
any such there were' was hearsay as far as he was concerned,
for Bourne had the counterpart of the lease. Bourne arrogantly
claimed what number of years in the premises he liked, paid

[1] P.R.O. C3/191/82.   [2] P.R.O. C3/204/17.

such rent as he pleased, and had allowed the premises to fall into ruin. The bishop had several times requested Bourne 'in very gentle manner' to hand over the lease or allow it to be copied, but Bourne had always refused. Although the bishop said that some 300 to 400 acres were in dispute, Richard Bourne rejoined that he held only just under 200 acres, namely, that part leased by John Mere the son, who was still living and who had conveyed his interest to him. He denied that he had the counterpart of the alleged lease from Bishop Bourne or that he held any part of the residue of the demesne—a direct contradiction this of the Bournes' defence in the Yonge case where they claimed a lease from Bishop Bourne. He added that he had paid for the registration of all leases made to him by his brother, so that he sincerely believed that they remained with the registrar of the dean and chapter of Wells. Obviously Bourne capitulated at this point, or the lease ran out, for during the vacancy following the bishop's death in 1581 Wiveliscombe was being administered directly by the episopal officers. But even when the bishop had regained control of the manor, and before it was lost again in Bishop Godwin's time, the Bournes kept their grip on a part of the demesne lands as under-tenants; accounts for 1592–3 give the holding of Richard Bourne in Wiveliscombe as worth £13. 6. 2d.[1]

The will of the notorious Richard Bourne, proved on 15 March 1593, confirms that the Bournes maintained their position, not only in Wiveliscombe but in Wells too, through the episcopates of Bishops Berkeley and Godwin:

I, Richard Bourne of Wells, gentleman . . . my body to be buried as nigh my late wellbeloved wife as may be within the Cathedral Church of Wells. I give my eldest son my lease of the demesnes of Wiveliscombe with the custody of the great house there demised to me by my reverend brother Gilbert, late bishop of Bath and Wells. I give him the lease of my now dwelling house situated within the liberty of Wells with my best furniture and tapestry and hangings belonging to the great chamber.

This son, Dr Gilbert Bourne, did not long outlive his father. His will was proved on 3 February 1595 and again there are references to the Wiveliscombe lease:

[1] P.R.O. C3/205/21, S.C.6/Eliz./2011, S.C.6/Add./3545/84.

my house in Wells to be sold and if it will not serve £80 a year to be paid out of my farm of Wiveliscombe until that sum be raised, I give to my son John Bourne the farm of Wiveliscombe. And if he chance to die I leave it among my daughters to be divided equally. . . . My will is that my executors have not in keeping my writings and my lease of Wiveliscombe, but that they commit it to the custody of the chamber of Bristol.

John Bourne was still at Wiveliscombe in 1623, and his family, strong Royalists, later suffered badly at the hands of the Parliamentarians.[1]

All these troubles at Wiveliscombe sprang from the fact that Bishop Bourne, although unmarried himself, was dominated by his brother and his family. In fact he had no sympathy for married clergy, and following the injunctions against them, he deprived eighty-two, including Dean Turner. Although he had generally the reputation of being humane, it is now accepted that nine clergy were burnt, presumably for heresy, in his diocese.[2] As a loyal supporter of the régime he was promoted towards the end of his episcopal career, on 29 October 1558, to become president of the council of Wales and the Marches. The queen wrote personally informing him of this appointment and urged him to repair to the council 'with all convenient speed'.[3] Although the death of his royal mistress on 17 November rendered his position, like that of all his fellow-bishops, extremely uncertain, he left Somerset to take up his duties and was with the council, presumably at Ludlow, at least until after 18 March 1559; because the warrants for diet money for the council had not been renewed, he had to keep house there at his own expense. The new queen did not allow his appointment to stand: Elizabeth I replaced him by Lord Williams of Thame, and made Sir Hugh Paulet, who was the bishop's chief steward of estates, vice-president. Sir Hugh did not hurry to his new post; he was still at his home in Somerset on 6 May 1559 when he wrote to Cecil that he hoped to be with the bishop at Bewdley in Worcestershire before Whit Sunday.[4]

---

[1] Hancock, pp. 237–9; Brown, *Wills*, v, 76.

[2] Hunt, *Bath and Wells*, p. 179; Ollard, Crosse and Bond, *Dictionary of English Church History* (1948 edn), p. 47.

[3] *Cal. S.P.D. 1547–80*, p. 108; C. Skeel, *The Council in the Marches of Wales*, p. 84.

[4] *Cal. S.P.D. Add. 1547–65*, pp. 489–90, *1547–80*, p. 123.

The bishop soon returned to Wells, for he instituted Thomas Hyne to the vicarage of East Pennard on 6 June.[1] By now the Act of Supremacy had been passed, the Protestants were in the ascendant and the Catholic bishops were expecting deprivation, for they could not in conscience take the oath required under the act. Back in Wells Bishop Bourne seems to have worked desperately to avert disaster, but he did not succeed in purchasing immunity. On 18 October Humphrey Colles (who had by now acquired a lease of the manor of Buckland from the bishop and was a notorious dealer in church lands in the west), John Horner of Cloford and two others were commissioned to take the oath of supremacy from the bishop.[2] Bourne was fortunate to have escaped so long. Bishops White of Winchester and Watson of Lincoln had been sent as prisoners to the Tower on 31 March and their goods had been sequestrated. The other bishops who were in London were put under duress on 10 May, and in June the authorities began administering the oath to them. They all refused to take it, except Kitchin of Llandaff whom the Spanish ambassador, the bishop of Aquila, described as 'a greedy old man with but little learning'. By 13 July Bishop Bourne's neighbour, the bishop of Exeter, had refused the oath and had been deprived.[3] Bishop Bourne must thus have been one of the last of the bishops to be proffered the oath. He had not attended the parliament which assembled in January 1559, and it is probable that after his recall from Wales he cowered in his diocese. He was certainly at Wiveliscombe on 15 August 1559, and that is presumably why the taking of his oath was entrusted to a local commission. The date on which he was formally deprived is not known, but it was before 11 January 1560, when the chapter at Wells sought permission to elect a new bishop.[4]

Bourne joined the other Catholic bishops in the Tower on 18 June 1560. Sir Edward Warner, the lieutenant of the Tower, who had charge of them, obtained permission from the council and Archbishop Parker for the bishops to have their meals in common at two separate tables; Bourne was to eat with Bishops

[1] S.R.S., LV, 156.   [2] *Syllabus of Rymer's Foedera* (1873), II, 800.
[3] *Cal. S.P. Spanish 1558–67*, pp. 48, 67, 69, 76, 79, 89.
[4] *D.N.B.*; *Wells*, II, 281–2.

Thirlby of Ely, Watson of Lincoln and Turberville of Exeter.[1] Although some bishops were still in the Tower in February 1563,[2] Bourne was released in 1561 and was committed to the care of Dr Bullingham, bishop of Lincoln, but he went from him to the protective custody of his friend Dean George Carew of Exeter in 1562. During these last years of his life, when Dean Carew was responsible for him, he may have lived with James Turberville, the deprived bishop of Exeter, in the manor-house now called Gaulden Farm (or Golden Farm) in Tolland in West Somerset. The hall of this house has a fine plaster ceiling and frieze with biblical scenes and a wooded screen separates a withdrawing room traditionally known as the chapel; the arms over the fireplace are those of the Turbervilles. If the ex-bishop lived here in the company of a fellow-sufferer, he was only three miles from his brother Richard at Wiveliscombe. He died on 10 September 1569 and was buried on the south side of the altar in Silverton Church in Devonshire.[3]

While Bishop Bourne and his colleagues were meeting their fate with fortitude ('England can never have had such bishops as these before' reported the Spaniard, de Feria),[4] the council was considering the problem of replacement and the terms on which a new breed of bishops should be allowed to take office.

BISHOP BERKELEY'S DIFFICULTIES

The turn of the wheel which brought Bishop Bourne deprivation and a not uncomfortable retirement, brought to Wells one of very different stamp. Bishop Berkeley was one of the Marian refugees from Frankfort who was not to be disappointed in looking to Elizabeth I for compensatory rewards. Bred a Franciscan of Northampton and York, and an Oxford B.D., he was merely rector of Attleborough in Norfolk when deprived by Mary. His ancestry is generally held to be uncertain, but the fact that the new reign brought him instant and remarkable preferment suggests either the favour of Matthew Parker, whom

[1] *Correspondence of Matthew Parker 1535–75*, ed. J. Bruce (1851), p. 121.
[2] *Cal. S.P. Spanish 1558–67*, p. 303.
[3] *V.C.H. Somerset*, II, 39; Brown, *Wills*, III, 25; *Murray's Somerset*, pp. 455–6; Pevsner, *South and West Somerset*, p. 186; Cassan, *Bath and Wells*, p. 464.
[4] *Cal. S.P. Spanish 1558–67*, p. 50.

he may have met in Norfolk where Parker held a living and found a bride, or a close relationship with the Berkeleys of Bruton in Somerset, a family who enjoyed favour with the Tudors and was later to receive patronage at his hands. He was already chaplain to the queen when on 20 March 1560 royal assent was given to his election as bishop of Bath and Wells; his temporalities were made over to him on 10 July.[1]

His administration of his diocese has been dubbed 'lax and venal', but this appears to be an unduly harsh verdict. He acquired a certain amount of unpopularity through a running dispute with his dean, Dr William Turner, originally the nominee of the Protector Somerset, who was restored in 1560 and who resisted Berkeley's attempts to discipline him into some kind of uniformity, so that the bishop was driven to appeal to Archbishop Parker and to Cecil in 1564.[2] In 1574 Berkeley was involved in a dispute with the burgesses of Wells over the renewal of their charter, and he waged victorious battle with the influential Lord Paulet over the tithes of West Monkton. Although he took the office of chancellor of his church into his own hands for a short time, between August 1560 and September 1561, and licensed a lad of eighteen to a living, these facts are not sufficient to label him 'lax and venal' by the standard of the age. More detailed study of his spiritual administration, outside the scope of this book, would be necessary to substantiate or disprove this charge.[3]

On the economic side he seems to have inherited a position of particular difficulty. Not only was there his struggle to dislodge the Bournes from three of his manors, but the endowment of the bishopric had by now been permanently depleted, and the bishop was so conscious of his poverty that he felt unequal to the burdens placed upon him. He wrote a querulous letter to Cecil about it saying, to use his own words, that since his promotion to the bishopric, although he knew himself unworthy, he had tried to answer the queen's expectation of him, but without further aid from her majesty he would be

[1] Garrett, *Marian Exiles*, p. 87; *D.N.B.*; Bates Harbin, *Members for Somerset*' pp. 118–19; *C.P.R. 1558–60*, pp. 408, 452.

[2] Garrett, *Exiles*, p. 87; *Wells*, II, 282; Hunt, *Bath and Wells*, pp. 189–90.

[3] Hunt, pp. 181–6; *Wells*, II, 282–3, 290.

unable to acquit his duty either to God or to her, because of the
great charge due to her and the little left to bear it. It would be
better for him to serve the queen as a poor chaplain in the
meanest degree than, having the name and the place of a bishop,
to be in need of those things requisite to it. He protested that
he did not mean great possessions, but necessary things for the
support of an honest family. The world expected bishops to be
hospitable, but he was left so destitute that he was denied his
very mansion house for residence, and the whole bishopric was
so depleted that whoever took up the office would be unable to
bear the cost. His predecessor Bourne, anticipating his deprivation, had tried, it seemed, to dissolve the whole bishopric, and
placed such officers under him as neither feared God or his word.
Unless the queen intervened he would be bound to resign his
title as bishop and become her poor chaplain again. He most
humbly besought Cecil's help, and asked for remedy, not for
any 'worldly respect' but 'for the zeal of Christ's true religion,
which now by vocation is my part to advance'. Complaints
that a predecessor had mortgaged the endowment by unduly
long leases were no new thing; Bishop Beckington had made
the same allegation a century before.[1]

Berkeley's reference to the need to support 'an honest
family' may connote his household, since there is little evidence
that he had a family in the narrower sense. Although Elizabeth I
disliked her bishops to marry, many of them did and thus
laid themselves open to attack by covetous courtiers hoping to
disgrace the episcopate and to acquire its lands. Such an unfortunate was Berkeley's successor Godwin. Episcopal wives in
Elizabethan times were in a particularly delicate position, their
social standing ill-defined, their legal status governed only by
the injuctions of 1559. The assumption that Bishop Berkeley
was married rests on a statement by Sir John Harington, who
was, however, apparently hostile to the bishops:

he was a good justicer, saving that sometimes being ruled by his
wife he swerved from the rule of justice and sincerity, especially in
persecuting the kindred of Bourne, his predecessor. The fame went
that he died very rich, but the same importunate woman carried it all
away, that neither the church nor the poor were the better for it.[2]

[1] P.R.O. S.P.12/16/27.   [2] J. Harington, *Nugae Antiquae* (Parks edn, 1804), II, 50.

Harington had reason to be grateful to Berkeley who had instituted his son, Thomas Harington, to the living at his home, Kelston, though only eighteen and a student at Oxford. But Harington's bias against the bishops was recognized even by his near contemporary Thomas Fuller:

A posthume book of his is come forth, as an addition to bishop Godwin's Catalogue of Bishops; wherein (beside mistakes) some tart reflections *in Uxoratos Episcopos* might well have been spared.[1]

Although there is no mention of a wife in Bishop Berkeley's will, he left the bulk of his property, and the lease of a house in Old Bailey, London, to Anne Smarthwett, the daughter of Roger Smarthwett of Dent in Yorkshire, who was the servant of 'old Mr. Field of Wakefield'. The son of that Mr Field, Matthew, a mercer of St Lawrence Lane in London, and James Smarthwett, brother of Anne, were made the supervisors of his will, and if it were challenged Anne Smarthwett was to bear the legal costs. A debt which James Smarthwett owed the bishop was cancelled, and a lad, Giles Smarthwett, was to receive £10 'to be paid by his aunt when he cometh at the age of one and twenty'.[2] It is therefore a question whether Anne was in reality the bishop's wife, married during Edward's reign when the marriage of clergy was allowed and perhaps 'put away' after Mary's accession. The Smarthwetts could have made Berkeley's acquaintance in the days when he was a Franciscan at York, and such a marriage would help to explain his flight to Frankfort. In that case Giles Smarthwett may well have been the bishop's unrecognized son. In 1580–81 a man of that name, otherwise unmentioned, was acting as the reeve of the bishop's manor of Huish, but by 1582, after the bishop's death, he had been replaced.[3] It was no position for a bishop's son to occupy, but there must have been many similar, sad stories in those changeful times. Yet a marriage between Gilbert Berkeley and Anne Smarthwett should not be too readily accepted as a fact; the registers of Dent in Yorkshire, which might have confirmed it, do not go back beyond 1611, except

[1] T. Fuller, *The History of the Worthies of England* (1840 edn.), III, 104.
[2] P.C.C. 43 Darcy.
[3] P.R.O. S.C.6/3545/82, S.C.6/Eliz./2011.

for one or two entries in 1596.[1] Other bishops' wills of the period openly acknowledge the existence of widows and of legal children, so that there is no obvious reason for Berkeley's failure to do so.[2] The relationship between him and Anne Smarthwett thus remains a matter of conjecture.

Anne does not seem to have been present at his deathbed. He had a severe illness in 1572 from which he never really recovered: he was confined to his room for a long period and suffered from sciatica for the rest of his life, which perhaps explains why he failed to tackle his problems more energetically. He eventually died of a 'lethargy' at the age of eighty.[3] His will was read over to him in the early evening of 31 October 1581 in the presence of John Middleham, notary public, and three others while he was still 'in perfect memory'. Two days later the man of eighty who had been Franciscan friar, Oxford scholar, country rector, Marian exile, and harassed bishop, passed away. Perhaps the bishop had been thinking of the Bruton Berkeleys, who, according to tradition, were always buried by torchlight, when he expressed this wish in his will:

my body to be buried where it shall be thought good to my friends according to my calling without torchlight or suchlike vanities

He was buried in his own cathedral.

[1] I am indebted to the Rev. Dr S. G. Bennett, formerly vicar of Dent, for this information.

[2] Professor W. M. Southgate has confirmed this point in the course of his study of Bishop Jewel and kindly gave me this information.

[3] Fuller, *Worthies*, II, 447.

CHAPTER IV

The Dissolution and Recovery

THE PROTECTOR SOMERSET'S
GAINS FROM THE BISHOP

BISHOPS' families were indeed an economic burden on episcopal estates, but they by no means account for the disasters which befell the Bath and Wells endowment in the mid-sixteenth century, when it was almost completely dissolved. The crucial time was the rule of Bishop Barlow (1547–53), and the crucial fact was his relationship with the Protector Somerset.

The reasons given for Barlow's promotion from St Davids were 'not only his singular learning' but also that he who had been faithful in little things should be promoted to greater.[1] Yet it is held that the Protector Somerset's personal recommendation achieved Barlow's appointment, and since Somerset's influence was predominant in the see until his fall, and he acquired much wealth from the episcopate during Barlow's tenure of it, this may well be so.

The Protector had a special reason for coveting the estates of Bath and Wells: he had already acquired many of the manors of dissolved houses in Somersetshire, of Glastonbury, Muchelney and Athelney, and he seems to have been trying to build up a solid concentration of power in the western parts. Had he maintained his position he would undoubtedly have been the mightiest man there. Barlow's extreme subservience to him is not surprising if one considers that Somerset's own power was so great, that Barlow had already lost two powerful patrons, Anne Boleyn and Cromwell, and could not afford to lose another, that his Lutheran opinions had already made him unpopular in one diocese, and that he was soon to become hated in another.

[1] *Wells*, II, 266.

To whom could such a man turn for support in the face of Somerset's demands?[1]

Moreover Barlow was not exceptional in transferring possessions to Somerset. Henry Holbeach, bishop of Lincoln, received his temporalities on 19 August 1547, and two days later he conveyed to Somerset the great manors of Thame, Dorchester, Banbury, Woburn and others. Other grants were made to the Crown, and the income of the bishopric of Lincoln was reduced from £1,962. 17. 4d. in 1535 to £828. 4. 9d. under Edward VI.[2] The ideas propounded under Henry VIII for the gradual disendowment of the bishops and the reduction of them to stipendaries were still fermenting. Ponet at Winchester in 1551 had to exchange the endowments of his bishopric for an annual income of 2,000 marks; a similar bargain was made with Hooper at Gloucester in 1552. The new see of Westminster was suppressed as superfluous. The Duke of Northumberland in 1553 was engaged on the dissolution of the rich see of Durham, which was to be replaced by two bishoprics of Newcastle and Durham with fixed stipends.[3]

No intelligible account has ever been given of the vicissitudes in the endowment of the bishopric of Bath and Wells in Barlow's time. The series of grants and regrants of manors is indeed at first sight confusing and apparently meaningless; the manor of Wells, an extreme example, changed hands no less than six times during Edward's reign. One historian takes refuge in a supposed scheme of refoundation, while the *Victoria County History*'s contribution to the argument, that some of these estates may have been transferred to the duke with a view to their being re-transferred to Bishop Barlow, is not very convincing.[4] Apart from the fact that the reduction of the bishoprics was a popular idea and that some of the manors would have gone to the Crown no matter who was in power, the clue to the fluctuations in the episcopal estates lies in the fluctuations of the career of Somerset himself. Only in the context of Somerset's story can meaning be found in them.

[1] *D.N.B.*; Collinson, I, B, 6, 39, 47.
[2] *Lincoln Chapter Acts 1547–59*, (Linc. Rec. Soc., xv) pp. viii–ix.
[3] T. M. Parker, *The English Reformation to 1558*, p. 138.
[4] Hunt, *Bath and Wells*, p. 175; *V.C.H. Somerset*, II, 37.

When William Barlow came to Wells in February 1548 he succeeded to twenty-four manors: they were Banwell, Bishops Lydeard, Blackford, West Buckland, Chard, Cheddar, Chew Magna, Claverton, Compton Bishop, Compton Parva (Berkshire), Congresbury, East Cranmore, Evercreech, Hampton (or Bathampton), Huish Episcopi (Hewish), Kingsbury, Pucklechurch (Gloucestershire), Wellington, Wells, Westbury, Westerleigh (Gloucestershire), Wiveliscombe, Wookey and Yatton. He also held the London property of the Minories; the site and lands of the dissolved Hospital of St John, Wells, which carried with it the advowson of the rectories of Evercreech in Somerset and Westdown in Devon; the townships of Axbridge, Chard, Wells, Wellington and Wiveliscombe; the palace and some rents in Bath; and the rights of the liberty of Wells and the hundreds of Chew, Kingsbury, Pucklechurch, Wells Forum and Winterstoke. Of this accumulation of property the only portions which the bishop was to retain untouched throughout his episcopate were the manor and hundred of Kingsbury, the manor of West Buckland and the manor and township of Wiveliscombe, although he was never at any one point reduced to holding these alone.

The first of the encroachments was made three months after Barlow came to Wells, when on 20 May 1548 he yielded to the king the lordships and manors of Claverton, Hampton, Lydeard, Compton Magna (Compton Bishop), Compton Parva,[1] Chard, Cheddar and Huish, the borough of Chard, the lordships and manors of Pucklechurch and Westerleigh, the hundred of Pucklechurch, and various lands in these manors and in Axbridge, Stoke Gifford, the city of Bath, the borough of Wells, Wells Forum, Westdown, Pynkesmore, Evercreech, East Walls next Wells, Southdever and London.[2] Cheddar, eventually, and Compton Bishop, went to the Protector Somerset, but most of these properties served to increase the wealth of the Crown, after the manner of the monastic lands; only the manors of Compton Parva, Chard and Huish, the boroughs of Chard and Wells, the hundred of Wells Forum and the rectory of Westdown were ever recovered for the bishopric.

[1] Of Berkshire, although described as 'of Somerset'.
[2] *C.P.R. 1548–49*, p. 128.

The manor of Claverton remained in crown hands until 1550 when on 1 August it was sold to Matthew Colthurst. The manor, with the advowson of the rectory and the closes called Bishops Park, Shortwood and Hampton Cliff, was valued at £24. 11. 5½d. and was sold to him for twenty times that amount, £491. 9. 2d.[1] The manor of Hampton was in the king's hands longer, but on 15 March 1553 it went to William Crowche of Wellow and Susan his wife. Crowche had been the Protector's receiver in Somerset, at least from 1542 to 1547.[2] He had to pay more heavily than Colthurst, being charged at twenty-six years' purchase on an annual value of £18. 11. 0½d., or £482. 7. 1d., but for that he also received the hundred of Hampton. Crowche was also liable for the fee of Robert Hemyngton the bailiff, at £1. 6. 8d., and that of the reeve, 9s.[3] One of the principal gentlemen of the privy chamber, Sir Thomas Wroth, acquired the manor of Bishops Lydeard, valued at £30. 15. 4½d., on 28 December 1551, and since there is no record of a purchase price, the grant was presumably by way of reward.[4] Compton Bishop (or Compton Magna as it appears in the episcopal accounts) was taken by Somerset himself, and after his fall it was granted to John St John for forty years on 2 February 1552 at a rent of £49. 3. 9d.[5] The other Compton, the Berkshire Compton Parva, was at some stage returned to the bishopric, which had recovered it by 1556.[6]

On 17 August 1548, a few months after the Crown received the manor of Cheddar, it was granted to Sir Thomas Heneage, Sir William Willoughby and Lord Willoughby. The value placed on it was £53. 9. 5¼d., a year and there is no record of the purchase price, so it may have been a gift.[7] Heneage and his friends did not keep it for long. On 20 December they sold it, together with the manor of Marshfield, which was not an episcopal manor, to the Protector Somerset, in return for the

---

[1] P.R.O. S.C.6/Ed. VI/420, E.318/1535; *C.P.R. 1549–51*, p. 426.

[2] MSS of the Marquess of Bath, Seymour Papers, IV, 124. I am indebted to Dr Marjorie Blatcher who kindly allowed me to use her transcripts.

[3] P.R.O. S.C.6/Ed. VI/420, S.C.6/P. & M./257, E.318/1560; *C.P.R. 1553*, p. 86.

[4] P.R.O. S.C.6/Ed. VI/420, E.318/2108; *C.P.R. 1550–53*, p. 188.

[5] *Forfeited Lands of the Duke of Somerset*, ed. D. T. Phillips, p. 11.

[6] P.R.O. S.C.6/P. & M./263; S.R.O. DD/CC/31523.

[7] P.R.O. E.318/567; *C.P.R. 1548–49*, p. 120.

manor of Stowe which he had just acquired from the bishop of Lincoln—a nice example this of the courtiers' traffic in church lands. When Somerset fell from power in November 1549 the manor escheated to the Crown; it was probably regained by Somerset with other lands on 4 June 1550, but after his execution in January 1552 it reverted to the Crown. When on the following 6 September some of Somerset's property was given to his son, Sir Edward Seymour, the manor of Cheddar and the hundred of Winterstoke were included in the grant. Eventually Sir Edward Seymour was licensed on 16 May 1558 to make the well-known grant of Cheddar to Sir John Thynne, who had been his father's steward.[1]

Over eighty years later Bishop Peirs, in going over his list of property, questioned the nature of the liberty enjoyed by the holder of the hundred of Winterstoke. Was it, he penned in his notebook, a liberty in gross and therefore held independent of the ownership of land, or was it a liberty appendant to a manor? The implication was that if attached to a manor it had gone with the manor of Cheddar and had indubitably been lost to the bishopric in Barlow's time. Had it legally passed to the king on the attainder of the Duke of Somerset, and had it been included in the grant to Sir Edward Seymour?[2] The bishop's doubt whether the hundred of Winterstoke was appurtenant to the manor of Cheddar was unfounded; it had been so annexed to the manor when granted to the bishop by Henry III in 1230. At that date, and much later, it was not uncommon for the lordship of a hundred to be attached to a particular manor.[3]

The bishop's rights in the town of Axbridge, Stoke and Draycot, the city of Bath and the Hospital of St John, Wells, were kept by the Crown throughout Edward's reign.[4] Although the Crown also acquired the manors of Pucklechurch and Westerleigh and the hundred of Pucklechurch, it is confusing to find that eleven days after the date of that grant Barlow gave a lease of these properties to Sir Nicholas Poyntz of

[1] Seymour Papers, Box I fo. 124 ff.; P.R.O. S.C.6/Ed. VI/420; *C.P.R. 1550–53*, p. 441; *1557–58*, p. 232.
[2] S.R.O. DD/CC/13324, fo. 347.
[3] H. M. Cam, *Liberties and Communities in Medieval England*, pp. 64, 66.
[4] P.R.O. S.C.6/Ed. VI/420, S.C.6/P. & M./257.

Iron Acton, Gloucestershire, a prominent courtier; the lease was to run for forty-two years at a rent of £80. 3. 3¾d. The discrepancy may be explained by the time-lag between London and Wells, but whatever the significance of the lease it is clear that both manors were being administered by the court of augmentations in Edward's reign. The subsequent history of the manor of Westerleigh is also clear: it was granted to Poyntz outright on 8 December 1552, and it was then worth £40. 16. 2d.[1]

The history of Pucklechurch is more confused; it seems that Sir Nicholas Poyntz and another courtier, Sir William Herbert, were jockeying to establish rights there. In 1550 Herbert was trying to get the manor and hundred of Pucklechurch from the Crown; he put in a request to purchase on 10 April 1550 at the same time trying to get the park at Evercreech which had also by now been taken from the bishop. He did not get the manor and hundred of Pucklechurch, but only the park of Evercreech on 7 May, and although the grant, as made out, included Pucklechurch Park, that part of it cannot have been valid, for Poyntz had somehow got hold of the park, which he retained until he sold it to the Crown at the end of 1552.[2] And a very pretty piece of enclosure Poyntz carried out while he had it. The transaction was summarized by Thomas Dutton, the surveyor, who wrote that the park was

now measured, divided and enclosed into several pastures and meadows by lugge[3] acres allowing to every perch or lugge 18 feet according to the covenants made between Sir Nicholas and the forenamed lessees as plainly appears by their indentures. I know not nor can learn the old rent thereof nor the improvement for that the same was always used to be replenished with deer and kept by a keeper and never let at any certain rent until now of late by the said Sir Nicholas . . . but now at this present the same is very good mead and pasture and the tenants offer to be bound to give a hundred pounds to fine for 40 years more than is in their leases.

The names of 'the forenamed lessees', the dates of their indentures, the amounts and names of their holdings, and the

---

[1] D.N.B.; Wells, II, 266; P.R.O. E.318/1889; C.P.R. 1550–53, p. 401.

[2] P.R.O. E.318/1687; C.P.R. 1550–53, p. 31.

[3] A lug is a pole or perch, varying according to local custom, usually 16½ feet, O.E.D.

duration of their interests are all set out. The great park was divided up into twenty-nine holdings of which eleven were let for three lives and eighteen for twenty-one years. There seems to have been no guiding principle of size or price to determine which holding fell into which category. The amount of each holding varied from five to twenty-five acres. The first enclosure took place on 27 May 1550, three more on 10 June, nineteen on 18 November, one on 10 December, one on 14 March 1551, three on 20 March, and the last one on 1 June. The total annual value to Sir Nicholas of this improvement was £87. 10. 6d., but there was an ancient rent reserved to the Crown of £5. 6. 8d., giving him clear £82. 3. 10d. The entire manor, inclusive of the park, had been worth only £43. 17. 7½d. in 1539. But Sir Nicholas was in debt to the Crown for £806. 18. 8d., and so it was in a strong bargaining position when on 8 December 1552 it acquired from him the manor of Westerleigh, and also the park of Pucklechurch. The Crown then had complete control of Pucklechurch manor, hundred and park; but it was Poyntz' old rival who was to prevail, for on 25 June 1553 Sir William Herbert, now Earl of Pembroke, acquired the manor and hundred, but not the park, which the Crown retained.[1]

On 13 January 1553, at a time when the Duke of Northumberland was planning to advance Lady Jane Grey to the throne, the Minories property which had come to the Crown with the grant from Bishop Barlow of 20 May 1548 went to Jane's father, Henry, Duke of Suffolk: it was a fitting residence for a prominent courtier. The grant covered the capital house called 'le Mynery House', a stable, three gardens, the great messuage or garden lately in the tenure of Elizabeth, Countess of Kildare, and eight messuages, including the Friars' Hall and the bakehouse, both leased to Ralph Pilkington. Other East London properties also went with the Minories: five messuages in St Botolph's parish without Aldgate, a messuage and garden in Tower Street, three shops in Old Fish Street, and a messuage in Paternoster Row: the value of it all was £37. 11. 5½d. Five months later, on 23 May 1553, Suffolk was licensed to grant the property to Lords Thomas and John Grey (his brothers), George Medley (his half-brother), and John Harington. The Greys lost their share

[1] P.R.O. S.C.6/Hen. VIII/3076; *C.P.R. 1550–53*, p. 406; *C.P.R. 1553*, p. 175.

when they were attainted after Wyatt's rebellion of January 1554, which perhaps explains why the Catholic Bishop Bourne was back in residence there from at least 30 April to 20 May of that year: he may have prevailed on the queen to return at least part of the property to the bishopric. But the next bishop did not keep it. On 24 April 1559 Lord John Grey recovered two parts of it and Medley still had his share. In 1562 they sold it to the Marquess of Winchester, who bought up certain remaining terms of leases which had been granted by the bishop of Bath and Wells for ninety-one years. On 22 September 1563, at Winchester's instance, the property was conveyed to the queen for the storage of ordnance, and in 1565 a keeper of the gate was appointed in anticipation of the receipt of stocks of arms, guns and other munitions.[1]

The lands included in the grant to the king of 20 May 1548 which eventually returned to the bishop were the manor and borough of Chard and the manor of Huish. Chard was among the properties still held by the Crown on 22 January 1550 and valued at £73. 5. 5½d., but on 15 February it was granted back to the bishop who, six days later, leased it away to his high steward, Sir Hugh Paulet, on a ninety-nine year lease at £50 a year for a fine of 100 marks. This was a real triumph for the Paulets, a long lease on favourable terms of a manor and township very near their seat, Hinton St George, and the lease was to hold good for its full term, until 1649. From the bishop's point of view this was probably not a bad deal. He was sure of an income, although a reduced one, from an outlying property and, more important, he could count on the patronage of the powerful Paulets. The manor of Huish, valued at £67. 15. 5½d., too, was returned to the bishop with Chard on 15 February 1550, and it never left the bishop's hands again.[2]

So much for the grant to the Crown of 20 May 1548 and the subsequent history of the properties involved. The next savage onslaught on the episcopal endowment came on 9 July of that year when the Protector Somerset was the beneficiary: he took

[1] *C.P.R. 1550–53*, p. 406; *1553*, p. 5; *1558–60*, p. 82; *1563–64*, p. 303; S.R.S., LV, 122, Tomlinson, *Minories*, pp. 112–19.

[2] P.R.O. S.C.6/Ed. VI/420, S.C.6/P. & M./257, E.318/1412; *C.P.R. 1549–51*, p. 180; Wells Museum Notebook, fo. 243.

the very heart of the see, Wells itself, six other manors, and further property. The full list comprised the manors of Banwell, Wells, Chew, Blackford, Wellington, Cranmore and Ever-creech; the borough of Wellington; the hundreds of Winterstoke (which had temporarily become separated from the manor of Cheddar), Chew and Wells Forum (and, it would seem from the grant of 15 February 1550 returning the property, the borough and liberty of Wells); the parks of Wells, Banwell and Evercreech; and all kinds of liberties belonging to those manors. This grant was confirmed by the dean and chapter on 12 July.[1] The bulk of this property was lost to the bishop for all time: only Wells and Banwell were eventually recovered. Of the manors which were lost for ever, that of Chew Magna came to the Crown on the attainder of the Protector Somerset in January 1552. It continued to be held by the Crown until Elizabethan times, although on 22 October 1552 it was leased to Richard Goodrich, attorney of the court of augmentations, for twenty-one years at a yearly rent of £101. 15. 5½d. and on 18 July 1561 this lease was renewed for a further twenty-one years to run from the date when the old one expired. In 1574 Elizabeth I granted part of the manor to Robert, Earl of Leicester, and in 1574–6 another part went to Sir Christopher Hatton. In 1591 the entire manor was granted to Lord Burghley, who in the same year sold it to Lord Lumley, and eventually it came to the Pophams and the Babers.[2] The manor of Blackford likewise came to the king on the attainder of the Protector Somerset, and then passed to John Dudley, Duke of Northumberland, his rival. The grant to Dudley was dated 2 March 1553, but his enjoyment of it was also transitory. When he in turn was attainted later in 1553 the manor reverted once more to the Crown, and eventually it was granted to a trio, Thomas, Duke of Norfolk, Sir Edward Fynes and Lord Clinton and Saye, on 22 January 1560.[3]

By now the depletion of the bishopric must have been apparent, and yet Somerset's demands were not satisfied. He was after the manor of Wookey, and he had his way. On

[1] *C.P.R. 1547–48*, p. 275; *Wells*, II, 266–7.
[2] *C.P.R. 1558–60*, p. 31; Wood, *Chew Magna*, pp. 37–8.
[3] *C.P.R. 1558–60*, p. 249.

10 October 1548 Bishop Barlow was licensed to alienate the manor (as it was disingenuously expressed) 'to whomsoever he will', although it was not until 4 February 1549 that the grant to Somerset was confirmed by the dean and chapter.[1] But because 'the possessions of the bishopric of Bath and Wells are now much diminished by reason of the above grant of manors and lands to the king and divers other grants from the residue of its possessions', Bishop Barlow was given some compensation. He was released from the payment of the first-fruits due in his translation to this new bishopric, and it was agreed that on all future appointments to the bishopric the first-fruits should be commuted for £479. 15. 1½d., and that the yearly tenth due on the bishopric should be fixed at £53. 6. 1½d. In addition the bishop was given certain rectories which had belonged to dissolved religious houses: St John Baptist and St Benignus in Glastonbury, Bradley and West Pennard, Northlode, East Brent, East Pennard, and Weston Zoyland, all of which had belonged to Glastonbury Monastery, and Corston, Compton Dando and Castle Cary which had belonged to Bath Priory. But even this grant was not unencumbered; a rent of £8. 3. 5d. was reserved to the Crown which was being paid in Stuart times.[2]

Even now the confiscation of the episcopal endowments was not halted. Two more manors, Congresbury and Yatton, went to the king on 24 January 1549, although confirmation by the dean and chapter was delayed until 1 March. How much one would like a record of the discussions of that chapter meeting; surely indignation and dismay abounded, and the chapter must have wondered if anything would be spared. The valuable manor of Congresbury with the advowson went on 4 July 1553 on a thirty-six year lease to one of the physicians who had been trying to save the king's life at least until a Protestant succession under Jane Grey or her son could be assured. Accounts show that George Owen, the grantee, paid £101. 16. 9d. a year for it, but he had to allow £4. 13. 4d. a year for the repair of the seabanks. Queen Mary, on 22 June 1554, granted a portion of this rent, £54, to Francis Hastings, Earl of Huntingdon,

---

[1] *C.P.R. 1548–49*, p. 128; *Wells*, ii, 268.
[2] *C.P.R., 1548–49*, p. 128; S.R.O. DD/CC/13324, fo. 355.

and Katherine his wife. On 7 July this grant was reworded: the Hastings were now to have 'the reversion of the said rent', that is, the reversion of the lands producing that part of the rent when the lease to George Owen should fall in in 1589. George and Richard Owen apparently bought out the Hastings' rights, and they sold their lease to John Carr, alderman of Bristol, who gave it to that city to the use of an orphans' hospital.[1]

The Crown retained the manor of Yatton for many years although it was already the subject of a lease made by Thomas Matthew, the bishop's auditor, to Thomas Semarke at a rent of £47. 6. 8d. In 1591 it was granted to Richard Lewkenor, serjeant-at-law, and nine others, who on 9 October 1598 sold it to Sir Nicholas Stalling.[2] Neither Congresbury nor Yatton ever reverted to the bishop. The traffic in these episcopal manors, the leases, sales and resales, was similar to the trade in monastic lands: in the first instance the grant nearly always went to a courtier or an official at the centre and only at the second or third stage did a local family, like the Pophams in gaining Chew Magna, acquire an interest.

With the aid of this enrichment, the chief beneficiary, the Protector Somerset, was predominant in the West as elsewhere. His servant Richard Fulmerston was able to write to him on 8 May 1549: 'I am near to Glastonbury, Wells and your other lands and parks in these parts.'[3] But in the autumn of that year the grasping Somerset fell from power. On 14 October the intrigues of the rest of the council landed him in the Tower. Somerset had yielded on being told that his rivals did not intend any hurt to him nor to take away any of his goods or lands. That last promise was not fully met. By virtue of an act passed on 4 November 1549 'touching the Fine and Ransome of the Duke of Somerset' certain lands were confiscated. Among these were the lands and rights in Cranmore, Evercreech, Wellington and Wells which had formerly belonged to the bishop and which now came to the Crown.[4]

---

[1] *C.P.R. 1549–51*, p. 180; *1553*, p. 304; *1553–54*, p. 187; *1555–57*, p. 283; P.R.O. S.C.6/Ed. VI/420; *Wells*, II, 268; Collinson, III, 585.

[2] P.R.O. S.C.6/Ed. VI/420; Collinson, III, 617.

[3] Seymour Papers, IV, 109.

[4] A. F. Pollard, *England under the Protector Somerset*, pp. 251 and n., 282 n., *Statute of the Realm*, 3 & 4 Edw. VI c.31, *C.P.R. 1549–51*, p. 180.

At this point in the career of Bishop Barlow, Somerset's first imprisonment, all that remained to support the bishop's family was the income from four manors, Kingsbury, West Buckland, Westbury and Wiveliscombe, and the eight rectories. Barlow was reduced to an income of £440. 18. 11d., but although his lands and rights in Wells had been taken, he still, presumably, inhabited the palace.[1] What must have been Barlow's feelings when, on 6 February 1550, Somerset was released from the Tower. But the duke was not to have any of his property restored until 27 May, and meanwhile, at least from 22 January, when a statement about the proposed deal had been drawn up, Barlow had been negotiating with the Crown to improve his financial position. The king had recently taken the manors of Yatton and Congresbury from the bishop, and, deducting their profits from the total of £440. 18. 11d. registered at the court of first fruits and tenths, he was now left with only £347. 15. 6d. So the manor and borough of Chard and the manor of Huish were returned to him, and he also recovered the manor of Wells, the hundred of Wells Forum, and the borough and liberty of Wells, which had been confiscated from Somerset. The total of that property was £332. 18. 11d., and it brought the bishop's income up to £680. 14. 5d.[2]

That was the best that the bishop could do to restore his position. On 4 June 1550 when, at his 'humble petition', much of Somerset's property in Somerset was restored to him, the grant included the manor and borough of Wellington, and the manors of Cranmore and Evercreech, old episcopal properties. The manor of Evercreech was no longer intact, as it had already been depleted by the grant of the park to Sir William Herbert on 7 May of that year. On Somerset's death in January 1552 the manor came once more to the Crown, which leased it to William Aylmer on 12 June for twenty-one years at £49. 17. 4½d. a year. In expectation of the reversion of that lease it was finally granted out to Lord John Grey on 24 April 1559.[3]

Although Somerset recovered the manor and borough of Wellington with the grant of 4 June 1550, he did not keep them

---

[1] P.R.O. E.318/1412.
[2] Pollard, p. 282; P.R.O. E.318/1412.
[3] *C.P.R. 1549–51*, p. 430; *1550–53*, p. 32; *1558–60*, p. 82; P.R.O. E.318/1687.

intact for long. On 2 December he restored the borough, the rent of certain meadows, the hundred silver and the demesne lands of Wellington to Bishop Barlow. The bishop in turn on 28 April 1552 granted his rights in Wellington *burgus*, that is the rents of certain free tenants worth £6. 9. 9½d., and the rents of demesne lands in Wellington worth £60. 2. 11½d., to the king, who on 2 March 1553 made them over to the Duke of Northumberland. When Northumberland, in his turn, fell they reverted to the Crown. This grant to Northumberland of 2 March 1553, after Somerset's fall, included, as we have seen, the manor of Blackford and the manor of East Cranmore. None of these manors, East Cranmore, Evercreech or Wellington, was ever recovered for the bishopric, and East Cranmore was on 13 April 1557 granted to Sir John Cheke and Peter Osborne.[1]

Unfortunately for Bishop Barlow, Somerset was interested not only in the bishopric, but also in the office of dean. Two successive nominees of his were deans of Wells in Barlow's time, and it was during Somerset's partial return to power in 1550 that trouble over the deanery came to a head. Dean William Fitzwilliam held the office at the accession of Edward VI, but early in 1548 he was persuaded to resign. The office of dean with all its dependencies was granted to Somerset, who had already received that of the archdeaconry of Wells, and John Goodman, who was a protégé of Sir John Thynne, Somerset's steward, was appointed. He was assigned, not the deanery, but a canonical house which had been occupied by Dr John Dakyn. An act was passed in the first parliament of the reign, as the chapter complained, by Dean Goodman and his friends, in other words the Somerset faction, for the re-erection of the deanery as a royal donative, endowed with the profits properly belonging to the archdeaconry, the sub-chantership, the prebend of Curry and the provostship. The archdeaconry was not restored until 1556 by Mary, and it was not until 1591 that the deanery and chapter were refounded by letters patent of Elizabeth I.[2]

---

[1] *C.P.R. 1549–51*, pp. 204–5; *1550–53*, p. 456; *1553*, p. 179; *1555–57*, p. 537; P.R.O. E.318/1412.

[2] *Wells*, II, 266, 269, 321; Hunt, *Bath and Wells*, p. 176; *Proc. Som. Arch. Soc.*, XII, 38–9.

The relationship between Bishop Barlow and a dean who was a creature of Somerset was not likely to be a happy one, and when, after his release, Somerset demanded the return of the lordship of Wells, with the bishop's own palace as well, matters became worse. They were complicated by the fact that Barlow was trying to remove Dean Goodman in favour of another Somerset protégé, William Turner. Dean Goodman started an action for damages in the court of kings bench and on 21 June a writ of *praemunire* was issued against Barlow and three of his officials. On 5 July 1550 the sheriff of Somerset warned Barlow that he must be ready to appear in court in the Michaelmas Term.[1]

It appears that, pending the hearing of the case, Dean Goodman maliciously tried to aggravate the differences between the Protector Somerset and the bishop. One of Somerset's dependants was John Berwick of Easton in Wiltshire, who had been his receiver in the county of Somerset from 1539 to 1549. On 2 August 1550 Goodman wrote to Berwick to urge him to go at once to the Protector and to tell him the truth about Barlow (whatever that might be), so that he might be the better prepared for an expected visit by the bishop. He also urged Berwick to be good to an honest poor man, presumably the bearer of the letter, whom the bishop had wronged. Berwick would see by the man's supplication how greedy the bishop was. Goodman added that the bishop was so uncharitable that the people no longer inclined to come to his sermons, and although in the past they had opposed the idea that Somerset might have the lordship of the bishopric, that is, the manor of Wells, they were now in such a mind that if Somerset had everything they would thank God heartily for it. He alleged that the bishop had expressed a derogatory opinion of Somerset: when Somerset was imprisoned a gentleman had asked the bishop what he thought of the affair, and, in the presence of Mr Heath, an acquaintance of Berwick, the bishop had replied that he had always thought that the duke would eventually be found a rank traitor.

Goodman also reported that the suffragan of Wells, who had returned after a long absence, went to the bishop and had a long conversation about the writ of *praemunire* and the palace,

---

[1] *C.P.R. 1549–51*, p. 211; Ridley, *Thomas Cranmer*, pp. 310–11.

which Somerset wanted. Finally, the bishop said that he would
not surrender the palace to the duke unless he were commanded
to do so by the king and council, for the duke had once made a
fool of him and deceived him, but he should never do so again.

Dean Goodman continued that now, however, Barlow was
content to let Somerset have the lordship and the palace,
provided that he was given an equal recompense. The bishop
had sent his wife up to London and was to follow himself shortly
by way of Reading, in order to obtain the duke's favour. He had
also despatched one of his servants in advance to Reading
(where presumably Somerset was staying) to prepare a household there, for he intended to stay in London and to make suit
to the lords of the council. Goodman urged Berwick that if
Somerset was not informed speedily of these things the bishop
would, on arrival, act generously about the lordship and the
palace and hope thereby to creep into Somerset's favour again.
The duke should be warned not to trust Barlow further than he
could see, or he would be deceived: 'you shall understand that
the praemunire sinketh sore in his stomach now and that is
one cause that maketh him to seek my lord's grace favour.'
Goodman had a favourable reply from Berwick and on
August 5 he wrote again from Wells saying that he hoped to be
with him soon. The bishop, he reported, had received letters
from the king and the council, and was resigned to the fact
that he must relinquish the lordship of Wells, but he was now
fighting for conditions. He declared that he would not depart
until he had received equal compensation, and that he trusted
neither the word of the king nor the council.

Goodman added that the bishop had little local support and
that if he were put out headlong the people would rejoice at it.

They hate him, and not only for religion, for those who favour the
reformed religion as much as he or more and used to come to his
sermons have now nearly forsaken him: for whereas the whole church
was too little to receive the congregation that used to resort to him,
now they might be received in a little chapel.

The cause of his unpopularity was that, although he had
been a great preacher on the theme of charity, inveighing
against the covetous, like many other powerful landlords

of his time he was seeking to improve his holding at the expense of his tenants. (Considering how much he had lost there was some excuse for him.) His critics alleged that since he had acquired the lordship of Wells he had acted very uncharitably towards many of them, ejecting some from their holdings although they had firm title to them; and although he promised others, before reliable witnesses, that they should retain their holdings, these too had been expelled, contrary to his promise and all good justice. Another example of his covetousness was the flock of sheep which he kept upon the common of Mendip, to the great hindrance of his poor tenants, about which they were shortly to make a suit to the council. If anyone incurred his displeasure he commonly used the pulpit for his revenge. For all these reasons the people hated him so much that they would gladly tear him with their teeth. Much of Goodman's report was probably malice and special pleading, but there must have been some truth in it.[1]

When the Michaelmas term came the *praemunire* case went forward. On 18 October 1550 Barlow was granted a special licence to send Thomas Gawdye and John Welshe as his legal representatives to appear before the king in chancery. Whether this was before or after Barlow had failed to appear on the appointed day is not clear, but in any case he and John Smythe of Wells, a clerk who was charged with him, were pardoned on 12 November and goods which had been forfeited were restored to them.[2]

Somerset now inflicted the unkindest cut of all and took the very heart of the episcopal estates. On 2 December the bishop's palace at Wells, with its buildings, orchards, gardens, ponds, fishponds and grounds, and the house for keeping convicted clerks, passed into Somerset's hands. A ducal home indeed! With it went the manor of Wells and the borough and hundred of Wells Forum, for the second time, and also the manor of Westbury, which the bishop had succeeded in keeping until now. These estates, at their 1552 values, and excluding the palace on which it was found to be impossible to put a value, were worth £171. 13. 2¾d., and with them Somerset also acquired the prebend of Dultingcote, which was not a part

[1] P.R.O. S.P.10/10/19 and 20.   [2] *C.P.R. 1549–51*, pp. 211, 222.

of the episcopal endowment but which the bishop presumably held at that time.

But Somerset had to part with some of his possessions for so rich a prize. In lieu of the palace the bishop received from him the deanery at Wells, which again could not be valued, and lands in Somerset valued at £124. 16. 2d. These were the manor and hundred of West Coker, value £13. 9. 9d.; the bishop's old borough of Wellington, value £6. 5. 5½d.; some rents of demesne land in Wellington, value £60. 2. 11½d.; rents coming from Wedmore Park with the woods there, value £7; rents from the park called Old Park in Wedmore in the tenure of John Mawdelyn; an annuity of £17 from the manor of Glastonbury; rents from the borough of Stogursey, value £7 19s.; the vicarage of Mark, value £13. 6. 8d.; and the rents from the meadows and the hundred silver in Wellington, value 12s. 4d. It was probably also at this time that the bishop received the lodge and park at Sharpham from Somerset, and perhaps the £400 which he afterwards confessed he had once received from him. This unhappy grant was confirmed by the dean and chapter on 10 December 1550.[1]

Early in the next year Barlow's enemy, Dean Goodman, was removed from office, but his place was taken by Dr William Turner, Somerset's physician, who was installed by the king's command on 24 March 1551. He was not yet ordained, but held the post as a layman, although as one of the early Cambridge gospellers and a pupil of Ridley he had gone about preaching in a coarse and witty manner. His extreme views had led to imprisonment in the reign of Henry VIII, and then to a period of exile when he studied physic and took a degree in medicine in Italy. He had already written a small herbal, but on his return to England he became physician to the duke and wrote the larger one by which he acquired some fame. Soon after his appointment as dean on 10 April 1551 Turner was licensed to be non-resident from Wells without loss of emoluments, so long as he was preaching the gospel in other parts of the kingdom. But his triumph was a short one. He could have been none too secure after Somerset's fall at the end of the year, and at Mary's accession he was deprived and once more went into

[1] P.R.O. E.318/1412; *C.P.R. 1549–51*, pp. 204–5; *Wells*, II, 272.

exile in Germany. At least by 6 March 1554 John Goodman was back in Wells acting as dean.[1]

There throughout 1551 the bishop lived, presumably in the deanery, biding the outcome of political manoeuvre at the centre. Eventually his persecutor Somerset was arrested a second time, on 16 October, brought to trial and executed on 22 January 1552. His lands were confiscated by an act of the parliament which met the next day. But his successor Northumberland was even less sympathetic to the episcopacy than Somerset had been: he was in fact proceeding with the dissolution of the bishopric of Durham for his own advantage, so that Barlow had to wait for restitution. In the meantime Sir John Gates, vice-chamberlain to the king and captain of the guard, and an intimate of Northumberland, is said to have acquired the palace and to have stripped the great hall of its timber and lead. He certainly received the king's permission on 21 June 1552 to take over the lady chapel with all its stone, lead, glass, timber and iron and to rid the ground of all rubble, leaving it fair and plain.[2]

Finally, the interest of the bishop prevailed: one would like to know by what considerations. A grand reshuffle of property was put in motion and details were drawn up on 4 July. Barlow gave back to the Crown all the property which he had received from Somerset in December 1550, including the dean's house. In return the bishop received back what he had parted with, his palace at Wells, the manor and borough of Wells, the hundred of Wells Forum and the manor of Westbury with the park, all valued, as before, at £171. 13. 2¾d. Yet the bishop was again the loser: a perpetual annuity of £10 was reserved to the king from the manor of Wells. One finds this item running through the accounts decade after decade: its origin obviously puzzled Bishop Peirs when making up his accounts in early Stuart times, for he noted: 'I do not know yet why this is paid.'[3]

Even now the bishop's humiliations were not ended. The

---

[1] *Wells*, ii, 273, 277; Hunt, pp. 177–80.

[2] Pollard, Somerset, p. 308; Seymour Papers, Box I; Phelps, ii, 91; *Wells*, ii, 274.

[3] P.R.O. E.318/1412; *C.P.R. 1550–53*, p. 456; S.R.O. DD/CC/13324, fo. 356.

manor of Wookey, which had been granted to Somerset on 4
February 1549, had apparently reverted to Barlow on Somerset's execution in 1552, for on 4 February 1553 it was granted
away by the bishop to the king, the dean and chapter's approval
being given on 8 April. This proved to be a permanent alienation, but the Crown did not retain it for long. On 16 April 1553
it was sold to William and Mary Dunch. The value put on it
was £48. 11. 2½d., which, at twenty-six years' purchase, cost the
Dunches £1,262. 11. 5d. They had to continue the customary
allowances of 8s. for the reeve, 8s. for the hayward, and 10s. to
the rector there for the pasture of a bull and eight oxen. Well-
wooded Wookey: the grant also carried with it fifty-six acres of
woodland and the timber in the closes belonging to the sixty-
two tenements there, all of which was worth £34. 10. 8d. and
shows that enclosure had been effected there. William Dunch
was another London bureaucrat filching episcopal lands: he
was an official in the audit of the mint during the reigns of
Henry VIII and Edward VI. His family retained Wookey
until 1 September 1626 when they sold it to the Rolles of
Devonshire. The bishop's granting away of the manor did
not apparently disturb Thomas Clerk's lease of the mansion
house for, it will be remembered, he died there two years
later.[1]

The bishop's enjoyment of his palace again was brief, but
to him must be given the credit, before he went into exile in
Mary's reign, of having achieved something towards the recon-
stitution of the episcopal estates, although he was guilty of the
last-minute lease to his son of the Glastonbury rectory. Then
for the winter of 1553-4 the bishopric was left vacant, and during that time, on 14 December, some of the Wells demesnes were
leased out by the Crown to William Tarry, a yeoman, for twenty-
one years. The lease covered the 40-acre close called Rowdon's
Close let for £4 a year and a 19-acre close of pasture called
Wykemead let for 40s. a year. Bishop Berkeley later on grumbled
about this lease.[2]

---

[1] *Wells*, II, 275; P.R.O. E.318/1589; *C.P.R. 1553*, p. 59; Scott Holmes, *Wookey*,
pp. 65-8. Scott Holmes gives a transcript of the grant to Dunch, but it is not
accurate.

[2] *C.P.R. 1553-54*, p. 319.

SOME RESTITUTION FOR BISHOP BOURNE

It was not Wells, in any case, which was to be the centre of interest of the new bishop, Bourne, but Wiveliscombe, where he 'made his most abiding' and where he was surrounded by the family of his brother Richard. On account of 'the tender zeal and love' which he bore to its inhabitants, as well as for the relief and comfort of the great multitude of poor people there, he made a special concession to them. As lord of the manor and borough of Wiveliscombe the bishop took certain profits from the markets and fairs there, and in 1559 he granted to Roger Bryckley and Richard Hill, churchwardens, and seventeen others in trust for ninety-nine years all his shambles, stalls and standings in the market-place lately in the tenure of Robert Story and Peter Prowes, and the ground on which the stalls stood, which was about sixty-one feet in length and eight feet in breadth. He also granted them the profits arising from those stalls on market days and fair days coming from persons who were not inhabitants of the town, and the site of a cross called Rye Cross with eighteen square feet of ground adjoining. The date of the grant, 3 January 1559, when Bourne must have realized that his episcopate was at an end, suggests that he may have wished to establish a memorial of himself there. He also left to the parishioners of Wiveliscombe the profits from weighing all yarn and wool coming into the market, which was presumably a form of toll assessed on weight. The proceeds were to be used to build a prison-house on the plot of ground at Rye Cross, and also a market-house 'for market people to stand dry in the market time': it was probably one on pillars so that the people could shelter underneath, like the one at Wells. The rights of Peter Gregory and his wife Alice in certain stalls were reserved, but they were to pay the bishop's lessees 12d. a year for them. The lessees themselves were to pay the bishop a small rent.

The lease was confirmed by the dean and chapter and the good folk of Wiveliscombe enjoyed the bounty of Bishop Bourne in peaceful and quiet manner until 1594 when Dame Winifred Bond, whose family had obtained a lease of the manor, challenged the existence of Bishop Bourne's lease. She alleged that the rent she received for the shambles did not cover their reasonable repair, which was probably true since prices had risen. The case came into chancery. The result is not known, but Dame Winifred may have been successful. There is no record of the lessees paying a rent to the bishop in Bishop Still's time.[1]

Bishop Bourne is credited with having done something to regain confiscated church lands. He recovered his London residence, the Minories,[2] but his most notable reconquest for himself was the second richest of the original episcopal manors, that of Banwell. Since the fall of Somerset this manor had been in the Crown's hands and had had imposed upon it at least two leases for twenty-one years each. On 17 December 1553 the queen's servant, Nicholas Singleton, was granted the parcels of land called Dayeslese (11 ac.), Hewares (6 ac.) and Redlandes furlong (7 ac.), excepting the woods and underwoods, at a total annual rent of 21s., and on 14 March 1555 William Huchynsen was given a lease of 8 acres in Cowley and 1 acre in Lordesmeade and all the lands called 'Gosee'.[3]

Earlier still, on 6 May 1552, not long after the execution of Somerset, the heart of the manor had been leased away to Sir William St Loe (Seyntloo), who already owned the nearby manors of Puxton and Churchill. He was given a twenty-one year interest in the bishop's palace at Banwell, all the houses and gardens within its site, and numerous lands and two mills in Westgarston, producing forty-four rents worth £53. 7. 5¼d. He was also given the keepership of Banwell Park and of the wild beasts there, and, allowing sufficient pasture for these animals, he was to have the rights of pasture and grazing for swine. But now on 23 April 1556 the lordship and manor of Banwell, which the Crown still retained, and all its lands and liberties, were made over to Bishop Bourne. The St Loe lease held good, of course, until 1573, but the reversion of it was specifically granted to the bishop, and meanwhile St Loe held it as of the bishop. It is probable that they came to some arrangement about the use of the palace, for Bishop Bourne was staying at Banwell for the first time in January and February of the next year.[4]

[1] P.R.O. C2/Eliz./S.12/38, S.C.6/Add./3545/84.   [2] See above, p. 90.
[3] *C.P.R. 1553–54*, p. 57; ibid. *1554–55*, p. 175.
[4] Bates Harbin, *Members for Somerset*, p. 116; S.R.S., LV, 148.

Yet high as the bishop and his uncle Sir John Bourne, the principal secretary, may have stood in royal favour, this restitution was dearly bought. The manor was henceforth burdened with a heavy rent resolute to the Crown. For the duration of the St Loe lease this was to be £113, but on its expiry the rent was to rise to £115. 8. 8d. The bishop also had to meet the fees of the manorial officers: 19s. 7½d. for the reeve, 12s. 3½d. for the beadle, 13s. 10½d. for the keeper of the water-courses, 11s. to the hayward and, a picturesque detail, 14s. 7½d. to the keeper of the swans. (Perhaps there were more swans at Banwell then than later, in Bishop Godwin's time, when there were two old swans, one of which was marked with the cross of St Andrew, and two young cygnets marked with the ragged staff.) In taking back Banwell Bishop Bourne also had to find a yearly pension of 6s. 8d. for John Hillacre and his son William, who looked after the park and the palace. The annuity to the Crown was an enormous liability, reducing the net profit of the manor to a negligible amount in some years, but the bishops continued to pay it to the Crown's receiver for Somerset through Elizabethan and Stuart times.[1] It is hard to reconcile with the usual view that Mary would have restored church lands if she could. The recovery of the episcopal estates, even the fraction that the bishops had regained, was costing dear. The manor of Wells was burdened with a reserved rent of £10, and now £115. 8. 8d. was loaded onto Banwell. Besides recovering one of his own manors, Bourne reacquired for the archdeacon of Wells all the lands properly belonging to him, and for the dean and chapter their parsonages of Dulverton and Long Sutton.[2]

Another interesting fact about Bishop Bourne's brief administration of the estates is that he brought the Waldegraves into it: Sir Edward Waldegrave was given the office of bailiff of the hundred of Wells Forum, although he exercised it through a deputy, the William Tarry who in December 1553 had acquired a lease of some of the Wells demesnes.[3] Sir Edward Waldegrave had been attached to the household of the queen

---

[1] *C.P.R. 1555–57*, p. 193; P.R.O. S.C.6/Add./3545/84; S.R.O. DD/CC/13324, fos. 355, 361.

[2] Phelps, II, 124.   [3] P.R.O. S.C.6/P. & M./263.

when she was but the Lady Mary, and on her accession he became a member of her privy council and master of the great wardrobe. He already owned lands in Somerset inherited from his grandmother, but on the attainder of the Duke of Suffolk he received the important manor of Chewton Mendip, right in the heart of the lead mining area. The Waldegraves were undoubtedly the most important Catholic family in Somerset in Bishop Bourne's time, but Sir Edward fell from power on his mistress's death and died in the Tower in September 1561. Although his descendants remained at Chewton Mendip, as they still do, they did not gain posts under the subsequent, Protestant bishops.

After the passing of the Act of Supremacy of 1559 and the consequent downfall of the Catholic Establishment, Bishop Bourne not only worked hard to bolster up the position of his brother Richard by giving him more leases of episcopal property, but he also appealed to one of the men who had swung into power with the new regime, a Protestant and one from Somerset who could be tempted with gleanings from the episcopal estates. That, at least, appears to be the significance of the grants made to Sir Edward Rogers in the autumn of 1559. Sir Edward was of Cannington in West Somerset, where he held monastic land. He had been imprisoned in Mary's reign, but was released in 1555 on a bond of £1,000. Immediately on her accession Elizabeth I made him a privy councillor and captain of the guard, and by the time Bishop Bourne gave him a lease of the manor of Wiveliscombe for twenty-one years at a rent of £78 7s. on 27 August 1559 he was also comptroller of the queen's household. Bishop Berkeley later referred to Bishop Bourne's having made this lease to Sir Edward 'immediately before his deprivation', but for some reason the lease was passed over to the bishop's brother Richard.[1]

Perhaps Rogers did not after all get Wiveliscombe because he was offered other compensation. On 12 October he was given three separate and consecutive leases of twenty-one years each, that is, until 1622, of the manor of Kingsbury at a rent of £111. 3. 1d. The hundred of Kingsbury was also leased to him for the first spell of twenty-one years for £7, and this

[1] Bates Harbin, pp. 120–1; *Wells*, II, 281. See p. 93 above.

lease was probably extended like that of the manor.[1] In the event the property in Kingsbury soon went to the Crown and Bishop Bourne had not succeeded in purchasing immunity.

THE PRICE PAID FOR RE-ESTABLISHMENT

With the deprivation of Bourne and the other Marian bishops came the question of the selection of the new establishment and of the terms on which the next generation of bishops should be appointed. The agitation against excessive episcopal wealth had not yet subsided, and the feeling that the prelates were too rich was not confined solely to the radical Protestants. The canons which Archbishop Pole made for the reform of the clergy in the convocation of 1555 had included the proposals that bishops should live strict and exemplary lives, not clothed in silk, nor having rich furniture, or large numbers of servants or horses. Episcopal tables should be frugal, with not more than three or four dishes, and, following the monastic idea of the avoidance of idle chatter, scripture and good books should be read during meals. Surplus revenues were to be spent on the poor or on breeding young scholars.[2] 'Surplus revenues' is indeed ironic in the context of the bishopric of Bath and Wells: one wonders if the reformers had any conception of the radical Edwardian reduction of revenues there.

Whether they had or not, the drive went on. On 11 April 1559 de Feria, the Spanish ambassador, reported that the question of depriving the bishoprics of their valuable possessions so that the queen could bestow them on whom she pleased had again been discussed in parliament. Fixed stipends for bishops coming from tithes and other small matters had again been proposed.[3] In fact a move had been made in that direction. Although in the spirit of the Elizabethan religious settlement it was a compromise, there was a very important act passed in the parliament of 1559 'giving Authority to the Queen's Majesty, upon the avoidance of any Archbishoprick or Bishop-rick, to take into her hands certain of the temporal possessions thereof, recompensing the same with parsonages impropriate

---

[1] *Wells*, II, 281.   [2] *Burnet's History of the Reformation*, ed. Pocock, II, 504.
[3] *Cal. S.P. Spanish 1558–67*, p. 50.

and tenths'. The Crown was authorized to appoint suitable persons to survey and value such estates 'as to your Majesty shall be thought meet and convenient to be taken into your Highness' Hands and Possession' and to return their clear yearly value by certificate into the court of exchequer. This bill was obviously popular with the laity: it passed rapidly through both houses. Introduced first in the Lords, it was read on three consecutive days, the third being 6 April when it was voted against by the archbishop of York, the bishops of London, Worcester, Coventry, Exeter, Chester and Carlisle and the abbot of Westminster. Bishop Bourne did not attend this parliament. The bill was brought from the Lords to the Commons the next day by Mr Weston and Dr Vaughan and read a first time. The second reading was the following day, 8 April, and the third and last on 17 April, when it passed, 134 being in favour and 90 against.[1]

This was the act which Elizabeth I used as a bargaining point with the new bishops who were to be elected, and it was by virtue of it that she gained her reputation as a despoiler of the church.[2] Not only did it sanction the Crown's taking temporalities, such as manors which could be improved and exploited, in return for parsonages and tenths, which were less capable of profit, during a vacancy, but it limited the granting of leases by bishops to twenty-one years or three lives, *except to the Crown*. Bishops could no longer grant unduly long leases, such as those granted by Bishop Barlow to the Paulets on the manor of Chard or by Bishop Bourne to Sir Edward Rogers for the manor of Kingsbury. This provision protected the interests of future generations of bishops and stabilized their economy, for the existing bishops were prevented from levying large fines for leases which could not be renewed for decades and which were a mortgage on the future. On the other hand, the power that the Crown now gained over bishops' lands was a profitable source of patronage, and the courtiers strove as vigorously as ever to acquire them.

The government certainly used its new powers cautiously, and the church was left leaderless while the details were settled.

---

[1] 1 Eliz. c.19; D'Ewes, *Journal*, pp. 26, 53–4.
[2] R. W. Dixon, *History of the Church of England*, v, 188.

In August 1559 Sir William Cecil and the lord treasurer, the Marquess of Winchester, were still poring over the 'book of the bishops' lands', doubtless debating what should be taken.[1] On 26 October the queen wrote to Winchester and the barons of the exchequer reminding them that the consecration of the archbishop of Canterbury and the other bishops was held up because the exchange of temporalities was not yet completed, and commanding them to proceed with all expedition. The bishop of Bath was specifically mentioned as one of those who could well spare some of his rich endowments.[2] The new churchmen were not entirely subservient, Protestant reformers though they were. Matthew Parker, archbishop elect of Canterbury, and four other bishops elect, Grindal of London, Cox of Ely, Scory of Hereford and our old friend William Barlow, now of Chichester, wrote to Elizabeth to protest against the 'present alteration and exchange'. They tried to buy her off with an annual pension of 1,000 marks from the province of Canterbury as long as they should hold office. They begged the queen, if the exchange must go through, to take account of eleven articles of petition which they appended.

The gist of the bishops' demands in these articles was that in making valuations for the proposed exchanges full account should be taken of the charges liable to fall to them as the new owners of impropriated benefices, such as the upkeep of chancels and mansions, and the pensions and the cost of chant books which also had to be met from rectorial incomes. In fixing the equivalent recompense for the manors, the queen should remember that the bishops would lose the casual profits, such as the perquisites of courts and sales of wood. They begged that even if manors were granted away, corn, sheep, fowl and fish, with carriage (presumably the right to claim carriage from their tenants in certain circumstances) and other commodities should remain to them for the maintenance of hospitality, a suggestion which would seem very impractical to operate. They also asked that arrears of subsidies incurred by their Marian predecessors should be forgiven, that they should be granted retro-

[1] *Cal. S.P.D. 1547–80*, p. 136.
[2] *Parker's Correspondence 1535–75*, ed. J. Bruce and T. T. Perowne (1853), pp. 101–2.

spectively the half-year's rents due at Michaelmas, and that their payment of first-fruits might be abated and spread over a longer period.[1]

Their prayers were not granted, their dioceses were ransomed, although the new bishop of Bath and Wells, Gilbert Berkeley, got off very lightly compared with the others, perhaps because he was the queen's chaplain and because his bishopric had already been seriously depleted. Sir James FitzJames of Red-lynch, Henry Portman of Orchard, John Mawdelyn of Wells, John Horner of Cloford, John Ayleworth of Wells and James Bysse of Stoke were appointed commissioners to survey his lands.[2] The result was that on 13 June 1564 the matter was settled: the manor and hundred of Kingsbury, which had recently been leased to Sir Edward Rogers, was taken from the bishopric: it was worth £113. 11. 4½d. In return, the bishop's own tenths, valued now at £53. 6. 1½d., were abated and he was granted other tenths arising in the diocese, including those of the archdeacon, the chancellor and the treasurer of Wells, making a total of £114. 3. 9¼d.[3] On paper the bargain looked even, but in a time of rising prices the manor of Kingsbury was capable of exploitation, while the tenths granted to the bishop were fixed in amount. There is no doubt that the queen gained by the deal. This was the famous 'Kingsbury arrangement', or the *nova dotatio*, which was adhered to, as Elizabethan and Stuart accounts show.[4] Other bishops made similar transfers: Parker lost lands of the archbishopric of Canterbury in Kent, Sussex and Shropshire worth £1,381. 10. 0⅝d. and received tenths, parsonages and rents worth £1,283. 15. 11¼d.; the bishop of Ely's deal involved £774. 11. 10¼d. worth of property; and the bishop of Worcester bargained with £483. 16. 10½d.[5] 'A pretty device indeed' was the scathing remark of Chyles, the Restoration historian of the bishopric, in considering the act of 1559. Although the legal niceties were not settled until 1564, Berkeley must have agreed to them in principle about four years before. On 10 July 1560, after his election as bishop, the relevant

---

[1] B.M. Eg. MS 2350, fo. 34 ff.   [2] *C.P.R. 1558–60*, p. 423.
[3] *C.P.R. 1563–64*, p. 164.
[4] E.g. S.R.O. DD/CC/13324, fo. 357; P.R.O. Rentals and Surveys, Roll 951, S.C.6/Eliz./2008.
[5] *C.P.R. 1558–60*, pp. 355, 441–2.

escheators were instructed to deliver the temporalities of the
see to him, 'except lands taken by the queen by virtue of stat.
I Eliz.', a reference to the forthcoming Kingsbury arrangement.[1]

LIABILITIES INHERITED BY BISHOP BERKELEY

Of all the problems that came to him with his new position
it was the depletion of his estates that seems to have worried
Bishop Berkeley most, and he was not alone among the Elizabethan bishops in this. In 1564 the new bishop of St Asaph,
Thomas Davies, was licensed to hold three other livings *in
commendam* to relieve his poverty because the bishopric was
worth but £187. 11. 6d.[2] On the other hand, although Bishop
Jewel of Salisbury also complained of the neglect of his property
and of his lands being leased out when he took over, yet in
general he approved of the reduction of episcopal wealth as
tending to lessen ceremony and to give the bishops more time
for their spiritual responsibilities.[3] From the hardships of exile
in Frankfort to the palace at Wells might seem indeed a fair
exchange, but the bishop was still 'lord bishop' and Berkeley
had enough wordly sense to realize that on his standing as a
local landlord depended much of his social and political
prestige: the new Elizabethan church needed support of all
kinds to become established.

Yet the lands remaining to the bishopric were, after the
Edwardian reductions, but a fraction of those which had supported it formerly. Eighteen manors and other rights and
liberties had gone for good and the remaining eight manors
were so encumbered with grants and leases that only Huish
Episcopi could be said to be really free for the bishop's full
enjoyment. The eight manors nominally remaining to him were
those of Banwell, Chard, Compton Parva, Huish, West Buckland, Westbury, Wells and Wiveliscombe; on the basis of 1539
figures, which represent the value of the episcopal estates just
before the cataclysm began, they were worth £664. 17. 1¼d. He
was also left with his rights in the city, forum and liberty of Wells
worth £22. 4. 0d., the eight rectories acquired in 1548 and one

---

[1] Ibid., 452.   [2] *C.P.R. 1563–64*, p. 177.
[3] W. M. Southgate, *John Jewel*, pp. 66–7.

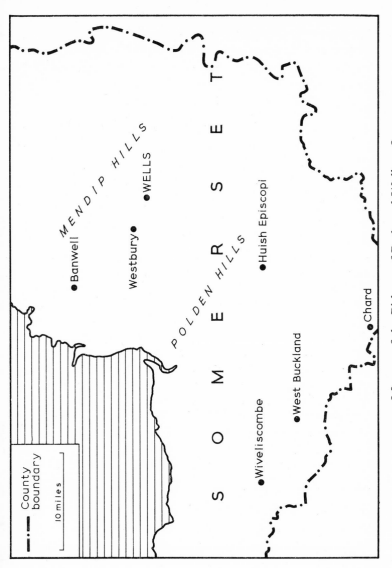

MAP 2. Manors of the Bishops of Bath and Wells 1560.
Not shown Compton Parva, Berks.

other, Westdown in Devon, which had belonged to the Hospital of St John in Wells, which were all worth £173. 11. 8d., and the newly acquired tenths of the Kingsbury arrangement worth £114. 3. 9¼d., which brought his total income to £974. 16. 6½d. Out of a gross income from land of £2,202 the bishop had lost £1,227, or 55 per cent, and out of the remaining £975 he had to meet the wages of his principal officers, the steward and the auditor and the like, and the expenses of administration, such as the purchase of parchment to keep the records. No lead royalties are included in these totals, but they were probably negligible before Bishop Berkeley's accession. By comparison, the average income of lay peers at this time was between £2,000 and £3,000.[1]

Not only did Berkeley have to meet the problem of this depleted endowment, but he also had to battle with the Bournes in his attempt to displace them from offices and leases. And it was not only their grants that burdened the bishopric. Berkeley allowed that Bishop Bourne had at first earnestly tried to augment the possessions of the bishopric, but that, when the change of régime became imminent, because of 'the hatred he bears Christ's true religion and her majesty's godly laws and statutes' he had overcharged it with fee-farm leases, annuities, reversions, offices and fees. Such great fees were paid out of the bishopric, Berkeley alleged, as when it was worth £2,000 more than it was then. This was done to defame the gospel and to discredit the successor of Bourne for lack of ability to keep hospitality: 'as they do not stick to say, here is a goodly prelate succeedeth my lord bishop Bourne.' Quite clearly Berkeley had to meet a certain amount of local malice.[2]

How far were the charges of Berkeley true? Four of his remaining manors were in fact leased out: three, Banwell, Westbury and Wiveliscombe to Richard Bourne, and the fourth, West Buckland, to Bourne's crony, Humphrey Colles, also for twenty-one years, for £47. 2. 5d. There is no doubt that the leasing of these manors meant a loss in hard cash. Berkeley reckoned that he received £167. 14. 5d. for them; the accounts show that he actually received £166. 5. 1½d. and that this was a

<hr />

[1] See p. 188; P. Ramsey, *Tudor Economic Problems*, p. 123.

[2] See p. 90 ff. The substance of all of Bishop Berkeley's complaints is taken from P.R.O. S.P.12/16/27.

consistent total rent. But according to the *valor* which has been taken as the standard throughout this study, that of 1539, they were worth £329. 10. 2d., and in the accounts for 1583 they are valued at £374. 13. 3¼d. Berkeley was in fact receiving less than half of what he should have received for these manors. The inclusion of the rent-free Banwell of course brings the total down.[1]

Another charge, for which there is no evidence either way, is that Bishop Bourne had capitalized as much as possible on the lands remaining to the bishopric but leased out before his time. Immediately on Bourne's deprivation, said his successor, he called in all his tenants and 'by compulsion for divers great sums of money' renewed their leases, reversion upon reversion, for many years to his great profit. Some of them were unable to pay immediately, so they took bond and obligation to do so and were still in debt to Geoffrey Upton, who was acting as Bourne's agent. No wonder that another of Berkeley's complaints was that many rents due at the Feast of the Annunciation 1559 were three or four months in arrear and could not be recovered without recourse to law. It irked him all the more that this Geoffrey Upton, who was acting for Bourne, was the keeper of his household, appointed for life with a fee of £14, and that he was not free to appoint another. But Bishop Bourne was not, in fact, responsible for the appointment of Upton as keeper of the bishop's palace and prison or as store bailiff. This was a choice dating from 1546, in Bishop Knight's time. Upton was certainly holding the post under Bourne, and Berkeley had to endure him for his lifetime, although by April 1581, the year the bishop died, Upton was sharing the responsibility with John Lunde. Upton died early in 1583 and by March 1584, when the accounts were made up, John Lunde was holding the post alone.[2]

Berkeley grumbled, too, about the perquisites of one William Grilles, who had been steward of the household in Bourne's time. He had been allowed a twenty-one year lease of some

[1] S.R.O. DD/CC/31523; P.R.O. S.C.6/Eliz./2011.

[2] *Wells*, II, 262–3; Wells Cath. Chapter Acts, Bk. H, 1571–99, fo. 16; P.R.O. S.C.6/P. & M./263, S.C.6/Eliz./2012; Brown, *Wills*, 1,7. Upton's will was proved on 4 May 1583.

common meadow which had been enclosed by Bourne for the maintenance of a school, and he paid a rent of only 3s. 4d., although it had previously been set at £3. 6. 8d. There is no evidence about this, but it is true as Berkeley complained, that he had been given an annuity of £6. 13. 4d., free of any service or duty. The payment of this pension runs through the accounts at least to September 1592. It would be interesting to know more of this William Grilles besides the fact that he was steward of the household in Bourne's time, when one of his jobs was to receive the cows paid as heriots for the use of the bishop's household. In 1554 with one Robert Hutchings he received a grant from the bishop of the next presentation to the prebend of St Decumans. The pension to which Berkeley objected may have been that of well-earned retirement.[1]

There was far more substance in the bishop's complaints about the diocesan registrar whom he inherited and whom he described as 'a manifest enemy to God and the queen's majesty'. This was William Lancaster, a native of Basingstoke, who settled at Milverton, which was conveniently near the Bourne household at Wiveliscombe, and who was probably hostile to the reformed religion: he described himself as 'a member of our Saviour Jesus Christ's Catholic Church',[2] and he was certainly a favourite of Bishop Bourne who once gave him a cup of silver. The appointment to the registrarship was in fact made by Bishop Bourne on 3 November 1558 and Richard Snow, a notary public, was jointly named with Lancaster in the patent.[3] Apart from Berkeley's complaints, there was so much trouble about this office later that the story is worth telling in full, and, although not directly concerned with estate administration, it well illustrates the scramble for office (which was regarded as a form of property), the competition to serve the bishop, and the corruption, the taking of bribes and fees, that went on at all levels in Elizabethan society.[4]

Apparently Lancaster overcame Berkeley's dislike, for he persuaded the bishop to confirm the grant of the registrarship

[1] P.R.O. S.C.6/P. & M./263, S.C.6/Eliz./3545/82, S.C.6/Eliz./2011, 2012, 2014, Rentals and Surveys, Roll 951; *Wells*, II, 277.

[2] Brown, *Wills*, III, 49.   [3] *Wells*, II, 281.

[4] J. E. Neale, 'The Elizabethan Political Scene', *Essays in Elizabethan History*, p. 59 ff.

to him, but this time his son Roger and John Bishop were named as the patentees with him. The grant was passed by the chapter on 1 July 1578. This arrangement was upset when the next bishop, Thomas Godwin, was prevailed upon on 22 September 1587 to give a new grant of the office to Robert Owen, a notary public and gentleman of Wells. Named with him in the grant for their lives were two other local men, Owen's father-in-law William Godwin of Wiveliscombe, a clothier, and another William Godwin, the son of John Godwin of Portbury. Robert Owen paid a fee of £6. 13. 4d. for the seal of this patent. These Godwins were not necessarily relatives of the bishop: there were Godwins in Wells before he came there. They probably represent a banding together of local interests to drive out the alien Lancaster of Basingstoke. However, the dean and chapter showed their wisdom in refusing to confirm the grant unless William Lancaster could first be persuaded to surrender his patent of the grant. They obviously wanted to avoid rival tenure of this vital office.[1]

Robert Owen then set about having talks with William Lancaster's other son, Edward, in the mistaken idea, as it seems, that Edward would be able to influence his father to give up the patent. After many discussions they came to agreement on Christmas Eve 1587: Edward Lancaster was to come in with Robert Owen and William Godwin, and to try to procure yet a new grant of the registrarship from the bishop for the three of them. The price at which Edward Lancaster sold his loyalty to his father was an annuity of £20 which Owen and Godwin were to pay to him as long as they lived, meeting for this purpose in the south porch of St Mary Magdalene Church, Taunton. Robert Owen also became bound to Edward Lancaster for 500 marks to keep to this agreement and he was held to a promise to keep the agreement secret by yet another £200 or £300. In return Edward Lancaster promised to get a surrender of the patent of the registrarship from his father by the next sitting of the chapter, which was on 1 April 1588.

Robert Owen professed that he had special confidence in Edward Lancaster, and he meanwhile made every attempt to

[1] Wells Cath. Chapter Acts, Bk. H, fos. 11, 48; Brown, *Wills,* I, 17; P.R.O. Req. 2/248/56 gives the full story.

persuade Bishop Godwin to grant the registrarship to the new trio. But their plan did not work out. The bishop, who had perhaps taken the measure of Edward Lancaster, replied that he would never grant him the office while he lived, and Owen alleged that Lancaster made no attempt to acquire the surrender of his father's grant. Owen managed to get what he wanted in the end, because on 1 July 1588 the chapter confirmed the grant of the office to him, and Owen later claimed that William Lancaster had originally made it over to him on 13 June 1586. It appears then that, in spite, of all his intrigues, Edward Lancaster was cut out, and that this is why he brought a case against Owen in the court of common pleas to establish his claim to the money held in bond. William Lancaster's disillusionment about his son is reflected in the wording of his will in 1596:

My son Edward Lancaster has most monstrously slandered me, has attempted to take away my living, disdained me in the presence of a great number of people, taken part with my enemies against me and by all sinister means procured my trouble and disquietude in this mine old age, for which offences I desire God's forgiveness and for my part will pray for him.

A family could be split by the competition to acquire a lucrative episcopal office.[1]

To return to the moans of Bishop Berkeley, another of them was that all the best advowsons in the diocese had been given to those who either refused to subscribe or fled the realm 'in the hope of a new day'. It is true that Berkeley found a good many recusants in the diocese, and it has been noted that Grilles had the presentation to St Decumans. Bishop Bourne had also on 12 June 1559 granted the next presentation to the prebends of Whitchurch and Whitelackington to his brother and Richard Snow, and on 15 August 1559 the next presentation to the prebend of Wedmore II to his old friend, Humphrey Colles.[2] Another of Berkeley's grudges was the lease of the demesnes of Wells to William Tarry, which he wrongly attributed to Bourne, for it was, of course, procured in the vacancy before Bourne came. The meadow called Wikmede, he alleged,

---

[1] Chapter Acts, Bk. H, fo. 48; P.R.O. Req. 2/248/57; Brown, *Wills*, III, 49.
[2] *V.C.H. Somerset.*, II, 39; *Wells*, II, 281.

had never previously been let, but had been reserved for the bishop's own provision, but now Tarry had it for twenty-one years at a rent of £2, although it was worth £10. He also had the lease of the brewhouse, which was within the bounds of the palace, so that the bishop had nowhere to brew his own beer. Tarry paid only £1 a year for the brewhouse with the barn yard, a fair green and a great garden belonging to the palace, but out of that the bishop had to provide him with food for a horse summer and winter for twenty-one years, although Tarry had sublet the lease for £8. Various implements that were the possessions of the office and not personal to the bishop were missing from the palace, and he was left without even a carriage-way to his house. The manor of Wells was charged with fees and annuities amounting to £100: of that £10 was, of course, the recent annuity to the Crown.

Berkeley did not hesitate to say that some of his difficulty was of the queen's own making. He reminded her that he had exchanged the manor and hundred of Kingsbury for spiritual livings. He begged for a commission of inquiry and for orders that he should enjoy the fruits of the bishopric without molestation, and he asked her to modify the extraordinary gifts and grants allowed by Bishop Bourne since the passing of the Act of Supremacy. There is no evidence that the queen did anything to relieve his distress, and the position in the diocese of Bath and Wells in fact amply corroborates Strype's strictures on the Catholic episcopate and his analysis of the economic position of the church in 1559:

although the church was replenished with gospel bishops, yet none had any cause to envy their wealth or greatness. For the revenues and incomes of the bishoprics had been so stript by their immediate popish predecessors, that the present bishops were in want even of convenience and necessaries for housekeeping . . . Their lands so reduced that they had scarce enough to keep them out of debt, and to maintain that hospitality that was looked for at their hands.[1]

Bishop Berkeley did not submit to impoverishment without question: his general policy, as in the battle with the Bournes, was to attempt to define his rights and to derive such profit as

[1] J. Strype, *Annals of the Reformation* (1824), I, 232 ff.

he could from them. Retrenchment and reform were the order of the day. In his quest for financial solvency the bishop's attention would naturally turn first to the work of his auditor, John Rawlins. Although Rawlins may have been an appointee of Bourne, Berkeley had such confidence in him that he extended his responsibilities and appointed him collector of all tenths and subsidies within the diocese as well as making him accountable for the episcopal rents. As early as 1563 the bishop realized that Rawlins' accounts were awry. His long struggle to bring him to order has already been described.

In general, such evidence as there is suggests that straitened circumstances were making the bishop a hard landlord, seeking ever to raise rents and to take advantage of the weak tenant. It will be recalled that at this time he possessed nine rectories, all farmed out. The two lowest rents accruing were those from Corston and Compton Dando, 40s. each, and the highest, one of £70, came from Weston. When the bishop brought action against William Horsington, lessee of the rectory of Corston, in 1564, it may have been in the nature of a test case; if Horsington could be ousted and the Corston rent raised, so could the other low rents.[1] The bishop's allegation was that the appropriation of the rectory, together with various other charters, writings and muniments, had come into the hands of Horsington, who detained them and wrongfully pretended title. Horsington's defence was that he had leased the parsonage in 1529 from the priory of Bath, to whom it then belonged, for the lives of himself and his brother Richard, with remainder to two others and at a yearly rent of 40s. After the dissolution of the priory in 1539 Horsington paid this rent to the general-receiver for Somerset acting for the Crown. The bishop's retort was that the parsonage was no longer Crown property, having been included in the grant to Bishop Barlow of 1548; he also denied knowledge of the lease which Horsington affirmed that he had had from the priory and demanded both that this should be produced in court and that Horsington should pay him the reserved rent. It is difficult to know which party to credit, because Horsington does not appear to have had unbroken tenure since 1529; accounts for 1555 show the rectory as leased to Thomas Taylor,

---

[1] P.R.O. C3/25/22. See Appendix C.

also at a rent of 40s. But Horsington was not ousted after the case of 1564: the accounts for the period 1566 to 1578 show him or his assignees holding Corston and still paying only 40s., and in the vacancy following Berkeley's death one Thomas Horsington still held it for the same sum. But the Horsington lease must have run out by 1587, when Bishop Godwin leased the rectory with the mansion place and all the houses and lands belonging to Thomas Godwin, his son, and Thomas Purfey, his son-in-law, again for only 40s.[1]

One gets the harshest impression of Bishop Berkeley's attitude towards one of his copyhold tenants, John Evans, a yeoman of Wells, in a case which came up in 1561. The property had become 'very ruinous and in great decay in housing, hedging, ditching and fencing', and part of Evans's dwelling house fell down, so that he was forced to live elsewhere while it was rebuilt. He was given some timber by the bishop's officers for this rebuilding, but it was not sufficient and he had to buy more, and also some stone, for the old was useless. This rebuilding, said Evans, had cost him at least 100 marks (£66. 13. 4d.), and because the new house had been built 'somewhat fair and more necessary and convenient' than the old one, the episcopal officers had persuaded the bishop to forfeit the tenement and eject him, on the pretext of the felling of trees and the failure to rebuild to the pattern of the old house.[2]

Wiveliscombe, that manor of much controversy past and to come, certainly felt the drive for increased fines from its tenants. Bishop Berkeley's Court Book records fines totalling £532. 15. 11d. for forty-eight new or renewed leases, giving an average of just over £11 each. Three of the leases called in question by Berkeley for technical faults and renewed for much larger fines dated only from the Bourne era, when they had cost a total of £10 in fines; the second fines imposed by Berkeley amounted to £55. These were expensive technicalities, especially since in one case 'the said Bishop thinks that the fault was in the officer'. Two of the recipients of the leases are especially interesting. William Edney, gentleman of the queen's chapel,

---

[1] P.R.O. S.C.6/P. & M./263, S.C.6/Eliz./2011; S.R.O. DD/CC/31523; *Wells*, II, 312.
[2] P.R.O. C3/58/1.

leased a cottage of old aster for a fine of only £2. He must, surely, have been an acquaintance of Berkeley in the days when the bishop was the queen's chaplain. Another grant of one toft, one barn and one half yardland of old aster went to 'John Lunde my servant in consideration of service', but it cost Lunde a fine of £20. Lunde was to become well known in the bishopric.[1]

There is further evidence of these fine-hunting activities in a *valor* of January 1582 drawn up in the vacancy following the bishop's death. Under the manor of Wiveliscombe is a note that the bishop made over £200 in copyhold fines (the exact figure is mutilated) and a further sum for the leasing of overland, or demesne, within the two years preceding his death. At Westbury, too, the bishop had made £46. 13. 4d. in copyhold fines and some (again not decipherable) fines for overland leases, besides some given to his servants. There is an interesting note that Mr Bourne had had a lease of this manor (further evidence, this, that his lease had expired about this time), but that he had made an accommodation with the bishop: they had agreed to divide the fines between them. Indeed, on the very day of the bishop's death his steward at the court at Westbury took several surrenders and granted them again for new fines, but the commissioners who drew up the *valor* had commanded the fines to be stayed until some order could be made for the security of the poor tenants. Surely this was a desperate attempt by the bishop to recoup the losses incurred during the validity of the Bourne lease.[2]

Illustrative, too, of the bishop's desire to improve his estates, despite their depletion, is the agreement which he made in 1564 with the tenants of his manor of Wells about the ditching and drainage of the large area of lowland contained in that manor. It was very necessary to define responsibilities for the proper cultivation of the land here, and so the duties of everyone who had rights of common within the manor of Wells were listed, hamlet by hamlet; these included the making of a new

---

[1] T.C. MS, PR 37. Land of 'old aster' seems to be a term indigenous to Somerset: it probably means land of ancient cultivation. 'Astered' means 'disturbed, stirred or moved', *see* J. Bosworth and T. N. Toller, *An Anglo-Saxon Dictionary*.

[2] P.R.O. Rentals & Surveys, Roll 573.

ditch at Polsham, beginning at Hartlake Bridge, eight tenants being made responsible for twenty-four feet each and two for stretches of twelve feet each. And it was probably no coincidence that the same manor, Wells, produced a four-fold increase in the value of lead royalties from the Priddy mineries in the ten years after 1567.[1]

Some details of Bishop Berkeley's administration of those estates which remained under his control can be gained from the account of 1566–78. There were, first, the farmed-out properties, five manors and nine rectories, which brought in a consistent income of £395. 16. 9½d. throughout the period.[2] The only properties remaining under the bishop's direct control and therefore capable of exploitation, were two manors, Wells and Huish Episcopi, and his rights over Wells *burgus*, Wells liberty and the hundred of Wells Forum. The manor of Banwell was let out rent free to Richard Bourne, but he apparently paid the rent reserved on it to the crown, £115. 8. 8d. One would expect to find that the hard-pressed bishop would wring a progressively higher income out of his estates, but, on the contrary, the profits varied considerably. There are complete figures for only five odd years: 1566—£645. 18. 0½d.; 1567—£704. 4. 10½d.; 1571—£633. 9. 10½d.; 1573—£875. 5. 2d.; and 1575—£695. 7. 0¾d.[3]

These are not figures of total income, for they do not include the fixed endowment which came to the bishop annually under the Kingsbury arrangement, £114. 3. 9d. With that figure added, the bishop's gross income, as far as ascertainable, varied from £747. 13. 7½d. to £989. 8. 11d., compared with a gross income of £2,202 in 1539. Moreover, the estates were realizing on the whole rather less than the 1539 yield of those still retained. For all his fine-driving, the bishop was not getting the improved rents which he might reasonably have expected in a time of price inflation. Again, the accounts drawn up just after his death—and Berkeley's groans—show that he was burdened with very heavy fees, annuities and reserved

[1] Wells Museum Notebook, fo. 314. See below, p. 190.
[2] S.R.O. DD/CC/31523. See Appendix C.
[3] As it happens, no lead figures are included in the totals given here, but it must be remembered that whenever figures for Wells manor are quoted they may or may not include lead figures. The method of accounting was not consistent.

rents.[1] Fees of the officers, including a new annuity of £40 to Lord Henry Seymour, and £6.13.4d. to William Grilles, amounted to £144; there were rents reserved to the queen of £10 from the manor of Wells and £11. o. o¾d. from the rectories of Glaston and West Pennard; and general expenses, for example of the annual audit and for repairs to the palace, might come to about £60. These general outgoings would take about £225 from the gross income. That left the bishop with about £522 in the worst year, 1571, and £764 in the best year, 1573. The reason why even a desperate bishop could not improve his income from the remaining estates consistently, and why one or two bad years invariably followed good years, was that for the two manors still in hand nearly all the sources of income, the rents of free and customary tenants and of those leasing pasture, meadow and mills, were fixed (the same figure recurs year after year), and of the casual sources of income, the two most important, heriots and fines, were dependent solely on chance. Some years there were none, but in 1573 the fines of the manor of Huish amounted to £105, and in 1570 those of the manor of Wells to £87. 6. 8d. The heriots from either manor might vary from 30s. to £19. They were usually paid 'direct to the use of the bishop', as in 1566 when a heriot worth £6 was paid on the death of John Plumley, and one worth £5 when Edward Hipplesley died.

In the manor of Wells there were at this time twenty-one free tenants, twelve holding by military service and nine by socage. Customary land and overland was divided into numerous small holdings, and it is true too of the leases of meadow and pasture that it was much divided among many tenants; for example, a meadow called Forelese of eighteen acres was held by six tenants with three acres reserved to the bishop. The homage of Wick was still paying vineyard silver, 3d. at Hocktide, and the homage of Westbury 4s. 10½d., but they accounted for it to the reeves of Wookey and Westbury respectively.

The list of payments against receipts was always headed by the acquitted rent allowed to the reeve and the hayward in lieu of wages. It is curious that while that allowed to the hayward never varied from 7s. 11d., except in 1577 and 1578, when

[1] P.R.O. S.C.6/Eliz./2011.

he was allowed an extra 9d., that allowed to the reeve fluctuated considerably: the lowest figure for the years 1566–78 was 7s. 1d. in 1571 and the highest was 18s. 5d. in 1575. Allocated and defective rents were the next item on the debit side, and these included the demesne lands kept in the lord's hand for his household needs, Wekemeade £1, Waterlese £3. 10s., Chaunters Close £1. 6s. 8d., Skinners Close £1. 4s., and the Camerhay 10s. Under this heading, too, was a house set aside for a stable for the use of the bailiff of the store and accounted as a loss of 5s., while the keeper of the bishop's park in Wells was allowed an allocated rent of £1. 6. 8d.

The last item on the debit side is always the most interesting, the non-recurrent expenses. These were often for the carriage of wood and hay within the manor of Wells and for the repair of the mills. Other examples of payments are to David Jones, understeward, for wax and court rolls, 12s. (1566); to the keeper of the lord's prison for convicted clerics for diet for five of them in prison, for his expenses at Chard, and for repairs to the prison house, £1. 2. 6½d. (1566); the diet of John Sprage clerk, kept in the convicts' prison for clerics in the absence of the bishop, 10s. 10d. (1567); repairs to the lord's pinfold, 1s. (1567).

Here, too, is evidence that although the bishop was financially pressed, and although he had his own brewhouse, he indulged in the luxury of imported wine from Bristol and the means of carriage had to be provided within the manor of Wells. In 1573 £1. 2. 11d. was paid for the carriage of two tuns of wine from Bristol to Wells; in 1575 13s. 4d. for one load of wine and other goods from Bristol; and again in 1577 and 1578 two tuns at 13s. 4d. a load. One wonders if the horses were subjected to the long haul over the Mendips, or whether they took the easier coastal route.

The normal income of the manor of Huish was £60–£70, because here again the rents had become formalized. They included fixed amounts for the rents of the three free tenants, of the overland, the dovecot let to John Higham for 5s., the wood let to John Bourne for 6s. 8d., the fishing to Thomas Baterm for 1s., the leases of pasture and meadow, and even issues of the manor, such as foldsilver at Hocktide, 1s. 6d., St Peter's Pence at

Lammas, 2s. 10d., and larder money, churchete and plough works. At Wells the bishop had kept some of his demesne in hand for his own use, but there is no evidence that he maintained a household at Huish, and so the demesne was let out. Some of it, 75 acres in Hillfield, had already been enclosed in two closes called Bishopsfield and let to John Worthy at £3. 2. 6d., and 75 acres of arable land in Derehill, Littlemore, Courtfield and Huish Hill had been let in four lots for £3. 1. 8d. Fines and heriots were the only variable sources of income; fines varied from £3 (1575) to £105 (1573).

In the absence of the lord, the reeve, John Marshal, managed the affairs of the manor, and perhaps to increase his authority and to maintain continuity in this place remote from Wells, he was not, like the Wells reeve, changed annually but retained his office at least between 1566 and 1578. He was assisted by a hayward, and as at Wells both officials received acquitted rents in lieu of wages. In addition they were allowed pasture for eight oxen in Oxenlease valued at 6s. 8d. and 3s. 4d. respectively. The expenses of the bishop's steward when he came to supervise the work of the reeve were usually about 10s.[1]

The income from the city of Wells was the only one which, except for a setback in 1570, rose steadily in the period under review; a large part of it came from the four annual fairs and the perquisites of the court, and assiduous supervision could improve it.[2] During the last year of Berkeley's life three of the leased manors returned directly to his control: Wiveliscombe produced £57. 7. 9½d., Buckland £43. 8. 7d., and Westbury £42. 0. 4½d. Banwell was still not free. The great decline in rents—Wells that year brought in only £91. 1. 4d. and Huish £67. 17. 4d.—must, one supposes, reflect the decline of their owner. The net income that year was but £440. 1. 4½d

And yet with so little at his disposal, Bishop Berkeley, like all the Elizabethan bishops, had to resist the pressure of courtiers ever alert to seize part of the episcopal estates. Sir Edward Rogers had failed to acquire the manor of Wiveliscombe and the hundred and manor of Kingsbury. Lord Henry Seymour also schemed to rob the bishop and he had the support of the

---

[1] All the foregoing details of Berkeley's estates are from S.R.O. DD/CC/31523.
[2] The perquisites of the court in 1566 were £8. 5. 4d., and in 1575 £26. 2. 2d.

queen acting through the privy council. On 6 August 1574 Elizabeth issued letters patent allowing the bishop to let the capital mansion, manor and park of Banwell to Seymour for twenty-one years. The chapter, not so weak as the bishop, tried to resist the council's demands, and late in December the council wrote to both bishop and chapter demanding confirmation of the lease. Three months later, finding them still obdurate, the council summoned some of the prebendaries and, after keeping them in attendance for several days, ordered them to obtain full authorization of the transfer from their chapter by St George's Day.[1]

Back in Wells the full extent of the queen's demands was discussed at a chapter meeting on 1 April 1575, and the bishop was made to promise that he would stand firm. The lords of the council, he was told, wanted to satisfy Lord Henry Seymour in one of three ways, namely, by giving him the lease of the manor of Buckland worth 1,000 marks, or £100 a year out of the manor of Banwell for twenty-one years, or of the whole of that manor with a reservation to him and his successors of £50 a year over and above the rent already reserved. The bishop said, subserviently, that he must keep to his promise to Seymour, since that had been approved by both the queen and the council, but the chapter, mindful of the long-term interests of the bishopric, still tried to hold out. Since the council had not received the reply demanded by St George's Day (23 April), it despatched a further letter to the bishop two days later. All that Seymour eventually obtained was an annuity of £40 a year from the manor of Banwell, and that he had to wait for. This payment appears in the accounts for 1582–3, in the vacancy following Berkeley's death, as having been granted by the former bishop and specially authorized, despite the vacancy, by a warrant from the lord treasurer, Burghley, of June 1583. The annuity was paid up to 1599, but how much longer it continued cannot be ascertained because of a break in the accounts until 1634, by which time its payment had ceased.[2]

---

[1] T. Rymer, *Foedera* (3rd edn 1741), vi (iv), 159; Dasent, *Acts of the Privy Council 1571–75*, pp. 328, 354, 370.

[2] *Wells*, ii, 295; P.R.O. S.C.6/Eliz./2009, 2011, 2013, 2014; S.R.O. DD/CC/13324, fo. 355.

There can be little doubt that Berkeley was one of the poorest holders of the see. To the end of his days he moaned and grumbled to the queen. When in 1580 he wrote to certify the number of trees felled in his diocese since his coming, he added that nineteen years ago when he arrived in Wells he had found the bishop's house left rifled and ruinous by his predecessor and had felled sixty-one trees for its repair. Some of the remaining trees had been sold by his officers to tenants, for the repair of their tenements, for £4. 5. 4d., but since then no timber trees had been sold within the episcopal estates, save for needful repairs, other than on the manors of Wiveliscombe and Buckland, where the tenants, Richard Bourne and John Colles, had grievously wasted the timber. Berkeley begged the queen to restrain their depredations or there would be hardly enough timber for repairs.[1]

THE WIVELISCOMBE LEASE

There is no doubt that, as a result of Bishop Berkeley's exertions and watchfulness, the estates were in a better condition when Bishop Godwin took over in 1584; but the newcomer's ill-health led to a slackening of control and to the abuses of his son Thomas Godwin and his son-in-law Thomas Purfey. Besides gaining offices in estate administration, these two acquired leases of the manor of Buckland, the rectory of Corston, lands in Banwell and on Mendip, and the four bishop's mills in Wells and the demesnes there. There were, moreover, other threats to be faced. Lord Henry Seymour had failed to get the manor of Banwell, but Sir Walter Raleigh was also interested in it, and Godwin might be expected to show tangible gratitude for his promotion. Godwin refused to part with Banwell, his favourite place of residence, so Raleigh asked for Wiveliscombe, another manor which had only just reverted to full episcopal control. Among the leases granted to Godwin's children at Christmas 1584 was that of a large part of the manor of Wiveliscombe to one of his sons, although the queen had already written to him requesting it for Raleigh. So on 13 June 1585 an urgent letter was despatched to the dean and

[1] P.R.O. S.P.12/137/33.

chapter of Wells, on the queen's behalf, urging them to stay confirmation of this lease and of any other which was for the bishop's own benefit. Godwin had to give way. On 4 November he leased the manor of Wiveliscombe to the queen for ninety-nine years at £80 a year—a good rent this, for the Bournes had paid £75. 18. 3½d. in Bishop Berkeley's time and the yield for 1581 had been only £57. 7. 9½d. There was a special clause about the woods: the tenants were to have firewood and 'timber for necessary reparations' and none other. Harington's oft-quoted verdict on the bishop's part in the business was that 'he neither gave Wilscombe for love, nor sold it for money, but left it for feare'.[1]

Yet Raleigh failed, after all, to get the manor. The queen turned the whole of the ninety-nine year lease over to Sir George Bond, an alderman of London. Sir George was a Somersetshire lad who had made good and had become lord mayor of London in 1588. He was born at Buckland, near Wiveliscombe, and his father was Robert Bond of Trull, a haberdasher. It is easy to understand the attraction which the Wiveliscombe lease had for him in offering him retirement to his native place. When he died in 1592 the property passed to his widow, Dame Winifred Bond, and she leased away Cottcombe Wood and other lands to Thomas Bereham for twenty-one years. Then the Colles family became involved: they became possessed of the main lease when in February 1596 the widowed Winifred married John Colles for the 'better advancement' of them both. After John Colles the father died about 1608, his son John, of Barton in Pitminster, inherited the remainder of the lease and continued to pay the annual rent of £80 to the bishop.[2]

Meanwhile Thomas Bereham's lease of Cottcombe Wood descended to his son Lawrence and his son-in-law, John Butcher, and it was against these two that John Colles the younger brought a case some time after 1610, on the ground that they were ignoring the clause in the lease which excepted the use of wood and timber. Colles alleged that, knowing that

[1] Harington, *Nugae Antiquae*, II, 151, 153; *Wells*, II, 307–9. The Wells Museum Notebook, fos. 246–7 and S.R.O. DD/CC/13324, fo. 363, both contain this lease in a survey of leases of c. 1635.

[2] Brown, *Wills*, III, 71; V, 55; Fuller, *Worthies*, III, 109. Brown is wrong in saying that Winifred was the daughter of Sir George.

their lease would shortly expire, they were despoiling the timber to the damage of the bishopric and thus rendering him liable to the forfeiture of his own lease. They had recently cut down many great oaks, elms and ashes and carried away about 500 of them; they had cut, topped and lopped 300 other trees and had used the timber for the erection of a new house. Since the serving of the injunction they had felled sixteen or seventeen more timber trees of a hundred years' growth and had threatened to cut down and carry away all the trees, although those already taken were worth £500. Even that was not the full catalogue of their misdemeanours; they had also plundered stone quarries in Cottcombe Wood and carted away 2,000 loads of stone, erected various limekilns where there were none before, sold the lime to foreigners, and neglected to do the usual hedging and ditching.[1]

The defence of Bereham and Butcher was that they were acting as the servants of Joan Bereham, the widow of Thomas Bereham, in her old age. They denied having cut any trees, except for necessary repairs, but they confessed to having lopped and topped certain oaks and ashes which had been lopped before. They maintained that the exception in the lease about the timber was void and that Joan Bereham could have hewed other trees for necessary repairs if she had wished. They accused John Colles of having more interest in his private profit than in the preservation of the inheritance of the bishopric. They denied having dug new pits for quarrying, but admitted having taken limestone from an ancient quarry there for Joan Bereham and at her command. Much of the limestone had been used on the land there to her great cost, and some had been sold to the inhabitants of Wiveliscombe, who had thereby improved the soil and produced better crops of corn. John Colles had refused Joan Bereham a licence to make these sales and she had then applied to the bishop, who, realizing that the spreading of lime would be an enrichment of his manor and of general benefit to the public, had licensed Joan and her servants to dig limestone and sell lime. The outcome of the case is not known, but it is probable that John Colles was successful, since he held the main lease and the Berehams were but transitory tenants.

[1] P.R.O. C3/303/15 from which all the details of this story are taken.

One version of the history of the Wiveliscombe lease is that the Bond family held it under the grant from Elizabeth I until it passed into the hands of John Coventry, the second son of Sir Thomas Coventry, the Lord Keeper. This cannot have been so since it had passed into the Colles family by marriage. When John Colles the younger, who had brought the action against Bereham, died in 1627 he bequeathed 'to my daughter Anne my lease of the manor of Wiveliscombe [and] to my daughters Anne and Dorothy, my plate, household stuff . . . in my houses at Wiveliscombe'. It was from the Colles that the Coventry family obtained the lease, and when it fell in they acquired a new one from Bishop Kenn in 1685; they continued to lease the manor from the see of Wells until 1813.[1]

Cassan and the other biographers of Bishop Godwin have overlooked the fact that, besides leasing Wiveliscombe, he also, in the end, partly gave way to the queen's importunities about Banwell. There are at least three extant references to a lease for 120 years made between the bishop and the queen on 20 March 1590, a few months before his death, of four tenements in Towerhead and 292 acres of land all within the manor of Banwell, together with Westbury Park and other lands within the manor of Westbury. (It is interesting to see the Crown taking advantage of its powers under the act of 1559 to exact long leases from bishops whereas those granted to other people were limited to twenty-one years.) The annual rent for the Banwell premises was to be £20 and for the Westbury lands £14. 14. 9d.; timber trees were excepted for Banwell, but not for Westbury; and a fine of 20 [s.?] was to be paid to the bishop every tenth year. This was the grant confirmed by the dean and chapter on 1 April 1590, when they charged the queen double the usual fee for the chapter seal; they also resolved that John Rodney of Pilton should enter into a bond of £100 to the bishop to ensure that whoever was assigned the queen's lease should not cut down any timber trees in the park of Westbury, except those allowed by the bishop and his officers for necessary house repairs. Why John Rodney should have been involved, except as a guarantor, is not clear, for the queen assigned the lease on

[1] Hancock, *Wifela's Combe*, p. 81; Brown, *Wills*, I, 33.

17 July 1591 not to him but to Sir Thomas Gorges of Wraxall, one of her gentlemen of the privy chamber.[1]

Another courtier who had already acquired something from the manor of Westbury was Sir Thomas Egerton, then solicitor general, who on 8 May 1587, was granted an annuity of £2 for life from the manor.[2] It is interesting to speculate whether a mutual connection with Brackley in Northamptonshire, whence Egerton took one of his titles and where Godwin had once been a schoolmaster, had led to an acquaintanceship between them.

No account of the problems arising out of the management of the temporalities in Bishop Godwin's time would be complete without mention of that veteran John Lunde who must have been an important and familiar figure in the streets of Wells for nearly fifty years. He was born about 1557, but it is not known whether he was a native of Somerset. He first came into prominence at the end of Bishop Berkeley's episcopate when, on 1 April 1581, he was associated with Geoffrey Upton in the episcopal offices which Upton held, as keeper of the bishop's palace, bailiff of the stores, and keeper of the woods at Wells. By July 1584 Lunde held these offices (worth £19. 13. 4d.) alone, and so he continued throughout the episcopates of Godwin, Still and Montague, and for the greater part of Lake's, until he retired in 1625 in favour of Walter Bushell.[3] Apart from his fees, there were other rewards for Lunde. In 1616 Bishop Montague granted him a garden plot in Wells, a hillock in Priddy Minery with the lot lead, or tithe, arising from it, and the storehouse there, all for the lives of himself, his son Maurice, and John Tricknell, who was probably his son-in-law. Lunde also held two copyhold lands in Wells, and leased forty-one acres of arable land and two water grist-mills; he had acquired the lease of the mills in Bishop Still's time, in 1597, at a rent of £12, although by 1635 their proper value was reckoned to be £20. For a brief time after the death of Bishop Godwin in

---

[1] S.R.O. DD/CC/28225; T.C. MS, P.R. 436; Wells Museum Notebook, fos. 249–53; Wells Cath. Chapter Acts, Bk. H, fo. 60.

[2] I am indebted to Professor S. T. Bindoff for this reference from Ellesmere MS 508 from the Catalogue of the Ellesmere MSS now at the Henry E. Huntington Library, San Marino, California.

[3] P.R.O. E.134/10 Jas.I/20, S.C.6/Eliz./2011, 2012; Chapter Acts, Bk. H, fo. 16; *Wells*, II, 383.

1590 Lunde seems also to have acquired the lease of Corston rectory, but he had lost it by 1594 to John Harington. John Lunde's wife, Anne (born about 1555) outlived him, and of their four children, Maurice, Sybil, Blandina and Frances, three bore names which appear in the Godwin family.[1]

The interest of Bishop Godwin's episcopate centres on the play of personalities. Of the rentals and surveys which would have told of the state of his endowment none survives, but the ministers' accounts for the vacancy following his death, when set against those which preceded his advent, show that, apart from the Wiveliscombe, Banwell and Westbury grants, the *status quo* at Berkeley's death was maintained at Godwin's. Leases to his family there might be but the bulk of the endowment remained unimpaired.

[1] S.R.O. DD/CC/13324, fos. 23, 234-5; Lunde's Will P.C.C. 1 Pile; P.R.O. Rentals & Surveys, Roll 951, S.C.6/Add./3545/84.

CHAPTER V

The Godwin Family

SONS AND SONS-IN-LAW

WHETHER Bishop Berkeley was married or not, his successor, Bishop Thomas Godwin (1584–90), is an outstanding example of the unhappy pass to which the liabilities of episcopal marriage could bring a prelate in the time of Elizabeth I. His appointment in 1584, after a three-year vacancy was, to say the least, ill-judged.

Whitgift's generation of bishops had need to be invulnerable, for the puritan attack against them was stiffening, few of them had much in common with their radical opponents, and the divergence between the right and the left wings of Elizabeth's church was growing.[1] Berkeley had shared the martyrdom of exile with the extremists in Mary's reign: Godwin had dodged the issue by becoming a temporary physician. When he was promoted to Bath and Wells from the deanery of Canterbury in September 1584 Godwin was already sixty-seven and a widower with a grown-up family. He had a history of trouble with his subordinates at Canterbury and he was a prey to gout and quartan ague: his superb portrait in the palace at Wells shows him leaning heavily on a stick. But he had enjoyed the patronage of Bullingham, bishop of Lincoln, of Archbishop Parker, and of the queen, and Bath and Wells may have been intended as a reward to dignify his declining years. Again, Whitgift, on taking up his appointment as archbishop of Canterbury in 1583, may have wanted to be rid of an awkward dean.[2]

---

[1] J. E. Neale, *Elizabeth I and her Parliaments 1559–81*, p. 273.
[2] I owe this suggestion to Sir John Neale.

Godwin's beginnings were humble. Born in 1517, he went to the free school at Wokingham in Berkshire, his native place, where he attracted the attention of Dr Layton, the zealous reformer; and it was at Layton's expense that in 1538 he was launched on a classical education at Magdalen College, Oxford, where he eventually became a fellow about 1549. When Magdalen founded Brackley School, Godwin, who had become unpopular through his Protestant views, renounced his fellowship and became the first master, and there in Northamptonshire he established those Midland affiliations which had so important an influence on his life. He married while at Brackley into the Purfey family of nearby Shalstone in Buckinghamshire, his wife being Isabel, one of the many children of Nicholas Purfey of Shalstone, who died in 1547.[1]

On Mary's accession he had to leave the school and he turned to the practice of medicine, which he had been studying in his spare time, as an alternative form of livelihood. He was licensed B.M. in 1555. It was only on the accession of Elizabeth I that he became ordained, about 1560, by Nicholas Bullingham, bishop of Lincoln, whose chaplain he was. Then began a series of changes from one post to another: he was rector of Kirkby Mallory in Leicestershire in 1560, rector of Hannington and Winnick in Northamptonshire in 1561, and in 1562 rector of Lutterworth, holding all these benefices in plurality with one or another of the prebendal stalls of Lincoln Cathedral. The year 1565 was an important year for Godwin: he then became dean of Christ Church, Oxford (where there is a portrait of him which may be a copy of the one in the palace at Wells), and he also became one of the Queen's Lent preachers, an honour which he retained for eighteen years. Two years later, in March 1567, he received further advancement by becoming dean of Canterbury; he stayed there for seventeen years, making his home at Chartham about five miles to the south-west of Canterbury.[2] He still held a prebendal stall at Lincoln and his appointment as Lent preacher which he kept until 1583.

---

[1] *D.N.B.*; Browne Willis, *History of Buckinghamshire*, pp. 262–3; B. Long, *Records of the Parish Church and Parish of Wokingham,*p. 65. I am grateful to the Rev. F. A. Steer for this last reference.

[2] I am indebted to Mr John Daeley for all the Chartham references.

In view of his later difficulties as bishop in Somerset it is interesting to note the trouble in which he was involved with the canons at Canterbury, who made constant complaints about him to Parker. One threatened to nail him to the wall with his sword, so that he had to appeal to the justices of peace. In 1573 Parker accused him of converting church goods to his own use, but Godwin was able to show that he had acted with the consent of the chapter and that the proceeds of the sale of prohibited church ornaments had been used in a legitimate manner, and not for his own benefit. The only preferment that he took for himself or for his family while dean of Canterbury was the office of porter of the South Gate, for his eldest son, Thomas.[1]

Wells was to be a different story. By now his family was grown up and getting married and, with establishments of their own to support, both sons and sons-in-law took advantage of the ill-health of the bishop to exploit his position. Since his powers were declining the bishop abandoned all other posts when he retired to lead the life of a semi-invalid in Somerset. In early August 1584 he presided over his last chapter meeting at Canterbury, and on 10 August he was elected bishop by the chapter at Wells: they had been urged to speed the election of Dr Godwin 'whom her majesty doth specially favour'.[2]

When the elderly bishop arrived in Wells he was already a widower; his wife Isabel had died about 1582 while he was still at Canterbury. Harington's statement that he was a widower is copied by all later biographers of the bishop, and it is confirmed by the evidence of two of the bishop's sons-in-law in a legal case on 21 October 1587. They referred to 'Mistress Isabel Godwin then wife to the said Reverend father and natural mother to this defendant's wife' lying upon her death-bed 'about five years past'.[3] There is, however, some controversy about the bishop's second wife. It is alleged by the unreliable Harington and others that he married her after he

---

[1] *D.N.B.*; J. M. Cowper, *Lives of the Deans of Canterbury*, p. 28 ff.

[2] Cowper, p. 40; *Wells*, II, 306.

[3] P.R.O. Req. 2/31/40. Unfortunately there is no reference to her burial in any of the Canterbury Registers which are in print, nor in F. W. Tyler's transcripts of Chartham Parish Register, 1558–1740 (1937, typescript) or the Bishops' Transcripts, No. 86 Chartham, both among the Canterbury Cathedral MSS.

came to Wells, when he was 'aged, diseased and lame of the gout', and that she was either a scheming girl of twenty who had acquired half the bishopric, or a widow of forty.[1] Cassan gives her surname as Boreman, but there is probably confusion here because a Margaret Bowerman of Wells indeed married a Thomas Godwin, who was, however, not the bishop but his son and namesake. The bishop's second wife is still something of a mystery. The sole reference to her is in the Banwell Parish Register recording her burial in 1587: 'Sibyll the wife of the Right Reverend father in god Thomas Godwen by gods providence [Bishop] of Bathe and Weles was buried the first of December.'[2] There is no evidence either for or against the statement that the bishop transferred half of his estate to this second wife, and he was clearly a widower again when he died in November 1590, for there was no wife with the other relatives around his deathbed and the packing of his household goods in Somerset was in the charge of his daughter Blandina and of his daughter-in-law, the wife of his son Thomas.[3] A will would have been helpful here, but the bishop did not make one.[4] In spite of the conflicting dates of the legal case (c. 1582) and of the Banwell Parish Register (1587), one is led to wonder, through the similarity of the names Isabel and Sibyll, whether Bishop Godwin had but one wife after all. Francis Godwin, the bishop's second son, makes no mention of a second marriage in his *Catalogue of the Bishops of Bath and Wells*; surely he would have mentioned his own stepmother had she existed.

Whether or not the bishop had a second wife who was a liability, the rest of his family were disastrous for the maintenance of his dignity and reputation. They obviously regarded his promotion as a ready opportunity for their own enrichment. Fearing that he might die before they had accomplished their ends, they were hard at it, pressing their wishes on him that first Christmas in Wells, in 1584.[5] He had five sons, Thomas, Francis, Robert, Matthew and Paul, and three daughters, Blandina, Joyce and Anne, and these midlanders soon began to

---

[1] Harington, *Nugae Antiquae*, II, 151; Cassan, *Bishops of Bath and Wells*, pp. 8–9; J. Rutter, *Delineations of N.W. Somerset*, p. 135; *D.N.B.*
[2] This is the correct reading which I have inspected.
[3] P.R.O. E.178/1966.   [4] *Wells*, II, 320.
[5] P.R.O. Req. 2/31/40.

exploit the western bishopric, with which they had no local affiliations or loyalties. There is no evidence of children by the second wife.

Thomas, the eldest son, was born before 1562.[1] His first wife, Frances, was buried at Banwell on 8 August 1588,[2] and he then married Margaret, the daughter of William Bowerman of Wells, who when giving evidence on 10 December 1590 about the disposal of the bishop's assets gave his own age as sixty-one and referred to his son-in-law as 'Thomas Godwin the bishop's son'. This is the William Bowerman whose will was made on 18 September 1590: since the will mentions a son Andrew and a daughter Margaret but no other daughter, it is clear that Margaret married Thomas Godwin the bishop's son, not the bishop himself. This second wife took an active part in packing up her father-in-law's goods at Banwell after his death. The return for the Bowerman family in the Visitation of 1623, which was made by Margaret's brother Andrew, shows that she first married a Godwin, and then William Martin; had she married a bishop her brother would surely have claimed the fact, so that again we may conclude that the bishop did not marry a Boreman or Bowerman as Cassan alleged.[3]

Thomas was a man of action. He was appointed a collector of benevolences and his father wrote to certify the appointment to Archbishop Whitgift in 1587; it was a position which Thomas used very much to his own advantage. When the question of his marriage arose, his prospective father-in-law William Bowerman was apprehensive about the financial commitments of this appointment. In his own reported words:

before he would give his consent to the marriage of his daughter unto Thomas Godwin the bishop's son . . . [he] asked the bishop whether his son was under collector and by means thereof answerable to the Queen for the collection of tenths and subsidies, who answered him that he was not, but dealt only as his servant and that the account was only chargeable upon the bishop, for other-

---

[1] P.R.O. E.178/1966, Thomas Purfey's deposition. The second son was born in 1562.

[2] Banwell Parish Register.

[3] Brown, *Wills*, I, 68; P.R.O. E.178/1966; *The Visitation of Somersetshire 1623* (Harl. Soc. XI), p. 11.

wise he would not have given his consent to the marriage of his daughter unto him.[1]

It was no doubt also through his father's interest that Thomas Godwin represented Wells as one of the two members in the parliament of 1586, being elected by the corporation on 3 October. He had to submit to the formality of being admitted a freeman of the city, on presentation of a dozen gloves, before he could take up this status. In 1587 the city tried to enlist his interest to obtain a new charter of liberties. At the convocation held on 1 March it was agreed that, in order to obtain the goodwill of the bishop, £100 should be paid to Thomas Godwin at the end of May and £10 yearly for three years; if the negotiations did not succeed Godwin was to repay all these sums with £10 interest, and he was to give an adequate assurance for the repayment. This financial opportunism is entirely true to Thomas Godwin's character, and since the charter was obtained he was presumably saved the embarrassment of repayment.[2]

Francis, the second son, born at Hannington in Northamptonshire in 1562, was destined for the church. He was educated at Christ Church, Oxford, where his father had been dean, proceeding B.A. in 1581 and M.A. by 1584, and in 1585 he was given a prebend of Wells, Combe VII, on the bishop's order. In 1587 he became the vicar of Weston Zoyland, the prebendary of St Decuman, another Wells post, and he was also made a canon residentiary, the bishop giving him a dispensation from the order which limited the number of canons to eight. In 1588 he was elected to capitular office as one of the two surveyors of houses and he was re-elected the following year. That same year he was given the prebend of Combe VIII, taking it over from his brother Robert, and in 1590 Porlock rectory. He lived in one of the canonical houses which had been leased to his brother-in-law, Thomas Purfey, by the bishop. Just before his father died, he married Susan, a daughter of Dr Woolton, bishop of Exeter, and became a sub-dean of Exeter. His marriage licence, dated 13 August 1590, described

---

[1] H.M.C. 10th Report, App. III, p. 265, n. 6; P.R.O. E.178/1966.
[2] C.W. Act Book 1553–1623, fos. 167, 172; S.R.S., xlvi, 186.

him as 'Mr. Francis Godwin, M.A., of the minor canons of Wells.'[1]

Francis was by far the most scholarly of the bishop's family. He later became a doctor of divinity and successively bishop of Llandaff and of Hereford, and he was the author of the *Catalogue of the Bishops of Bath and Wells* (1595) and other learned works. He was skilled as a Latinist, a mathematician and an antiquary, enjoying the friendship of the antiquary William Camden, and he made a study of the motion of the moon.[2] His scholarly inclinations were apparent in his Wells days, for he acquired the greater part of his father's books, including the works of Cicero and St Augustine. He claimed that these books had been given to him about fifteen months before his father's death, and this statement was supported by a fellow cleric, Thomas Manton, chancellor of the cathedral, but he was made to pay at least £40 for them by those clearing up his father's estate. Since his wife 'did earnestly request it', Francis also acquired his father's portraits of Burghley, Hatton, Walsingham and Whitgift.[3]

The death of his father did not sever Francis's connexion with Wells. As a canon he took an active part in cathedral administration; he was elected steward and auditor in 1594 and surveyor of houses again in 1598. He settled disputes and was given leave of absence for about six weeks, with full allowances, in 1594 to go to Oxford to take his B.D. He stayed at Wells until he was consecrated bishop of Llandaff in 1601, and then began a dispute with the chapter at Wells about the retention of his emoluments as a canon residentiary. In 1602 he claimed allowance for sixty-seven days, which the canons refused. This provoked him to appear personally seven days later, armed with the documents of his appointment, to ask not only allowance for past absences, but 'that all the rest of his days for residence in his absence may be allowed him hereafter'. Decision was deferred to the next general chapter,

[1] F. O. White, *Lives of the Elizabethan Bishops*, p. 408; *Wells*, II, 307–15; *D.N.B.*; H.M.C. 10th Report, App. III, pp. 266, 267, 270; Wells Diocesan Registry, Marriage Licences (Phipps transcripts, 1946); Bishop Woolton's Will P.C.C. 37 Dixy.

[2] Duncumb, *County of Hereford*, I, 488.

[3] P.R.O. E.178/1966; Wells Cath. Chapter Book H, fo. 57.

but the matter was presumably settled amicably, for in 1606 the chapter gave him permission to take six timber trees off their lands for the repair of a house in Congresbury. There is record of his being formally excused residence for one year in 1607, and in 1609 the chapter went further and agreed that he should be allowed the profits of his residency without making annual petition for them. Finally in 1617 he resigned his place of residence and his office of canon residentiary in favour of Paul Godwin, M.A., prebendary of Holcombe, his youngest brother.[1]

So ended Francis Godwin's formal connexion with Wells, except that he still held the rectory of Kingston Seymour.[2] Later, as bishop of Hereford, he gained the reputation of being a gross nepotist and of providing for his sons and daughters out of episcopal estates: in this he was being a true son of his father. Some of his children were certainly well entrenched in the church in the western parts: his eldest son, Dr Thomas Godwin, became chancellor of the diocese of Hereford, Morgan Godwin was archdeacon of Salop, Charles Godwin held a benefice at Monmouth, and a daughter married Dr John Hughes, archdeacon of Hereford. Fuller, however, lauds Francis Godwin on account of his scholarly achievements: 'the church of Llandaff was much beholding to him, yea, the whole church of England.' He died in his moated palace in the remote Herefordshire manor of Whitbourne, where his son, Thomas Godwin, was rector, and he was buried under the nave in front of the chancel on 29 April 1633 in the red sandstone church. His tomb, now gone, was inscribed with the family motto 'Win God—win all'.[3]

The third son of Bishop Thomas Godwin, Robert, was also destined for the church, but he apparently lacked his elder brother's ability and he became nothing more than a country parson. He was born in 1563, while his father was rector of

[1] *Wells*, II, 329, 330, 331, 334, 350, 359, 372.

[2] He was presented to the rectory of Kingston Seymour on the death of his brother Robert, and was instituted on 27 July 1613 when already bishop of Llandaff. The patron was Elizabeth Bowerman, the mother-in-law of his brother Thomas. He had previously held three livings in turn: F. W. Weaver, *Somerset Incumbents*, p. 274.

[3] White, *Elizabethan Bishops*, p. 408; Duncumb, p. 489; *D.N.B.*; A. G. Matthews, *Walker Revised*, p. 193; *A Guide to Whitbourne Church* (1963).

Lutterworth. He was already a B.A. when he was ordained a deacon by his father in the bishop's chapel at Banwell on 29 October 1587, and it was there again, nearly a year later, that he was admitted to the priesthood. His father watched his interests. In 1588 he was given the prebend of Dinder and the rectory of Kingston Seymour. He married, in 1591, a widow of that parish, Thomasin Snowe, the marriage licence being recommended by the justices and by his brother Francis, in his capacity as a canon residentiary of the cathedral. His father had died and the bishopric was vacant at the time, so this was in conformity with the injunctions of 1559 about clerical marriage. Since the previous incumbent of Kingston Seymour had been a John Snowe, Robert may have married his predecessor's widow. He gave evidence about the disposal of his father's goods in December 1591 and died, while still parson of Kingston Seymour, some time before July 1613. Unlike his brothers he spent his life there, in the parish, rather than in the cathedral close.[1]

Francis was not the only son who had connexions with Exeter Cathedral. The bishop's fourth son, Matthew, was born in 1569 and was baptized at Chartham, while his father was dean at Canterbury.[2] Matthew had musical inclinations and became assistant to the aged organist there before moving to Exeter, perhaps in 1584 when his father also moved west, to become master of the music in Exeter Cathedral. But he died young, on 12 January 1587, when only seventeen, and a wall slab on the north side of the nave of the cathedral bears witness to his memory. The memorial shows the same arms as his brother, Francis, who as sub-dean may have been responsible for its erection, and the arms include a martlet which indicates that Matthew was indeed the fourth son. The claim on the monument is that Matthew held the degree of Mus.B. at Oxford, and also that he was previously master of the music at Canterbury, which is probably an inflated title.[3]

[1] P.R.O. E.178/1966; Wells Marriage Licences (Phipps Transcripts); H.M.C. 10th Report, App. III, pp. 266, 268, 270.

[2] F. W. Tyler, Transcripts of Chartham Parish Register 1558–1740, p. 6.

[3] I am grateful to Mrs A. H. Erskine, Archivist of Exeter Cathedral Library, for information about this monument. The degree claimed for Matthew has not been traced.

There is little information about the early life of the bishop's youngest son Paul except that he was born in 1575 while the family was at Canterbury, that he matriculated at Oxford in 1589 when fourteen, and that he was with his father in Wokingham, Berkshire, the morning before he died. That night the bishop instructed his clerk, Thomas Middleham, to pen a lease of the manors of Westbury and Huish to John Boys 'to the use of Paul the bishop's son', but before it was fully written the bishop died and the lease was burned. All this suggests a belated attempt by a fond father to make some provision for his youngest son who was but a boy. Paul was certainly the only member of the family who did not join the scramble for property at the bishop's death. Not until 1596 was he preferred by the next bishop to the rectory of Long Sutton, which he held until 1618, for a time in plurality with the rectory of Burnham. He also held the livings of Chilton Cantelo (1607–8), Netherbury with Beaminster in Dorset (from 1608), and Kingweston (from 1619), the last two until his death. He was admitted to cathedral society in 1617 when he acquired his brother Francis's place as a canon residentiary on payment of 100 marks caution money. Now he began to take an active part in cathedral affairs: from then until the cataclysm of the 1640's he was much employed as auditor, surveyor of houses, steward, communar, and preacher extraordinary, and he voiced his opinions in chapter meetings.

By 1623 he had become, like his father and his second brother, a doctor of divinity, and a man of influence. He was one of the leaders in a dispute with the dean, Barlow, in 1625; he dared to resist, unsuccessfully, the election of Robert Creighton as a canon residentiary in 1633 although Creighton was a royal nominee; he again differed from the dean when discussing the number necessary to form a quorum to validate a lease in 1636 and in 1640 he was involved in a dispute with Bishop Peirs. The bishop disliked the sermons preached by him and Dr Wood, another canon, and through his registrar he pronounced an inhibition against their preaching any more. The dean and chapter supported their fellows against the bishop and by October 1640 the differences had been settled.

From 1629 Dr Paul played an important part in county affairs as a J.P., and he had sporting interests. In July 1633 he leased from the dean and chapter their fishing, hunting and hawking rights within the hundred of North Curry for twenty-one years, with the reservation that the other canons were to take their pleasure in fishing, hawking and fowling there if they so wished and to have the use of Godwin's servants and nets. Those summer days by the river Tone were rudely ended. On 1 April 1639 Dr Godwin, as communar, was paying £80 out of the capitular purse towards the king's war expenses. He attended a chapter meeting on 30 September 1643 but not the last recorded one of Charles I's reign on 28 January 1644. He was sequestered from Kingweston by the Somerset Committee for Compounding in 1646 as 'a known delinquent and an idle and scandalous minister' who left his curate, Baber, much in want. The next year he was involved in a chancery case. He was then seventy-two and feeling his age, and he did not live to be restored to Wells with his fellow canons. He died some time before May 1652.[1]

So all Bishop Godwin's sons were safely ensconced in ecclesiastical office. His sons-in-law it was who caused most embarrassment, notably Thomas Purfey, who married the bishop's daughter Blandina. He was born about 1556, the son of William Purfey (and this must surely be the William Purfey of Hollingbourne in Kent who received some of the bishop's goods at his death[2]). William was one of the Purfeys of Shalstone in Buckinghamshire and a nephew of the bishop's wife; it is significant that he gained a lease of the demesne lands of Hollingbourne, which belonged to the dean and chapter of Canterbury, in 1576 while Godwin was dean of Canterbury. He died in 1595 leaving at least two sons, Thomas, the bishop's son-in-law, and Edward, who married Joyce, the sole heiress of his distant kinsfolk, the Purfeys of Fenny Drayton in Leicestershire: by this marriage Edward acquired the manor of Fenny Drayton.[3]

In 1588 Thomas Purfey replaced his brother-in-law, Thomas Godwin, as one of the two M.P.s for Wells, but his great achievement was to acquire the office of bailiff of the bishop's liberty,

---

[1] Weaver, pp. 39, 58, 119, 195; S.R.S., LXV, 2, 8, 16, 31, 41, 45; *Wells*, II, 335, 372–88, 414, 421–7.

[2] P.R.O. E.178/1966.

[3] E. Hasted, *History of Kent*, v, 464; G. F. Farnham and A. Herbert, 'Fenny Drayton and the Purfey Monuments', *Trans. Leics. Arch. Soc.*, XIV, 1, 88 ff.

ousting the tenacious Richard Bourne. There was trouble over this grant: it was made by the bishop on 27 September 1590 to Thomas Purfey and his assigns for the lives of George Purfey, William Purfey and Edward Purfey, the sons of Thomas's brother Edward Purfey of Fenny Drayton, or the longest liver. But the chapter were unhappy about the matter and stayed their approval of this and other grants of the bishop, and Dean Herbert, who was in London, conveyed their doubts to members of the council, Whitgift, Fortescue and Hatton. He wrote back to Wells on 5 October giving their opinion that it would be difficult to withhold approval of the grants as long as they were in the usual form and did not impair the state of the church. When the chapter debated the matter on 19 October it was in the knowledge that the bishop was not expected to live, and they decided to give Purfey a temporary grant. If the bishop were still alive and *compos mentis* on 2 January this temporary grant was to be surrendered and Purfey given a new one for three lives on delivery of a bond of £1,000; should the bishop die before that date, Purfey was to give bond for £500 that he would not assign the patent to the corporation or borough of Wells. Accordingly, on 23 October, less than a month before the bishop died, the dean and chapter confirmed the patent to Thomas Purfey on conditions. The office was not to be assigned to any burgess of the city of Wells, or to any other for the use of the city; Purfey and his assigns were from time to time to take a corporal oath to uphold the liberties and privileges of the bishop; and he had to enter immediately into a bond for £100 to the dean and chapter that he would observe these articles.[1] The old struggle for power between the cathedral authorities and the borough, as well as distrust of Thomas Purfey, are reflected in these provisions.

The bishop's other two daughters, Joyce and Anne, married two brothers, Thomas and Dennis Emylie. Thomas held the manor of Helmdon in Northamptonshire and was near neighbour of the Purfeys of Shalstone in Buckinghamshire, his mother-in-law's family; moreover, Godwin had probably known the Emylie family in his Brackley days, while the Purfeys of Shalstone had intermarried with the Purfeys of Fenny Drayton,

---

[1] *Wells*, II, 318–20; P.R.O. C3/262/7; Wells Chapter Acts, Bk. H, fos. 65d, 66.

whose neighbour Godwin had been when at Kirkby Mallory.[1]
These connexions explain why this group of midland gentry
formed part of the entourage of the bishop when he came to
Somerset. Thomas Emylie was older than the rest of the bishop's
family. He was born about 1536 and he must have been quite
twenty years older than his wife, Joyce Godwin. They had four
children, two sons, Maximilian and Edward (b. 1586), and
four daughters, Judith, Mary (b. 1577), Anne and Joyce (b.
1591).[2]

By that first Christmas of Bishop Godwin's in Wells (1584),
Thomas had acquired the key post in the administration of the
episcopal estates, that of under-steward and clerk and recorder
of all the courts of record, although confirmation by the dean
and chapter did not come until 1 April 1585. Thomas Emylie
was to retain the post until 1596.[3] He was then about sixty and
presumably retired to Helmdon (where his family seem to have
remained all the time, for there is no record of their being in
Somerset), and there on 27 April 1607 he made his will 'being
diseased in body but of good and perfect remembrance'. He
wished to be buried in the church at Helmdon, towards the
repair of which he left 6s. 8d. To his youngest daughter,
Joyce, he bequeathed a messuage or tenement with the appurtenances and three yardlands in the town field of Helmdon,
and to his brother Dennis and Anne his wife the remainder of
the lease of the 'college house' in Helmdon which they occupied,
together with the barn and close, all leased from Magdalen
College, Oxford. His servants were remembered and all the
residue of his estate was given to 'Joyce my beloved wife and to
Maximilian my eldest son'. He died the next year and was
buried in Helmdon Church on 30 March 1609. His wife,
Joyce, lived until 1622 and, described as 'gentlewoman widow',
was buried on 17 May. Her sister Anne, wife of Dennis Emylie,
had died the previous year and was buried on 11 April. So these
two Godwin sisters, survived perhaps only by their brothers

[1] P.R.O. Req. 2/31/40; Thomas Emylie's will P.C.C. 57 Windebank; Browne
Willis, *Buckinghamshire*, pp. 262–3.

[2] P.R.O. E.178/1966; J. Bridges, *History of Northamptonshire*, 1, 173; Helmdon
Parish Register (1572–1704) which I was able to consult by the kindness of the
Rev. R. J. Rowbury.

[3] Chapter Acts, Bk. H, fo. 30; P.R.O. E.178/1966, S.C.6/Eliz./2009.

Francis at Hereford and Paul at Wells, died within a year of each other at Helmdon.[1]

Although Thomas Emylie exerted much influence at Wells he did not indulge in the blatant peculation of which Thomas Godwin and Thomas Purfey were to be guilty. While they fled from Somerset when inquiries were instituted into the purloining of the bishop's goods after his death, Emylie was retained in his post as under-steward, and he was a member of the second commission of inquiry of 1591 which investigated the disposal of the bishop's estates. He seems to have been a conscientious officer: in 1586 he compiled a rental of the bishop's estates which became a 'domesday book' for future reference, and between 1592 and 1596 he was commissioned by the Crown, with William Watkins, to collect debts owing to Bishop Godwin before his death. Although in 1597 he was involved with William Watkins in a dispute about the lease of the demesnes of the manor of Wells, which Watkins claimed, he seems to have been acting in the interests of the bishop and to have tried to ensure that the demesnes, which had always supported the bishop's household, should not be separated from the rest of the estates.[2]

LEASES FOR THE FAMILY

Yet Emylie's integrity in administering his father-in-law's estates was not above question, as is shown by the case which Bartholomew Haggatt, a gentleman of Wells and communar to the dean and chapter, brought into the court of requests in 1586.[3] Haggatt's complaint concerned the renewal of his lease of some demesne land, one messuage and seventeen acres of arable land, meadow and pasture, and a further twenty acres of arable land, pasture and wood known as the Vineyards at Wick. Bishop Berkeley had granted this land to him about twenty-one years previously and, his lease being due to expire, at Christmas 1584 Haggatt made suit to the

---

[1] P.C.C. 57 Windebank; Helmdon Parish Register.

[2] P.R.O. S.C.6/Eliz./2009, E.178/1966, C2/W.18/50.

[3] The entire story of this dispute is contained in P.R.O. Req. 2/31/40, Req. 2/223/1 and Req. 2/96/42; Wells, II, 301–15.

new bishop, Godwin, for its renewal. The bishop received
Haggatt lying in his bed in his bedchamber at the end of the
gallery in the palace. Dr John Day, his chancellor, and others
were standing by, and in their presence he promised Haggatt a
renewal of the lease for three lives and longest liver for a fine of
£20. He then called Thomas Emylie and instructed him to
draw up the appropriate lease. During the following weeks
Haggatt had several discussions with Emylie about the matter,
but Emylie was evasive and by 'dilatory answers' prolonged
the negotiations until Shrovetide 1585, when Haggatt named his
three co-lessees and earnestly requested both Emylie and the
bishop to complete the lease.

Meanwhile Emylie had cunningly forestalled him. According
to Dennis Emylie, when Mistress Isabel Godwin was lying upon
her deathbed she entreated her husband the bishop to make provision for the maintenance of Dennis and Anne Emylie and their
children as soon as convenient, and he promised to do so. After
Godwin's promotion to the bishopric Dennis Emylie wrote reminding him of that pledge, and Emylie also solicited the help of
his brother Thomas and his brother-in-law Thomas Godwin in
bringing pressure on the bishop to obtain a lease of lands for him.
Mindful of the interests of all of the bishop's children, Thomas
Emylie went through the records and compiled a short list of
those leases which had nearly expired. He then penned five or six
of them to be granted to several of the bishop's children, including a lease of Haggatt's land which was to go to Dennis and Anne
Emylie and their children. The bishop rejected some of these
leases, including that which covered some lands in Wiveliscombe, because they contained no clause excepting the woods.
They were then redrafted.

The crucial time was a January evening in 1585, immediately
after dinner, when the bishop was sitting in his chair at the upper
end of the table in the 'cracking chamber',[1] or audience chamber, in his palace at Wells. He was 'sickly of the disease of the
gout whereof he had long been pained', and many of his entourage obviously thought he was 'like to die'. Among those standing
by were Robert Whithorne, a notary public of Wells, and
Thomas Emylie's servant Richard Vincent, who had followed

[1] Crack = talk, chat. *English Dialect Dictionary*, ed. J. Wright.

him down from Helmdon. To the bishop in this vulnerable condition Emylie produced 'divers and sundry writings in parchment', the second versions of the leases, and to each one of them the bishop set his seal and signature, Whithorne and two others witnessing them. But did the bishop read the leases before signature? Was he sufficiently composed to understand their contents? That was the point on which the case hinged, for the lease of the ex-Haggatt lands was one of them. Witnesses were not unanimous in the matter, but Emylie's servant Vincent was positive that the bishop 'did read privately to himself the said lease'. Whether or not the bishop did so he was obviously incapable of understanding its contents. His faltering memory and confusion were apparent when he was questioned about it four years later, on 3 January 1588, by William Bowerman and William Jones, who went to him at his Banwell home to take the statement. He agreed then that Bartholomew Haggatt was the tenant of the land in question; he recalled promising Haggatt a renewal of the lease in return for a fine and instructing Thomas Emylie to draw it up. He did not know what action was taken on these instructions, and he was not aware of writing or sealing a lease to Dennis Emylie, even at the time of his sickness, when Thomas Emylie on one occasion brought him many writings to be sealed. Had he known of any lease prejudicial to the interests of Bartholomew Haggatt he would not have passed it.

Against this there is the explanation, given on 21 October 1587, by Thomas and Dennis Emylie of the circumstances in which the bishop made the original lease. Since he was aged and sickly he feared a sudden death, but because of his 'continued great housekeeping' both before and since coming to the bishopric, he had not made any provision for the advancement of his children. He therefore arranged that leases of some small parcels of lands of the bishopric, which were void, or nearly void, should be made to the children, and among these was the one to Dennis Emylie. The Emylies admitted that the bishop may not have known in detail the lands contained in the leases, but he was well able to read and he did read the greater part of Dennis Emylie's lease. Dennis himself was a stranger to Wells when the lease was made, and he knew nothing of it until it was handed to him by his brother, as the gift of the bishop.

When Dennis later asked the bishop for a new and longer lease he seemed to have forgotten the original one, and Thomas Emylie had to remind him that he had already endowed Dennis and Anne his wife. Then the bishop 'seemed nothing discontent therewith . . . but delivered words of natural piety towards his daughter'. They agreed that the bishop had intended that Haggatt should have preferment of the lease after them, and they would have honoured this wish. Bartholomew Haggatt did not succeed in dislodging the bishop's sons-in-law, although it was decreed that the lease granted to Dennis Emylie should be lodged in court and that the bishop should make a new lease to the complainant. The old lease was handed in, but Haggatt died, the new lease still undrawn, and in November 1589 his widow Margaret renewed the case against the bishop.

There are details of some of the other leases which the bishop's children acquired. The most interesting is the lease of the Towerhead estate at the eastern end of Banwell, where the bishop built a new house, 'known by the name of Towerhead or Ockingham House in Banwell', for his son Thomas, who seems to have shared this property with Thomas Purfey. There is no doubt that this house was originally called Ockingham House, and not merely Towerhead House, by the bishop, who obviously felt an exile from his native Ockingham (the modern Wokingham) in Berkshire: there are many references to it under this name.[1] Lying three-quarters of a mile to the east of the church, it was a large, substantial structure in the Elizabethan style with a front porch, over which were the bishop's arms impaling Bath and Wells with the family motto (the one which appeared on the tomb of Francis Godwin at Whitbourne in Herefordshire), *Godwyn—wyn God wyn all*. The house contained a hall, a great chamber, a parlour with a small chamber above, two more little chambers, a study, a kitchen, a larder, a bakehouse and a dairy; there was a well which served it outside, and a causeway was constructed from it to the church for the convenience of the bishop's family. The house was pulled down about 1840 and a new building erected to the south-west of it. This modern house had some remains of the bishop's house incorporated in it: some old

[1] P.R.O. E.178/1966; Long, *Church and Parish of Wokingham*, p. 17n.

stone doorways, an oaken iron-studded door and the sculptured stone bearing the bishop's arms.[1]

The lease of this messuage carried with it a virgate of land and one other tenement with a fardel of land to the value of £16; but Thomas Godwin and Thomas Purfey, described as 'of Banwell, gentlemen', acquired other lands in Banwell— 19 acres of meadow at Way Wick and 4 acres at Westgarston— all for a rent of 35s. This lease, dated 30 December 1587, also included the four grist mills in Wells known as the Out Mills and In Mills at the normal rent of £24: in other words, the lessees were given the monopoly of milling in Wells which Thomas Clerke had once enjoyed. At the same time they were given a lease of the parsonage of Corston for twenty-one years.[2] These were not all the benefits of Godwin and Purfey. On 28 September 1587 they gained a lease of an entire manor, that of West Buckland, in theory for twenty-one years: it had only just come back to direct episcopal control after being leased to the Colles family for most of Bishop Berkeley's rule. The rent, however, was quite a fair one by past standards: they paid £48 a year, whereas the Colles had paid £47. 18. 5d. For some unknown reason, however, the manor was retaken by the bishop, perhaps through pressure of local interests, and granted to John Allott on 14 September 1589.[3]

Another family transaction was that of the reversion of a property called Whorwalles (?) and a decayed lodge upon Mendip, which was confirmed to Dennis Emylie after the bishop's death, when he gave bond for £40 for it at Michaelmas 1597. Even the demesne lands of the manor of Wells, or a large part of them, came into the hands of those two adventurers, Godwin and Purfey. On 27 April 1588 the bishop granted them a lease of these for twenty-one years, which he was able to persuade the dean and chapter to confirm, although the five closes involved were normally kept in hand for the maintenance of the bishop's household. Godwin and Purfey 'for a great sum of money' assigned the lease to William Watkins and John Marshal; Marshal soon died, and in 1597, after Bishop Godwin's

---

[1] P.R.O. E.178/1966; F. A. Knight, *The Seaboard of Mendip*, p. 425.
[2] *Wells*, II, 312; Chapter Acts, Bk. H, fo. 45d.
[3] *Wells*, II, 311; Chapter Acts, Bk. H, fos. 43d, 50d.

death, Thomas Emylie entered into dispute with the survivor, William Watkins, about the lease. Emylie alleged that after Purfey's death, Godwin, the surviving lessee, assigned it to him by deed; Emylie denied that the lease had ever been passed to Watkins and Marshal, and he seems to have been acting on behalf of the bishopric rather than for his own benefit. Accounts for 1590–92 indeed confirm that the demesne land 'formerly held in the bishop's hand' had been leased out. Some of the Banwell demesne, the Lord's Meadow and the Court Orchard, was also on lease—one suspects to Godwin and Purfey, but there is no proof.[1]

THE BISHOP'S LIFE AT BANWELL

Banwell was in fact the centre of the bishop's interest. Wells saw little of him. No doubt the moated palace aggravated his gout, for it was allowed to fall into decay and part of it was pulled down and the stone carted away to Banwell to assist in building the new house. After the bishop's death John Mayne, a plumber and tiler, estimated that it would cost more than £100 to repair the plumbing and tiling, and Richard Counsell, one of the workmen at Wells, spoke of the 'great waste and spoil' in the bishop's woods, where 200 oaks had been felled every year since the bishop's coming.[2] The bishop lived instead in his old palace at Banwell. This manor house is generally supposed to have been despoiled by the Protector Somerset during his tenure of the manor and it has been said that no bishop lived there subsequently. This is incorrect. After Godwin's death the house was said to be in a reasonably good state of repair and better than the bishop had found it: £5 would repair the tiling and plumbing. There is no description of the appearance of this old palace in the last decade of the sixteenth century; the only references are to its external surroundings, to the barn, the stable, the slaughterhouse, the fowl yard and the beerhouse with its furnace of copper, a keeve (or large tub) standing under a leaden cooler, and a vat. There was a great nut tree in the Court Orchard there.

[1] P.R.O. E.178/1966, C2/W.18/50, S.C.6/Eliz./2013 and 2014.
[2] P.R.O. E.178/1966. The subsequent description of life at Banwell is also built up from this source.

We must imagine Bishop Godwin living a life of almost retired ease in his palace at Banwell, for the evidence of his register shows that he spent most of his time there.[1] At the same time he earned a reputation for hospitality: 'he was a man very well esteemed in the country, beloved of all men for his great housekeeping; of the better sort, for his kind entertainment and pleasing discourse at his table.'[2] His household was certainly well equipped to meet these demands. Apart from the hierarchy of officers who looked after his estates, there were at least twenty-two other lesser servants besides the common labourers. They included Thomas Williams, the coachman, who drove the bishop's cushioned coach drawn by two great horses. The most important of these lower officers was perhaps Thomas Middleham, a notary, who acted as the bishop's private secretary; whether he was related to the John Middleham who had witnessed Bishop Berkeley's will is not known.

The palace was comfortably furnished: the bishop's guests gathered round a fair drawing table of walnut and there was a choice of chairs. The bishop probably occupied one of black leather, but there was another leather one, two green cloth ones, one of silk, and twelve joined stools. There were hangings and tapestries, the best one depicting St Dunstan, and three green curtains of a linen-woollen mixture adorning the walls, over forty velvet and tapestry cushions, and carpets, one of silk with imagery on it, which were not necessarily used on the floors. Storage space was provided by six livery cupboards and seven chests. Many guests could be invited to sleep, for the palace contained at least twenty-eight beds, ranging from several good ones of wainscot worth 30s. each to plain ones at 4s. One would sleep well, because it was the practice in the bishop's spacious household to use two feather beds to each bedstead: there were at least sixty feather beds, forty pairs of sheets, some of fine linen, thirty-two blankets, fifty bolsters and pillows, and tapestry coverlets, some lined with blue linen. The amount which the bishop invested in linen and soft furnishings was indeed remarkable: at his death it was valued at twice as much (£156) as furniture, pewter and brass. Besides the candle-sticks of pewter and brass and the pewter dishes adorning the

[1] H.M.C. 10th Report, App. p. 266 ff.   [2] Harington, *Nugae Antiquae*, II, 156.

damask cloths on his table, there was some impressive silver-
ware: two great standing pots of silver and gilt, a great salt of
silver and gilt weighing 39½ oz., and several other silver pots,
some with covers.

The bishop could also dress well to receive his guests, in a
chymmer, or loose upper robe, of silk grosgrain. He had at least
three of these, two of them faced with calever and lined with
squirrel; his rochet was of holland with cambric sleeves, and all
could be topped with a velvet coat and taffeta hat. On more
formal occasions he would wear a satin cassock lined with
squirrel, a tippet of rich taffeta, and his doctor's hood of scarlet
lined with taffeta. His parliament robes were at Banwell too,
probably never used.

There at Banwell he must have watched the erection of the
handsome mansion at Towerhead, and out to him would ride
Thomas Emylie, his steward from Wells, to show him the great
rental which he drew up in 1586 and which revealed a grati-
fying increase in the number of pigs of lead which the Priddy
miners were sending down to Wells as their royalties to the
bishop. Clerics came to him there at Banwell to be ordained in
his private chapel, thus saving the bishop the journey to Wells,
as did Edmund Wattes, his domestic chaplain, to ask to be made
a canon residentiary, a matter which the bishop was able to
arrange on 1 October 1588.[1] His son Francis, the canon of Wells,
would ride out bringing him the latest gossip of the cathedral
which his father so much neglected, and they would share the
joys of scholarship together, sampling the contents of the bishop's
library. Now it would be a topical work, 'Sermons against the
Puritans', or a much-worn book which had lost its cover, entitled 'The Power of Priesthood to forgive sins'. Or they might
take down from the shelves the works of Cicero or St Augustine,
'a great book of cosmography' in Latin called *Theatrum Orbis*,
a herbal, or some of the religious pamphlets the bishop
owned. These they would discuss together, the portraits of
Whitgift, Burghley, Walsingham and Hatton looking down
from the walls to remind the aged bishop of his great days at
court.

[1] H.M.C. 10th Report, App. p. 265.

THE DEATH OF BISHOP GODWIN
AND THE SEIZURE OF HIS PROPERTY

At last, about 7 October 1589, the bishop left Banwell, either in his coach drawn by two sumpter horses, or perhaps in the great chair in which he was sometimes carried, and suffering the agonies of gout as he jogged along on the journey from which he never returned, to go to his native Wokingham, where he had started life in humble circumstances. The bishop was a trained physician and probably knew that his life was in decline. Just over a year later, at four o'clock in the morning on Thursday 19 November 1590, the crisis was reached, and he sent young Nicholas Clunne, his servant, in haste to Reading to fetch some medicine. While Clunne sped through the darkness the members of the household gathered round the bishop's bedside. Thomas Purfey and his father, William Purfey, were there, as were the bishop's youngest son Paul, his confidential clerk Thomas Middleham, Thomas Manton, and another cleric Joseph Colliar, who lived at Nunney in Somerset and was a friend of the bishop's eldest son Thomas.

The thoughts of those present perhaps strayed to a certain black box or casket where the bishop kept his money and which he guarded most jealously. Robert, the third son, had seen it opened, but the bishop had refused to allow him to look inside. Thomas Purfey managed to get control of the casket, but there were conflicting versions of what took place. Purfey himself later said that the bishop opened the box while Clunne was away at Reading and divided the contents, £41. 11s. in gold and two or three gold rings, between him and Paul Godwin, whereas according to Joseph Colliar the key of the box was handed to William Purfey by Thomas Purfey two hours before the bishop died, 'the which key he willed his father to keep very safe', and it was not until two days after the bishop's death that the box was opened. Thomas Godwin had thought that his father had at least £500 there, but great was Purfey's anger when he found only three crowns of silver and fifteen shillings of white money, one piece of gold and three seals.

The bishop was buried on the following Tuesday, 24 November 1590, in the south chancel of Wokingham church, where he

is still commemorated by the floor slab now in the choir vestry
and by a tablet on the north wall of the north aisle.[1] For the
funeral the church was 'hanged with blacks'; altogether about
£61 was spent with John Johnson, a merchant taylor of London,
for 'blacks for the funeral of the bishop', although this sum
probably covered funeral apparel as well as drapery.

During the last year of the bishop's life Thomas Godwin and
Thomas Purfey had gained control of the management of his
affairs down in Somerset. At the same time they were both
getting into personal debt, for they jointly owed about £430 at
the bishop's death, and Thomas Godwin was defaulting in his
payments as collector of the clerical subsidies and tenths to the
exchequer. The trouble over the payment of subsidies had been
brewing for some time, for as early as 27 October 1587 his
father had written to Lord Burghley from Banwell asking for
respite for one term for a tenth already due. In great distress
he pleaded:

> process is too terrible to me, and so disgraceful to my place the
> credit whereof I would fain maintain, for the bettering of my
> service, hath forced me to be thus bold with your Lordship. It shall
> be the last time that I will trouble you with this kind of suit.[2]

Obviously Godwin and Purfey saw their financial salvation in
the bishop's death. They had sold some of his property before
he died, such as the two livery pots of silver all gilt weighing
144½ oz. for £35, and three bowls of silver with a cover of silver
all gilt weighing 100½ oz. for £25, which went to Henry
Kindersley, a citizen and merchant taylor of London for cash.
Peter Robinson, a citizen and salter of London, had bought
from them a standing cup of silver gilt for £10 14s. and also, a
month before the bishop died, his parliament robes for £9.

As soon as the news of the bishop's death reached Somerset
his relatives and hangers-on scrambled to seize his personal
property, for the bishop had died intestate and in debt to the
Crown and others for £3,000,[3] and the family knew that the
sheriff or a special commission would soon arrive to seize the
late bishop's property to meet his debts. Margaret Haggatt had

---

[1] Long, *Wokingham*, p. 66, gives the full inscription.
[2] B.M. Add. MS, 25460, fo. 204.   [3] *Wells*, II, 320.

something to say about this when she revived her case against the Emylies about January 1592: she blamed their 'fraudulent and indirect dealings' for the pillaging of the bishop's estates. They put up a vigorous defence, blaming Thomas Godwin and Thomas Purfey 'who, many have since thought, were too long and too near about the bishop for his part while he lived'. The Emylies alleged that these two were trusted by the bishop with all that he had, namely with the receipt of all his rents and revenues, and of all the tenths, subsidies and benevolences of the clergy of his diocese due to the queen. They had failed to pay this money into the exchequer, as they should have done, so that the bishop 'as a sheep led to the slaughter' was brought into debt unawares. Thomas Emylie claimed that he 'never had so much as a black gown or a mourning coat, or otherwise the worth of one penny of the said bishop's goods after his death'.[1] There is no evidence to the contrary.

It was the Godwins and Purfeys who were busy seizing clothes, household linen, silver, pewter, furniture, pictures, books and farmstock, in fact all the late bishop's movable goods of value. Thomas Purfey was with the bishop in Wokingham, but his wife Blandina was at Banwell. Joan Came, a local widow, described how by the light of the candle she carried she saw Mistress Purfey pack up all the best carpets and coverlets that were in the house at Towerhead, all the best hangings and apparel, except those taken to Wokingham by the bishop, and all the sheets, except seventeen or eighteen pairs of the worst ones which Thomas Godwin and Thomas Manton told Mistress Purfey to leave there so that the sheriff might find something when he came. All the linen was made up into four great packs and Mistress Purfey had an inventory of the contents made for her husband's use. Widow Came added that these packs were carried away by night two days later. Mistress Godwin, the wife of Thomas Godwin, also assisted in the disposal of the bishop's pictures and in packing up his linen, his four best feather beds and other furniture and bedding which were carried to Francis Godwin's house at Wells. Then there was the pewter, which, according to Alice Nebbes, was hidden in the ground at the Towerhead house after the bishop's death by William

[1] P.R.O. C2/W.18/50.

Baker before Purfey came there; on his arrival Purfey had told Baker to carry all the pewter into the study, but Alice did not know what became of it.

The bishop's store of arms, acquired no doubt against the perils of the Armada scare two years before, and consisting of thirty-six calevers (large pistols or blunderbusses), with their powder flasks, touch boxes and head pieces, were also hidden underground in the bishop's hop garden. All the pigs were delivered out of the gate of the bishop's palace at Banwell by the same William Baker and his helpers on the Saturday or Sunday after the bishop's death (that is, even before his burial), before Thomas Purfey came down from London and probably unknown to him. Several wagon-loads of goods were brought out, some to Wells, and Edward Quarre of Banwell remembered a cart driven out late in the evening and covered with mats, presumably to conceal the contents.

What was remarkable about the seizure of the bishop's goods was the speed with which it was effected and the wide area over which they were dispersed. The chief beneficiaries were the relatives and friends of the Godwin circle, but the local parsons had their share. Robert Woolfall, the parson of Wanstrow, acquired a mare worth 30s., and bedding and table linen. Thomas Manton had a feather bed, a bolster, a pair of blankets, a coverlet of tapestry, a cupboard, and some of the bishop's books; and the parsonage house of Middlezoy, where Peter Rawlins was vicar, had four packs of apparel and linen. One of Peter's sons, John, had a board cloth of damask out of this hoard, and another, Matthew, acquired the bishop's scarlet hood which he had made into a waistcoat. Outside the immediate locality the geographical distribution of the goods was very wide. George Purfey of Drayton in Leicestershire, the high sheriff of that county, had twenty-five horses, although the cost of these was afterwards charged to Edward Purfey. Thomas Purfey's father, William Purfey of Hollingbourne in Kent, acquired goods to the value of £10. John Walsall, a doctor of divinity of Easling in Kent, selected the kind of goods which marked him as a special friend of the bishop, perhaps of his Canterbury days: a college pot of silver with a cover worth £6 and the bishop's great chair in which he had been carried.

The full story of the episode would be tedious, although the Crown was much concerned to reconstruct all its details. In brief, the queen and her council acted promptly after the death of the bishop on 19 November; within ten days a commission had been issued out of the exchequer to Sir Henry Berkeley of Bruton, one of the deputy lieutenants of Somerset, Thomas Horner of Mells, J.P., and two of the chapter at Wells, Philip Bisse and John Langworth, doctors of divinity, to inquire into the matter.[1] Thomas Fanshawe, the queen's remembrancer, provided them with instructions. They were to seize all the late bishop's goods and chattels and to value and store them towards the satisfaction of the debts due to the crown; to discover what debts were owed to the bishop and to seize the bonds made to cover them; to ascertain what corn was sown upon any of the demesnes or lands possessed by the bishop and to assess its value; and to inquire who held the revenues due to the Crown before the bishop's death and what sums remained unpaid. The commissioners were to lease the demesne of the bishopric for the profit of the Crown during the vacancy and to certify what timber trees had been felled upon the episcopal estates in Godwin's time and for what purpose. Lastly, they were to report on the state of the bishop's house and on the condition of the woods.

By 10 December 1590 the commission was at work taking evidence from thirty-one witnesses. They were all from the locality—from Banwell, Wells, Westbury and Hewish—and they were all interested parties, relatives, officers or servants of the bishop. The Crown was obviously not satisfied with the result. On 30 November 1591 a second commission was given to Thomas Emylie, the late bishop's under-steward and son-in-law, and to William Watkins, to pursue inquiries further. Their action was more thorough than that of the first commission: they called forty-eight witnesses, against the previous thirty-one, and only seven had previously given evidence. These seven in general, and Nicholas Clunne, William Blake and John Warren in particular, gave much more detailed evidence the second time. The new commissioners also called their witnesses

---

[1] Bates Harbin, *Members for Somerset*, pp. 129–30; *Wells*, II, 308, 315. My article *Proc. Som. Arch. Soc.*, XCVI, 78–107.

from a much wider area: they went to Middlezoy and examined eight of its inhabitants about the activities at the parsonage house there, and they questioned four of the London merchants, Henry Kindersley, John Johnson and John Young, merchant taylors, and Peter Robinson, a salter, about the goods they had purchased from Thomas Godwin and Thomas Purfey.

Elizabeth kept the see void for nearly three years, and during the vacancy the Crown received the revenues through Thomas Sherwood, who was appointed the receiver-general on 12 February 1591.[1] In a way this was a fair device, since the bishopric owed the Crown so much. The next bishop, John Still, was not consecrated until 11 February 1593, but the miserable inquiries went on into his episcopate. On 28 November 1605 a third commission was issued to Francis Godwin, the bishop's second son, now bishop of Llandaff, Sir Henry Poole, George Escott and others, to go yet more closely into the matter. They were ordered particularly to examine what goods, chattels and lands the bishop had possessed since 9 October 1589. (This was probably the date on which he had left Banwell to retire to Wokingham, for Samuel Pettingale, the curate of Banwell, said that he left about 7 October the year before he died.) The commissioners were also to discover what property Thomas Godwin and Thomas Purfey, here described as 'the factor and dealer of the bishop', had then and since, to seize all lands possessed by either of them then, and to ascertain if any goods found by the former commissions had been sold under value, and if so by whose authority. Yet another commission was issued in June 1607 to Francis Godwin, bishop of Llandaff, Robert Robotham, his archdeacon there, Paul Godwin, the late bishop's youngest son, and others, and there is evidence that they concentrated on mopping up the outstanding debts.[2]

While all these inquiries were going on the two individuals most involved had fled from Somerset, which was obviously too hot for them. Thomas Purfey went to Youghal in Ireland to join Sir Walter Raleigh's other west country settlers there, and

---

[1] P.R.O. S.C.6/Eliz./2013 and 2014.
[2] All the details of the death of Bishop Godwin and the commissions of inquiry are taken from P.R.O. E.178/1966.

died about 1591;[1] one wonders if he took his wife Blandina with him. Thomas Godwin went first to Waverley in Surrey, presumably to visit the Mr Pike who had acquired some of Bishop Godwin's plate.[2] He was still there after the death of Purfey in Ireland, because it was from there that he wrote to Thomas Emylie assigning to him a lease which he had held jointly with Purfey.[3] Margaret Haggatt said that they had both fled overseas and Godwin may eventually have gone to Ireland; he died before 1623, for his wife Margaret had married again by that date.[4]

The Elizabethan bishops were themselves often to blame for the profiteering of their families: one such was Bishop Sandys of Worcester who made a very good thing for his family out of the possessions of the see, giving them lands on very long leases at inadequate rents, and who stripped the episcopal residences of everything he could carry away when he left Worcester for London.[5] Bishop Godwin seems rather to have been the victim of ill-health and covetous children. How much, we may wonder, did Harington know when he wrote that Godwin was 'used like a leaden conduit pipe to convey water to others, and drink nothing but the dregs and dross and rust itself'.[6]

---

[1] P.R.O. C2/W.18/50. A. L. Rowse, *The Expansion of Elizabethan England*, pp. 142–3. The registers of Youghal do not begin until the 1660's, but they show the burial of two widows of the name of Purfey in 1676 and 1696, evidence that there was a family of that name settled there. There are also several Godwins in the register.

[2] P.R.O. E.178/1966.   [3] P.R.O. C2/W.18/50.

[4] *Visitation of Somerset 1623*, p. 11.

[5] A. L. Rowse, *The England of Elizabeth*, pp. 410–14.

[6] Harington, *Nugae Antiquae*, II, 154.

CHAPTER VI

Bishop Still: Firm Administrator

THE STILL FAMILY

THE sad condition in which Bishop Godwin left the bishopric is reflected in a dispute which came to court in 1590. Robert Owen, the bishop's registrar, had paid William Lancaster £52 a year for the office, but both his own authority and episcopal jurisdiction were being challenged by David Sarney and Thomas Bartlett, the registrars of the archdeacon, who, he alleged, had issued licences to marry and probates of wills and pocketed the fees.[1] Obviously episcopal office was regarded as a form of property to be bought and sold and to be made to yield its profit.

Such incidents as this dispute, and Bishop Godwin's indebtedness to the Crown for clerical taxes, gave the puritans easy arguments in their attacks on the establishment, which had reached their peak in the parliament of 1586. Dr Peter Turner, the son of Dean William Turner, who had been Somerset's protégé, was one of their leaders in demanding a revised prayerbook on the Genevan model, and now Anthony Cope and the 'root and branch' extremists were advocating the abolition of all existing statutes, laws and institutions of the church. In parliament the cry rang out 'Let cathedral churches be utterly destroyed.'[2] In this revolutionary atmosphere it was indispensable to the discipline and repute of the diocese to send a man of the highest character and learning to the West. There was much speculation about the possible nominee and the price he would have to pay for promotion: the plunder of the church by

[1] P.R.O. Req. 2/248/57 and 58.
[2] J. E. Neale, *Elizabeth I and her Parliaments 1584–1601*, pp. 62, 147.

the court had not abated, and it was generally held that the manor house and park at Banwell would be awarded to some courtier. Harington reported that Sir Thomas Heneage, vice-chamberlain and chancellor of the duchy of Lancaster, was thought to 'have an oar in the matter' and that he might acquire a bigger booty than Banwell; 'but', continued Harington, 'when it was notified once who was named to it, I had better conceit, and straight I wrote to him, as an old Cambridge acquaintance, and in such rusty Latin as I had left, gave him warning of this rumour, which he took exceeding kindly at my hands, though some other frowned on me for it, many months after.'

The 'old Cambridge acquaintance' was Dr John Still, Harington's old tutor, for whom he had a high regard expressed in that memorable tribute: 'to whom I never came but I grew more religious; from whom I never went but I parted better instructed . . . his breeding was from his childhood in good literature, and partly in music . . . I have heard good music of voices in his house.'[1] Still was very much a man of the eastern counties, born at Grantham in Lincolnshire and bred up at Christ's College Cambridge, of which he was a fellow from 1562 to 1572. He replaced Thomas Cartwright, expelled for his puritan teaching, as the Margaret Professor of Divinity in 1570. He had a high reputation as an historian, philosopher and divine, and as a redoubtable opponent of the puritans. Archbishop Parker was impressed by him and in 1571 collated him to the rectory of Hadleigh in Suffolk, to which in 1572 was joined the deanery of Bocking; he also appointed Still as his chaplain. Still was master of St John's in 1574, then of Trinity in 1577, and twice vice-chancellor.[2] He was clearly marked for promotion, for he was a client of the Earl of Leicester, and the subject had been raised as early as 1579 when Gabriel Harvey wrote to Leicester from Trinity Hall:

Your lordship hath a very learned and wise chaplain, Mr. Doctor Still, a man of very good government, and in all respects very meek, and sufficiently furnished to such a place as your lordship of your singular wisdom can judge (which did evidently appear by making

---

[1] *Nugae Antiquae*, II, 157–165. [2] *D.N.B.*

choice of him for the voyage to Smalcaldy etc.) and the common opinion and special liking of all men doth testify. If your lordship thought good to prefer him to the bishopric (as is already desired of many, especially of us university men, and such other of judgement, who find a great want of such able men in like places of authority) I know of all men my old tutor and continued friend would make choice of no other.[1]

Still's known hostility to the puritans would commend him also to Archbishop Whitgift, and it is not surprising that once his election had been decided on it was hustled through, thus ending the long vacancy. Elizabeth I was anxious that he should take his place with the other bishops in the parliament summoned for 19 February 1593. He was installed and enthroned that day.[2] Not an acre had been sacrificed to ambition, and there was never any suggestion that it had been.

Dr Still was yet another married bishop with a family. During his sojourn as rector of Hadleigh in Suffolk he had married Anna, the daughter of Thomas Alabaster, a clothier of that town.[3] There were nine children of this marriage, but three of them had died young, while Still was at Hadleigh. When the doctor and his wife moved to Wells they were accompanied by Sarah, a young lady of eighteen; the eldest son and heir, Nathaniel, aged thirteen; Anne aged eleven; Elizabeth who was nine; Mary who was seven; and John who was just five. Anna, the mother, lived only two months longer to enjoy the promotion, and was taken back to her native Hadleigh for burial. There in the church, very largely obscured by the organ, is the brass to her memory. Some of it is no longer decipherable, but it appears to read:

'In obitum Anne Still uxoris Joh'is E'pi Bathon' et We(llensis) quae obiit Apr. 15° A° 1593.

Hic matrum Matrona iacet pietatis imago

---

[1] P.R.O. Bath II/Dudley II/202. In 1578 Still was the Cambridge delegate at the Diet of Schmalkald.

[2] *Wells*, II, 326–7.

[3] Several pages of the Hadleigh Register are missing between 1568 and 1575, so that the date cannot be ascertained.

Exemplum vitae speculum virtutis honestae
verus Alabaster meritis quae vivit in aevum
Et quam certa fides coelo super astra locavit.'[1]

Beneath this inscription is etched a full-length portrait of Anna
Still. (Is it the only extant picture of an Elizabethan episcopal
wife?) She wears a hat with a rounded crown and a fairly wide
brim. Her costume is in every respect typical of that of an Elizabethan lady: an embroidered underkirtle shows through her
farthingale in front.

The bishop did not long remain a widower. He now strength-
ened his position by marrying into county society. His new wife
was Jane, the daughter of the late Sir John Horner of Cloford
near Frome in Somerset. The Horner family had in their turn
married into that of Sir John Popham, the lord chief justice,
and the names of Horner's sons-in-law reads like a roll of
leading county families: Sir John Mallet, Edward Rogers, Sir
Richard Champernowne, and Roger Warre.[2] Well might
Harington say that the Horners had much local influence:
'a kind of alliance with Judge Popham that swayed all the
temporal government of the country.' The bishop's second
marriage was held to be much more 'justifiable' than the
first, he being not too old, nor she too young, and she was
well provided for by her father's will of 1571 by which he left
300 acres of wood within the manor of Cloford towards the
advancement of his daughters in marriage.[3] Indeed, Jane
brought with her a dowry of £1,050 which was invested in the
manor of Mourton Wroughton in Compton Martin, but by
indenture dated 15 October 1603, this property, which included Mourton Farm and the water grist-mill in Compton
Martin, was held in trust for her by her brother Thomas
Horner of Cloford and his son John.[4]

The bishop's marriage with Jane Horner took place at Ston

---

[1] 'In memory of Anna Still wife of John Bishop of Bath and Wells who died on
April 15 1593. Here lies the best of mothers, the image of piety, an example of
goodness throughout her life, a mirror of virtue and integrity, who by her good
deeds lives a true Albaster for ever. Her unshakable faith has given her a place in
heaven beyond the stars.'

[2] Brown, *Wills*, v, 108, 161.

[3] P.C.C. 33 Rutland; TC MS, Sherwood Transcripts, F.A.22.

[4] Bishop Still's Will P.C.C. 33 Windebank; S.R.S., LI, 166.

Easton on 16 December 1594. Harington alleged that the queen, with her usual impatience of episcopal marriages, was not very well pleased with the match but that she let it pass with a jest to Sir Henry Berkeley, playing on the name of the bishop's wife, that 'it was a dangerous name for a bishop to match with a Horner.'[1] There is an odd story about this second wife, reported to be a woman of uncommon probity. One summer's day about 1596 a thunderstorm occurred during divine service in Wells Cathedral and the lightning left the sign of a cross on the bodies of many, including the bishop and his wife.[2]

Although there was only one son of this marriage, Thomas, who was still a minor when his widowed mother died in 1608, there were also the children of the first marriage to provide for, and Bishop Still was faced with the problems of Bishop Godwin in securing the future of his offspring. All his daughters married. Sarah, the eldest, married William Morgan, variously described as woollen draper and gentleman of Worminster, a hamlet on the outskirts of Wells; they had six children, but the mother died young, just before her father, and was buried in the cathedral. Another daughter, Anne, married Robert Eyre of Wells; Elizabeth chose Richard Edwards of London; and Mary's husband was Sefton Jones. All had children, but how many is unknown. When the bishop died he left to each family the sum of £100, and £20 for each of the grandchildren (William Morgan did not receive £100, for he was then a widower, but he was forgiven debts amounting to £54); in addition they all received a silver-gilt cup. The bequest to Robert and Anne Eyre ran:

one standing gilt cup of silver with a cover meaning the same to be one of them which I had of the late Queen's Majesty for a New Year's gift to be kept by them without selling or exchanging of the same as a token of my love.[3]

[1] *Somerset and Dorset Notes and Queries*, xii, 158; *Nugae Antiquae*, ii, 161.

[2] H. Pigot, *Hadleigh*, p. 60. Pigot attaches the story to Anna Alabaster, the first wife, in the year before her death, but she was not alive in 1596 and she did not live through one summer in Wells, only from February to mid-April 1593.

[3] Pigot, pp. 130–9, but he erroneously gives Worminster as Westminster and Sefton Jones as Caston Jones; P.C.C. 33 Windebank; Brown, *Wills*, iii, 113. A. J. Jewers, *Wells Cathedral: Its Monumental Inscriptions and Heraldry*, pp. 147–9 erroneously calls Mary Still's husband Seston Jones, not Sefton Jones.

As well as the four daughters there were the sons, Nathaniel and John, and now by the second marriage, Thomas. The bishop's constant care was to extract the maximum profit from his temporalities in his lifetime, and to provide for his children, and especially his sons, out of that accumulated fortune; in this he succeeded, leaving a dower for his wife and a suitable estate for each son. Harington, well informed about his Somersetshire, knew the chief source of the bishop's personal fortune: it was the increased profits from the Mendip lead mines.

God hath also blest him many ways very greatly, to see his children well brought up, well bestowed, and to have an unexpected renew out of the entrails of the earth (I mean the lead mines of Mendip) greater than his predecessor had above ground.[1]

THE PROFITS OF THE LEAD MINES

When in 1930 J. W. Gough wrote the standard book on the now defunct Mendip lead-mining industry, he was unable to make any assessment of the output of the mines, although he stated that there had been a marked increase from the mid-sixteenth century and that the maximum was reached between about 1600 and 1670. Of the four liberties or mineries into which the mining area was divided for purposes of jurisdiction, he was able to give figures of production running for a series of years for only one, the Chewton minery. These figures were derived from the court rolls of the hundred and manor of Chewton Mendip and the lead-reeves' accounts among the Waldegrave papers at the Estate Office at Chewton Mendip; they were not figures of the total annual production of lead within the Chewton minery, but of the royalty of lot lead, or tenth pound of lead, due to the holder of the manor of Chewton Mendip, who was one of the four lords royal of Mendip. Of the other three mineries, Priddy, Harptree and that usually known as the West Minery, Gough said that no accounts survive.[2]

Priddy Minery, attached to the episcopal manor of Wells and claimed by the bishop of Bath and Wells as a lord royal, is of particular interest in view of Fuller's famous statement:

[1] *Nugae Antiquae*, II 162.
[2] J. W. Gough, *The Mines of Mendip*, p. 114.

It is almost incredible what great sums were advanced to the bishops of Bath and Wells by the benefit of lead, since the latter end of Queen Elizabeth. Bishop Still is said to have had the harvest, bishop Montague the gleanings, bishop Lake the stubble thereof; and yet considerable was the profit of lead to him and his successors.

Again Fuller corroborates Harington's statement of Bishop Still's wealth:

In his days God opened the bosom of the earth, Mendip Hills affording great store of lead, wherewith and with his own providence (which is a constant mine of wealth) he raised a great estate and laid the foundations of three families, leaving to each of them a considerable revenue in a worshipful condition.[1]

Prebendary Coleman, writing in 1909, although not realizing that Fuller was the source of the legend about the bishop's wealth from the mines, was inclined to discount it. Using only two fifteenth-century court rolls of the manor of Wells to glean a few figures of lead production, he concluded that these were 'entirely opposed' to the claim that the bishops acquired great wealth from their mining rights.[2] He estimated that the average annual revenue of the bishops from the mines in the fifteenth century was but £5 10s.; Gough put it as low as between £1 and £3. For the sixteenth century the only figure for any mining liberty quoted by Gough or Coleman is that of the bishop's revenues from lead taken from the *Valor Ecclesiasticus* of 1535: £3. 5. 8d. in an average year. So the question of the bishop's profits, and whether Fuller and Harington exaggerated the Tudor yield, has remained to tease the mind.

Some of the missing detail can now be supplied. Gough's searches took him to the offices of the Church Commissioners, and he used a record of the Code of Mendip Mining Laws deposited there, but not a similar and later copy of the code with additions. He failed, too, to find the account book of Bishop Berkeley's time which covers the years 1566–78, and a court book which contains accounts for 1634–40, both providing figures of the episcopal lead royalties.[3] Again, ministers' accounts of the temporalities of the see, compiled

---

[1] Fuller, *Worthies*, III, 85, 276.   [2] *Proc. Som. Arch. Soc.*, LV, 155–7.
[3] S.R.O. DD/CC/13331, DD/CC/31523, DD/CC/13324.

during vacancies and now in the Public Record Office, include the income from the manor of Wells and supply a few stray lead figures for the sixteenth century. When all this information is brought together, deficient and disjointed as it is, a little more is revealed about the bishops' profits from the mines, at least in Tudor and Early Stuart times, and it suffices to prove a remarkable increase in production in the period covered, the years from 1567 to 1640.

The fourth of the ten basic mining laws which were common to all four Mendip liberties, but to which each liberty made its own additions, makes it clear that the lord royal's tithe was based on the amount of crude lead ore raised within his liberty irrespective of where the ore was actually extracted:

Item that when a workman has landed any ore he may carry the same to cleansing and blowing to what minery he shall please for the more speedy making of the same so that he do truly pay the tenth thereof to the Lord of the soil where it was landed.

The bishop's dues were collected by two lead-reeves who were immediately responsible to his steward. There are many references to their duties, for example, the obligation to keep a register in the storehouse at the minery to record all pledges, pawns or mortgages on pain of £5.[1] One or two names of lead reeves have survived: in the 1580's William Berry and Richard Cocke were performing these duties, but by 1590 Richard West had replaced William Berry and he and Richard Cocke were still lead-reeves in 1593.[2] The Priddy lead-reeves were paid £5 a year each in two instalments at Midsummer and Christmas, yet the lead-reeve at Chewton was paid only 6s. 8d. a year plus 8d. for seizing the goods of disputants. There is evidence that the Chewton job was unpopular on account of its low reward.[3] The lead-reeves kept a separate account of lead dues received, although the total profits were also sometimes entered in the general accounts.[4] No lead-reeves' accounts for the manor of Wells seem to have survived. The general estate accounts were made up annually at the general audit at

[1] S.R.S., xlv, 4, 100, 102–3, 107, 116, 122.
[2] P.R.O. S.C.6/Eliz./2011, 2012, 2013, 2014, S.C.6/Add./3545/84.
[3] S.R.O. DD/CC/13324, Accounts for 1634; Gough, p. 103.
[4] S.R.O. DD/CC/31523, Account for 1567.

Michaelmas and they normally run from the third quarter of each year. The accounts in the court book of 1634 also show quarterly fluctuations in price. The storehouse attached to the Priddy minery not only housed the records but also, of course, the lead tithes. During the years 1582–3, when the bishopric was vacant and the temporalities were being administered by the Crown, £7. 12. 3d. was spent on making a storehouse 'for the safe keeping of the lead of the lady queen called the lot lead within the manor of Wells'.[1]

Whether the hard-pressed bishops were looking for fresh sources of income, or whether it was the general industrial activity of the period which supplied the local impetus, the amount of lot lead climbed steadily from the time of the first Elizabethan bishop, Berkeley, during whose episcopate it quadrupled in just over a decade. The bishop's royalties, which in 1567 were 2 tons 8 cwt. 37 lb., had risen by 1578 to 9 tons 12 cwt. 7 lb.[2] There was a significant drop to 6 tons 15 cwt. 40 lb. in 1592 during the vacancy following Bishop Godwin's episcopate, when the supervision of the estates was probably less careful. For the years 1593–1634, during which time six bishops, including Bishop Still, came to and departed from the palace at Wells, there are no figures. This is the more unfortunate because Gough provides some figures of royalties from the Chewton Minery, where there was a marked increase in production in the early seventeenth century, and comparison of the two would have been interesting.[3] These Chewton figures, available for only three complete years after 1620, are worth noting: in 1620, 22 tons 16 cwt. 12 lb., in 1623, 13 tons 8 cwt. 67 lb., and in 1628, 18 tons 9 cwt. 24 lb. The 'gleanings' which Fuller attributes to Bishop Montague (1608–16) must have been considerable, for Fuller also says that he spent 'vast sums' on the repair of Bath Abbey.[4] It was Montague, too, who drew up afresh the code of mining laws for Priddy Minery in 1612, which in itself suggests that there was much activity needing careful regulation.[5] For the years 1634–40, in Bishop

---

[1] P.R.O. S.C.6/Eliz./2011.

[2] See Appendix D for all figures of royalties. Measurements then were 100 lb. to 1 cwt. and 25 lb. to 1 qr. (Gough, p. 59). This scale has been adopted throughout.

[3] Gough, p. 82.   [4] *Worthies*, III, 89.   [5] S.R.S., XLV, 4.

Peirs' time, there are again figures of the bishop's royalties and they have by now climbed to an annual average of almost 13 tons; in the peak year, 1634, they reach 17 tons. Defective though the evidence is, it suggests that the lord of Chewton slightly outdid the bishop in royalties.

As production rose in Elizabethan and early Stuart times, so did the price. In the fifteenth century it had fluctuated between £4 and £5 a ton, in 1492 dropping to £3. 6. 8d., but by 1572 the bishop's lead was worth £6 10s.[1] Two years later it was fetching £8, and in 1637 it reached the top figure of £11. 13. 4d. Thereafter the price dropped, doubtless in part by reason of the political troubles. When the contractors for the sale of bishops' lands sold the episcopal lead royalties to the corporation of Wells in April 1647, they were valued at £80 a year. Although we may wonder that they were still worth as much as that, it was less than half their net value in the peak year 1634, when they had brought the bishop an income of £177. 6. 11d.[2]

Other evidence of the value attached to the bishop's mining rights on Mendip is the dispute arising out of a grant to one of the episcopal officers, John Lunde, who had been appointed to the key position of store-bailiff, keeper of the palace and woodward in 1590, in Bishop Godwin's time. His subordinate, Cocke the lead-reeve, was given a lease of one-tenth of 'those plots of ground called the hillocks or slagheaps lying in Priddy mineries' together with the lot lead arising. That grant was made by Bishop Still in 1598 and Cocke assigned it to his superior, Lunde, who apparently persuaded the next bishop, Montague, to confirm it to him in a new grant which included a little property in Wells, a garden plot and a small house, and 'also one new erected house lately builded by the Reverend Father in Priddy mineries for the weighing and keeping of lead there with a proviso that the lord and his officers shall weigh lead and keep it there as formerly it hath been done'. By this new grant of 1616 Lunde paid a rent of 7s. 8d., but when a

[1] Gough, p. 62. By comparison the almoner of Westminster Abbey was paying £8 a ton for lead which he bought for repairs in 1473–4. He may, of course, have purchased through a middleman. Institute of Historical Research, Price History Material, P.8/No. 19080.

[2] Wells Museum Notebook, fo. 286; see Appendix D.

rental of Wells manor was drawn up about 1635 the property was valued at 16s. The dispute which arose, sometime before January 1636 when probate of Lunde's will was granted, was between Lunde and John Clarke with his ally William Smaleridge. These two alleged that Lunde's lease was void on several grounds, the most interesting of which were that a bishop cannot grant away the lot lead for longer than his own lifetime, and that Lunde claimed these hillocks as a chattel 'which cannot be, for chattels are things certainly known, this is altogether unknown for it is incorporated into the earth soil freehold of the bishop and lieth some time three feet, six feet, nine feet and more and now less than three feet under earth'. The outcome of the dispute is unknown, but when Lunde made his will on 11 May 1635 he seemed to assume that his title held good. He left his interests in his hillocks to his cousin Edward Hippesley and bequests amounting to £30 to be paid out of the profits.[1]

THE FAMILY ACCUMULATE OFFICES AND ESTATES

Although no lead figures exist to prove Fuller's contention that Bishop Still made a personal fortune, evidence of his wealth survives in his will.[2] This lengthy and detailed document confirms Fuller's remark that Still was able to lay the foundations of three families, those of his three sons, Nathaniel, John and Thomas. Nathaniel had been raised up in his father's Cambridge days to become a fellow of Trinity, and he was bequeathed houses and land in Hadleigh, Suffolk, where he was born in 1579.[3] This property had been purchased by the bishop from his father-in-law, Thomas Alabaster the clothier. Nathaniel also inherited an estate at Hutton in Somerset including the manor-house Hutton Court, which had a fifteenth-century hall and a defensive tower. He settled at Hutton as a country gentleman and became a justice of the peace for Somerset in 1613. He married Jane, the daughter of William Whitmore an alderman of London, and when he died on 2 February 1626 he

[1] S.R.O. DD/CC/13324, fos. 234–5; P.C.C. 1 Pile.
[2] P.C.C. 33 Windebank.
[3] Pigot, *Hadleigh*, p. 137; *D.N.B.*; S.R.S., xxiii, 24; Jewers, *Wells Cathedral*, pp. 147–9; Brown, *Wills*, v, 32.

was buried in the chancel of Hutton Church. John, the second son, born in 1588, was also educated at Trinity and he too adopted the life of a country gentleman. In 1605 he received from his father an estate at Fodington in the parish of Babcary in Somerset: it had been leased back to the vendor, Oliver Lottisham, for £70 a year. John's wife, Ann Baynard, also had a farm, Henbury Farm, in Gloucestershire, but he made his home at West Bower Manor House near Durleigh in Somerset, which he bought from Henry Halswell. This was a splendid home for a bishop's son with its two polygonal towers flanking the gateway and a particularly fine window, all secured by a moat: it is still, in Professor Pevsner's words, 'an impressive survival', now fronted by a reservoir. John Still left this family home to his son John, with an annuity of £50 to his wife during the son's minority. He asked, when he died in 1633, to be buried in the chancel of Durleigh Church.[1]

By his father's will the bishop's youngest son Thomas, the son of 'my well beloved wife Mrs. Jane Horner', being a minor, received only £50 immediately, but after his mother died he was to inherit the £1,420 estate settled on her in dower. This estate consisted of lands in Somerton recently bought by the bishop of Robert Webb of Beckington. The farm-house there was 'now newly reedified' at the bishop's expense. The impropriation of the parsonage of Milton Clevedon also came to his widow and afterwards to his son Thomas. Like his two brothers, Thomas was enabled by his father's wealth to become a country gentle-man: it is curious that none of Bishop Still's sons entered the church. Thomas eventually purchased the manor of Shaston next Shaftesbury in Dorset in 1613 and settled there until his death in 1640. His wife, Bridget Champernowne, died before him, and they were both buried in St James's, Shaftesbury.[2]

There were also monetary bequests in Bishop Still's will to his grandchildren and friends, to the poor—including £200 to augment the £300 already given to the almshouses at Wells —and to Trinity College Cambridge. They amounted to about £3,000, and there were legacies of household goods, furniture,

[1] Bishop Still's will; *D.N.B.*, Jewers, pp. 147–9; Brown, *Wills*, v, 81; Pevsner, *South and West Somerset*, p. 159; *Murray's Somerset*, p. 279.
[2] Bishop Still's will; Jewers, pp. 147–9.

linen, pewter and tapestries, all derived from the bishop's accumulated fortune: it was of some magnitude. Clearly the bishop had made provision for his family by careful investment. His two predecessors had shown signs of financial strain. Granted that Still had twice married wealthy wives, one the daughter of an apparently well-to-do clothier and the other of a Somerset gentleman who endowed her with nearly £1,500, it may yet be concluded both that this bishop was a skilful manager of his affairs and that Fuller was correct about the profits of the lead mines.

Bishop Still had been a benefactor to his family in other ways: as opportunities for gain arose within the episcopal estates he was as prompt as Godwin to give them to members of his family. There is no evidence that the terms on which they got them were better than an outsider would have secured, but the family had the advantage of these means of advancement at a time when there was keen competition among the gentry for fee-bearing offices and lands. From a bishop's point of view there was, as Hill has pointed out, much to be said for surrounding himself with dependants bound by family loyalties; that was the traditional method of carrying on administration and it helped him to retain independence of the local gentry.[1]

The three senior posts in the episcopal estates, those of chief steward, auditor and surveyor, were still the monopolies of the Paulet, Berkeley and Hopton families, but fortunately for the bishop, the two offices which carried the most active responsibilities became open for new appointment. Thomas Emylie, Bishop Godwin's son-in-law, still held the post of steward, but the new bishop 'showed himself well natured and courteous to the kindred of his predecessor', and presumably made no effort to deprive him.[2] Emylie was acting as steward at least until 1596, although apparently maintaining a domicile at Helmdon at the same time; perhaps wanting to retire to a less active life in Northamptonshire, he relinquished the stewardship finally in 1598.[3] Here was the bishop's opportunity. He gave the post to Robert Eyre, who was possibly his favourite

---

[1] C. Hill, *Economic Problems of the Church*, pp. 21–3.
[2] Harington, *Nugae Antiquae*, II, 161.
[3] Northants Rec. Soc., III, 29–30, 55.

son-in-law (Eyre was mentioned before the others in the bishop's
will and was given the choicest of his cups). The grant to
Eyre was made in 1598, but its duration was not specified.
Eyre was a good choice, a barrister-at-law and an active and
efficient officer, to judge by the many references to him in the
accounts. He retained the office under six subsequent bishops,
but by then he must have been an old man and not really
fit for the job, for about 1634 Bishop Peirs noted that he was
steward of his courts at £3. 6. 8d. and 'I use[d] to give him
more for wood and hay but he comes not now to do his office
but hath a deputy that serveth him'. He died in August 1638.[1]

The other post which became available was that of receiver-
general. During the vacancy following Bishop Godwin's death
it had been held by Thomas Sherwood,[2] and then in 1593 by
Adam Wynthorpe, but for some unknown reason no general
accounts were drawn up for the next two years and Wynthorpe
was certainly not receiving the revenues paid in by the reeves.
For the year 1596 the bishop acted as his own receiver,[3] and
it was perhaps as much to prevent another relapse as to reward
his kin that he decided to keep the post in the family. In July
1599 the dean and chapter, only Dr Powell dissenting, confirmed and sealed the letters patent granting the office of
receiver-general to Dr Francis James.[4] But the bishop's
full intention in making this grant is explained in his will: he
wrote there that when he made the patent to Dr James and his
assigns it was on trust for the three lives of Edward Horner
(his brother-in-law now deceased), John Still and Thomas Still
his sons, and he went on: 'now my meaning is that my son
John Still, being the elder, shall enjoy the whole benefit of the
yearly fee thereof (which is ten pounds yearly) during his life.'
Thomas was to succeed to the office if he survived John. There
were repercussions from this grant as late as the episcopate of
Peirs. In Bishop Lake's time the office passed to Ezechiel
Barkham in 1621, as confirmed by the dean and chapter, again
for a fee of £10, but the Stills disputed this grant. When Bishop
Peirs drew up a list of his officers about 1634 he noted that

---

[1] *Wells*, II, 336; S.R.O. DD/CC/13324, fo. 357; Jewers, pp. 147–9.
[2] P.R.O. Rentals and Surveys, Roll 951.
[3] P.R.O. S.C.6/Add./3545/84.   [4] *Wells*, II, 339.

the patent had been granted by Bishop Still for three lives to Dr Francis James for the lives of Edward Horner of Leigh and John and Thomas Still, and added: 'only Thomas Still is living and claimeth the patent. Mr Barkham sayeth it is not good because it was granted for 3 lives.'[1] Much more was at stake, of course, than a mere stipend of £10: the generally accepted practice of offering gratuities to officials of all kinds would greatly enhance the value of the post. Ezechiel Barkham's protest was prompted not only by cupidity, but also by the Still family's attempt to establish hereditary office, which was a distinct tendency in episcopal administration.

Apart from offices there were profits from the episcopal estates for the Still family. First there was the rectory of Compton Dando which was, at least by 1596, 'in the hands of the bishop' and was still valued at 40s.[2] Once more the bishop's will makes the position clear:

I declare that my son John Still has his life as the third life if he live so long in a lease made by me to my wife Mrs. Jane Still during her life of Compton Dando in Somerset reassigned to her by my lease thereof to her brother Mr. Edward Horner.

Then there was the manor of Buckland, or West Buckland, which Thomas Godwin and Thomas Purfey had held for so brief a tenure: in 1599 it was granted to Nathaniel Still for twenty-one years. Again the bishop explained his true intention in his will: although the lease was in the name of his eldest son Nathaniel, the bishop planned that he should have but one half of it, and that the other should be reassigned to one of the bishop's other sons. Now, by his will, the bishop confirmed that his youngest son Thomas should have half of the manor, and he charged Nathaniel to make the lease to Thomas within six weeks. The Stills did not hold the lease beyond 1627.[3]

BISHOP STILL'S CLOSE SUPERVISION

There were no significant changes of officers during Still's administration beyond those already described. Anthony Paulet

[1] S.R.O. DD/CC/13324, fo. 244.   [2] P.R.O. S.C.6/Add./3545/84.
[3] Wells Chapter Acts, Bk. H, fo. 121d; S.R.O. DD/CC/13324, fos. 332, 363.

remained the chief steward, Robert Berkeley the auditor (with Hugh Sexey as his deputy) and Arthur Hopton the surveyor, and John Lunde still retained his lucrative post (worth £17) as keeper of the bishop's palace and bailiff of the stores. The one change concerned the bailiff of the liberty. Thomas Purfey, whose acquisition of the post in September 1590 had been challenged by the chapter, assigned it on 9 December 1590 to Leonard Crosse in recompense for £400 which Crosse had lost by giving bond to Sir Henry Portman for the debts of Bishop Godwin. Crosse held the office with a fee of £14. 6. 8d. for the lives of George, William and Edward Purfey, and he acted as bailiff during the vacancy and after the coming of Bishop Still, on whose behalf he collected the Green Wax profits amounting to about £300. But he soon became involved in a dispute with the new bishop who withheld his fee, refused to allow him his expenses, and accused Crosse of defrauding him. The matter came to a head at an audit held on 3 December 1595 before Hugh Sexey, the deputy auditor, who had travelled down from London to Wells by night at the bishop's special request. The bishop alleged that Crosse had embezzled some of the Green Wax profits, had failed to keep proper accounts, and had been unable to produce the receipt from the exchequer for the amount which he owed in the bishop's name. The bishop also maintained that Thomas Purfey had invalidated his patent from Bishop Godwin by assigning it to Leonard Crosse, as the dean and chapter had confirmed it strictly on condition that it did not go to a citizen of Wells, and Crosse was thereby ruled out. The bishop tried to pass the office to John Lunde and Richard Mogg, but Richard Crosse, Leonard's son, intervened as a mediator, and the quarrel was apparently settled on the understanding that he took the office over from his father, for he exercised the right of bailiff from 1597, a year in which, in any case, his father was otherwise occupied as M.P. for Wells. Leonard Crosse lived on till 1611 and was buried in St Cuthbert's Church on 18 February.[1] The post of bailiff became hereditary in the Crosse family at least until the bishop's estates were confiscated. In 1616 Bishop Montague confirmed it

[1] P.R.O. C2 Eliz./C.14/4, S.C.6/Add./3545/84; *Official Return of Members of Parliament 1213–1702*; Parish Register of St Cuthbert, Wells; P.C.C. 37 Wingfield.

to John Crosse and his assigns for three lives, and the dean and chapter ratified the grant on 13 September. So the Crosse dynasty was established in the office in their own right: they were no longer acting as the assignees of Thomas Purfey, and by 1634 they had acquired the farm of the Green Wax for only £40.[1]

Some assessment of the condition of the episcopal estates just after Still's accession is possible through the fortunate survival of accounts covering, although not completely, the first four years of his episcopate.[2] They throw most light on the year ending Michaelmas 1594, that is, the first full year after Still came to Wells. For the following year, ending Michaelmas 1595, no audited accounts were drawn up, except for the issues of Wells *burgus*. The bishop was presumably getting to know his diocese and attending to more important spiritual and political matters; but in the year ending Michaelmas 1596 he obviously turned his attention to his estates. The result was a great hurrying to and fro of bailiffs and reeves, a searching out of income that had gone by default, and an increase of rents and dues for that year. In 1597 the bishop in no way relaxed this new vigilance, for the reeves of Wells, Hewish and Westbury were made to account directly to him, so that their profits do not appear in the general accounts, and again in the next year the Wells reeve at least had to render account directly to his master. In 1599 there is once more a complete account, which shows the result of the bishop's close supervision: one of the highest net profits yet earned since the Edwardian depletion, £1,337. 8. 3¾d., and this without the inclusion of any revenue from the lead mines or from the Green Wax.

Clearly Bishop Still's wealth accrued not only from the lead mines but also from the exploitation of the estates. How was all this extra income extracted? Although small in amount, that which came in increased rents from the rectories was symptomatic of the bishop's attitude. By virtue of the agreement of 10 October 1548 a reserved rent of £8 was paid to the Crown out of the income of the eight Somerset rectories held by the bishop. In the year 1596, when Still carried out a complete overhaul of his estates, he tried to pass this imposition

---

[1] *Wells*, II, 371; see above, p. 39.
[2] P.R.O. S.C.6/Add./3545/84, S.C.6/Eliz./2008 and 2009.

on to the farmers of the rectories, whose rents had remained unchanged since they were first leased. A new agreement was forced on four of the lessees: John Harington by agreement dated 24 January 1596 had to pay 2s. 7½d. extra for Corston, William Wigmore on the same date £1. 3. 7½d. for East Pennard, Andrew Bowerman on 18 April 3s. 4d. for Northlode, and Thomas Cook on 1 June £1. 3. 0¾d. for East Brent. To this additional income of £2. 12. 7¾d. the bishop hoped to add an imposition of 15s. 9d. wrung from James Kirton, who held the rectory of Castle Cary, as the following note made somewhere between 1595 and 1599 shows: 'M^d it is promised that the like composition shall be made as for the other parsonages after the rate of 15s. 9d. per annum promised to be paid for this parsonage.' This intention was not realized, for the accounts for 1634 to 1640 show the lessee of Castle Cary free of this sum.[1] The three remaining rectories of Glastonbury and West Pennard, Weston and Compton Dando also escaped; it was, of course, unlikely that Still would charge Compton Dando with an additional rent, because it was held by his own family.

Other evidence of the flogging of the estates lies in the heavy fines taken for the renewal of leases, especially from the manor of Banwell; they were far heavier than those taken in Bishop Berkeley's era. Where the figures for fines are separated from the other receipts from the manors, these examples of the bishop's severity can be found: in 1599, £135. 13. 4d. from Wells and £187. 1. 8d. from Huish; and from Banwell £371. 3. 4d. in 1597, £278. 4. 0d. in 1598, and £327 10s. in 1599. Exactions such as these cannot have commended episcopal rule: one wonders how many of the Banwell tenants supported the puritans when the testing time came.

Nothing in the way of feudal dues was relaxed. Heriots were still taken: in 1599 they amounted to £5. 12. 8d. in Wells, £4 10s. in Huish, £10. 13. 4d. in Westbury and £31. 13. 4d. in Banwell. Even a fine for a licence to marry was extracted from a Westbury tenant, Agnes Young, in 1599: it cost her £3. 13. 4d. The *Valor Ecclesiasticus* had shown the bishop receiving an annual rent of £1 a year in lieu of a stork from the lord of the manor of Badgworth, but in subsequent accounts

[1] S.R.O. DD/CC/13324, fo. 365 ff.

this was omitted, and it might have been inferred that the bishopric had been deprived of this item with so much else of its property. Not so: the rent must have gone by default and have been overlooked. Bishop Still presumably did some research on the subject, and in his accounts for 1599 he noted that there was a debt of £7 due 'from the lands and tenements lying in Badgworth called Hampsons who hold of the Lord Bishop annually for 20s. or one *ciconem* [a stork] at the will of the lord, and so liable for 7 years ending at [the] Feast of St Michael and All Angels'. Later bishops were presumably not so assiduous as Still in chasing a quit rent of £1, for by the accounts for 1634 the item had disappeared.[1]

The result of the bishop's inquiry in December 1595 into Leonard Crosse's handling of the Green Wax profits was that he was able to extract these arrears for three years, amounting to £550. 9. 10d., from the respective three undersheriffs. With this windfall the revenues from the bishopric that year reached the peak of £1,434. 12. 5¾d. There is evidence of some new rents gathered in 1596 or after, such as 'the new rent of a house called Court House' in Huish, 5s. first paid in 1595; but these are insufficient to suggest a real drive to create new tenures. Nor, despite some fluctuations, can one say that there was any reduction in wages for the reeves and haywards, save in two instances. There was the drastic cut from 16s. 6d. to 6s. 2d. for the reeve of Westbury in 1598, and in the same year the fee of John Browning, the hayward of Huish, was reduced from the usual 11s. to 5s. 6d. because he neglected his office in not driving the prey off the fields. So closely did the bishop watch the performance of his officers' duties.

So much for income. On the expenditure side one of the relatively heavy items was the cost of carrying timber to the bishop's palace at Wells from within the manor there and from Westbury. This charge was only for carriage, nearly always 6d. a load, and not for timber, which was a capital loss not appearing in annual accounts. In 1593 £28 3s. was spent in bringing timber from Wells alone, in 1596 £14. 7. 11d. from both Wells and Westbury, and in 1599 the cost of 409 loads of timber and wood was £12. 17. 8d.; this figure of 409 loads,

[1] Ibid.

presumably waggon-loads, gives some idea of the immense task of heating the bishop's large household, surrounded as it was, in Bishop Berkeley's plaint, by 'cold airs'. The provision of wood for the bishop's other home at Banwell was on a smaller scale; the carriage of fourteen loads to the mansion house there cost £2. 1. 3d. in 1599.

Comparison of the financial position under Bishops Berkeley and Still is possible and instructive. Berkeley had kept only two manors, Wells and Huish, under his control; the other six, Buckland, Wiveliscombe, Westbury, Banwell, Chard and Compton Parva, were all leased. Bishop Still had four in hand, Wells, Huish, Westbury and Banwell, and the remaining four were still leased, Buckland and Wiveliscombe being in new hands, those of Gilbert Prynne and Winifred Bond respectively (Buckland soon went to Still's sons). The nine rectories were also leased as before, but again with some changes of tenant. John Harington's tenure of the rectory of Corston is especially interesting. His lease must have been a new one, perhaps that of January 1596, for during the previous vacancy, up to September 1592, the rectory had been held by John Lunde.[1] Harington was a great friend of Bishop Still, and his acquisition of the rectory of Corston, so near to his home at Kelston, perhaps conduced to his more favourable portrait of Still than of the two previous bishops, Berkeley and Godwin. One wonders if it was about this time that Harington wrote the following retraction of what he had previously written about those who acquired church rents:

> Of late I wrote after my wanton fashion,
> That favourites consume the Churches rents:
> But mov'd in conscience with retraction,
> Ile shew how sore that rashness me repents.
> For noting in my private observation,
> What rents and schismes among us dayly grow:
> No hope appears of reconciliation,
> By help of such as can, or such as know.
> My muse must sing, although my soule laments,
> That Favourites increase the Churches rents.[2]

[1] P.R.O. S.C.6/Eliz./2014. See p. 199 above.
[2] N. McClure, *The Letters and Epigrams of Sir John Harington*, nos. 92, 103, 183, 188.

Apart from saddling the lessees of rectories with a share of the rent reserved to the crown, as Berkeley had tried to do, there was nothing that Still could do to increase the income from the leased properties. It was from the casual and variable sources of income, lead royalties, fines, heriots and other perquisites of the manorial courts, that any increase must be sought, although a limited number of new rents might be created. Even the tolls from the four annual fairs and from the market at Wells seem to have become formalized by now.[1] To take the manor of Wells, the rents collected by John Hall the reeve in 1596 were, with two exceptions, identical with those gathered thirty years earlier by his predecessor John Huchins; the exceptions were the palace mill, not previously mentioned and therefore presumably kept in hand, which was now let for £4, and some new rents, two of them of canonical houses, amounting to £1. 1. 4d. In Huish, too, where John Marshal's place as reeve had been taken by his son of the same name, the position had not altered save for a new rent of a house let to John Sawtell. Yet Huish was flogged as hard as any manor in the drive for fines. One of the reasons that 1599 was a bumper year was that the net income from Huish was £255. 15. 2¼d., whereas the peak year in Berkeley's time, 1573, had produced only £174. 10. 5½d., and an average year's income was £60–£70.

In Banwell the mill was now let for the high rent of £15. 13. 4d. Not all the demesne land had been taken back into the bishop's hands after the vacancy: his holding still included a dove-cot, a big garden called the Court Orchard, three gardens, some common pasture in Crosse Moore with tenements in Axbridge and herbage of the park, but some of it was newly let out and brought in an extra £7. 18. 10d. The income from fixed rents reached £133. 8. 1½d., but it was the enormous increase in casual sources in the 1590's which gave the bishop a net income fantastically in excess of that of 1539 when it had been £21. 11. 4d. In 1596 the total was £162. 19. 2¼d. and in 1599 no less than £483. 8. 6d., but against this the bishop now had to meet the reserved rent to the crown, £115. 8. 8d. (There is no record of the Towerhead rent of £20 from the Gorges, an odd omission.) Banwell presents a good illustration of the bishop's policy of

[1] See Appendix A.

exploiting the remaining manors to compensate for the loss of so much of the original episcopal endowment. The income from Westbury also showed an increase above the 1539 figure of £40. 1. 0d., but not commensurate with that from Banwell. The rents, free and customary, were fixed as in the rental drawn up by Thomas Emylie in 1586, so that only through the perquisites of the court could additional income be obtained: in 1596 these amounted to almost half the gross income. The net yield of the manor was £85. 5. 0¾d. in the year ending 1596 and £56. 0. 1d. in 1599.

ATTEMPTS TO LEGISLATE ON CHURCH LANDS

Bishop Still's abilities as an administrator, evident in the management of his estates, are also reflected in his activities in parliament: in the parliament of 1597 he was a member of no less than seven committees.[1] The most parliamentary-minded of the bishops of Bath and Wells of this period, he must have watched attentively the campaign in the last decade of Elizabeth I's reign to legislate afresh on episcopal temporalities. There seem to have been two separate, and perhaps contrary, lines of attack. The first was Whitgift's attempt to halt the unofficial dissolution of the heritage of the church. The alarming depredations of church property had to cease and its dignity to be safeguarded if true religion and social order were to be maintained, but Whitgift had to wait for the accession of James I before he acquired support from the Crown for a policy which threatened its powers of patronage. James I saw more clearly than Elizabeth that if episcopacy was to survive its economic position must be conserved, and as late as 1601 an act had been passed which ratified grants made to the queen by corporations and by her to individuals. (The lessees of Wiveliscombe and of the lands at Banwell and Westbury must have been relieved.) It was not until 1604 that a halt was called to the alienation of episcopal lands by the passage of the act which forbade this even to the king, on the ground that the possessions of archbishops and bishops must be protected from diminution 'for the better

[1] D'Ewes, *Journals*, pp. 531–45.

mainteinance of God's true religion, keeping of hospitality and avoiding of dilapidations'.[1]

The other line was the attempt to restrict the bishops' powers of leasing land and taking fines; this may have been puritan in inspiration, although there is no adequate account of it. The first, abortive, effort was made in the parliament of 1597. On 23 November the 'bill concerning leases made by archbishops and bishops' was rejected after a second reading in the Commons. It came up again in the parliament of 1601, was read in the Commons for the first time on 2 November and drew such an impassioned speech against it from John Boys that it was rejected on the second reading.[2] Boys was the member for Canterbury and he spoke with knowledge of his subject, for he was Archbishop Whitgift's steward and he may have been the John Boys of the Middle Temple whom Bishop Godwin had intended to act in trust for his son Paul and to whom he granted an annuity of £2 from the manor of Westbury.[3]

Something of the gist of the proposals of the draft bill may be gathered from his arguments. The bill would be harmful to bishops present and future, to their servants, farmers and tenants. The reigning bishop maintains his position only by continual fines: if these are taken away he will be unable to keep that hospitality and retinue which are proper to his dignity. It will be still more hurtful to his successor who, when he comes in, will be bound to pay first-fruits and yet not be allowed to profit by fines, while he may have no power to make leases for twelve or sixteen years. As to the servants and farmers:

> We know very many good gentlemen's sons serve bishops, and how can they reward their long and faithful services, but only by means of granting over of these fines or some other means out of their spiritual function. But this Act is good for the courtier; but I may speak no more of that point.

> Lastly, Mr. Speaker, myself am farmer to a bishop, and I speak this as in my own case (on my knowledge) to the house, that it is ordinary upon every grant after four or five years, ever to fine and take a new lease.

[1] Hill, *Economic Problems of the Church*, pp. 31–2.

[2] D'Ewes, pp. 562, 623, 625 ff.

[3] Neale, *Elizabeth I and her Parliaments 1584–1601*, p. 416; H.M.C. 10th Report, App. III, p. 265; P.R.O. E.178/1966.

Perhaps in that last sentence Boys got to the heart of the matter: the proposed bill would have prevented bishops from altering leases or conditions of tenure at short intervals, maybe to insert other lives on payment of a fine, as was the practice at Banwell in the 1620's.[1]

Christopher Hill has written: 'We know all too little about the relations of ecclesiastical landlords with their humbler tenants', and he inclines to the older view that churchmen were conservative in their outlook.[2] The evidence of Bishop Still's government of his estates and the tenor of these parliamentary debates alike suggest that opinion was rising against the financial exactions imposed on episcopal tenants. With other 'improving' landlords the bishops were trying to beat inflation and, in the case of Bath and Wells, to overcome the handicap of a reduced capital endowment. It seems a fair inference that these economic tensions, like the conflict over tithes, fed the root and branch movement and have their place in the causes of the civil war.

Bishop Still did not live to see that crisis: he died in the palace at Wells on 26 February 1608. Much use has already been made of that long and interesting document, his will, but there is another portion of it worth noting, the provision which he made for his wife and for his funeral. His bequest to his wife begins 'to my wellbeloved wife Mrs. Jane Still the sum of £500'. Then in touching vein, obviously referring to a joke they shared about a goblet, he bequeathed her 'my great gilt bason and ewer, and that gilt wreathen cup or "nutte" [?] (so used to be called by us) with a gilt cover thereunto belonging which my brother Mr. Edward Horner gave unto us at the day of our marriage'. She was left, also, two of his best and largest drinking bowls, one dozen silver spoons, her apparel and jewels, a salt, the complete furniture of any one bedchamber she chose, two other good feather beds with their bolsters, pillows, sheets and blankets, various chests, a fourth part of his table linen, pewter, brass and candlesticks, and one of two suites of tapestry. The other suite of eight pieces of tapestry hangings was left in the palace at Wells, and in September 1608 Nathaniel Still gave them to the next bishop, Montague.[3]

---

[1] See below pp. 236–7.   [2] *Economic Problems*, pp. 6–7.
[3] B. Halliday, *Catalogue of Books on Topography*, (1952), no. 1013.

Still's wife was also to have some of his livestock: two of his best milch kine, his best gelding or mare, and one other gelding for her servant. All these goods were the necessary equipment of the modest household of a dowager. The bishop also left lands to bring in the revenue to support it.

Bishop Still was not concerned only with the material welfare of his children. He left his books to be equally divided among his three sons,

charging them upon my blessing but especially in regard of God and better blessing of them, that (so far as their occasions can conveniently permit) they will be studiously occupied in the reading and studying thereof especially in the divine books of God's Holy Scripture and duly to meditate thereon, and to express the same in their Godly life, and virtuous conversation.

The bishop left 400 marks for funeral expenses and £30 for a 'decent and comely' monument or tomb. The tomb is there at Wells still, near the chapter steps, topped by a coloured effigy of him in the scarlet glory of his robes. It is one of the finest in the cathedral.

Jane Still did not long outlive her husband. She was buried at Cloford on 29 September 1608, and her will was proved in January 1609. She left bequests to her step-children, friends and servants, but the bulk of her property went to her only son, Thomas, to be held in trust for him until he was twenty-one or until he married. He was to be 'brought up in learning'.[1]

---

[1] Jewers, *Wells Cathedral*, pp. 147–9; P.C.C. 12 Dorset.

CHAPTER VII

Bishop and Borough

THE ELIZABETHAN BISHOPS AND THE CITY

RELATIONS between the bishop and the city of Wells had been a perennial source of conflict. The exercise of his rights over the city's trade and of his special baronial jurisdiction had always been resented, and co-operation became even more difficult from the Elizabethan period when the bishop was pressed for money. This is not to say that harmony never prevailed: there were several instances in Stuart times of the city fathers courting the bishop's good will.

Bishop Berkeley seems to have had an uncommonly vexatious time. Trouble started in 1561, the year after his arrival in Wells, over the opening of the palace gate. This was doubtless the main gate in the outer enclosure, known as the Bishop's Eye, which gives access to the moat. It was customary to keep the gate open, and the bishop had agreed that it should remain open on condition that no rubbish was carried inside and that no harm was done to the grass or ground there; yet at the meeting of the city council of 8 July the burgesses complained that the gates remained closed.[1] Five years later it was the respective jurisdictions of the bishop's court and the borough court which were in question, a matter which touched pocket as well as prestige. The citizens were not to be bullied, as the minutes of their meeting on 11 March 1566 show. The bishop forbade them to keep any three-weeks court for action between burgess and burgess according to their old custom, or to take any bond of the tailors of the town for the reformation of apparel and the making of 'great hoses' according to the requirements of

---

[1] C. W. Goodall's Book, fos. 110–11.

the law; he also disputed the town council's customary right to sit at the High Cross when the bailiff was reading a proclamation. The burgesses for their part unanimously agreed to ignore these restrictions on their authority. The subject was still warm on 8 August the following year when it was confirmed between the bishop and the council that the constables should punish all malefactors within the town.

Then relations eased for a while—in 1568 the city paid £3. 3. 3d. for a dinner for the bishop, Hugh Paulet and other justices—but by 1574 discord was again apparent. The new charter which the burgesses had contrived to obtain from the queen on 5 March giving them additional privileges was challenged by the bishop, so that on 3 August the borough council agreed to appeal to the queen.[1] In October Sir Maurice Berkeley and other justices had the dispute before them and early in 1575 the case was taken to law; the burgesses lost, and their new charter was cancelled. Their subsequent attempts in 1577 and 1581 to obtain privileges beyond those of their ancient charters were not successful until the advent of a new and weaker bishop.[2]

A sure indication that Bishop Berkeley was exercising his rights to the full, to the aggravation of the citizens, is the fact that his revenue from the *burgus* of Wells was the only part of his income which, apart from a setback in 1570, rose steadily; it started at £12. 14. 9d. in 1566 and reached £65. 2. 1d. in 1575. Success here was largely dependent on the activities of his bailiff, or rather of the deputy-bailiff, for the office itself seems to have been held by Richard Bourne and executed by a deputy. (John Bridge, who was doing the work in 1582, was certainly Bourne's deputy.) John Lane was the deputy-bailiff in 1566 and 1567, but his account for 1568 was unfinished and by 1569, still owing the bishop 16s. from the St Calixtus Fair, he had been replaced by David Jones. In 1572 the account is again incomplete, and by the next year Jones had been replaced by John Harwood, who although described as 'gentleman' and also 'bailiff' must also have been a deputy.[3] One gets the impression that Harwood

---

[1] Ibid., fo. 117; C.W. Act Book 1553–1623, fos. 55d, 103d; C.W. Serel MSS, Recorders, Mayors and Clerks.

[2] S.R.S., xlvi, xx–xxi.

[3] S.R.O. DD/CC/31523 and P.R.O. S.C.6/Eliz./2011.

was one of the more efficient of the bishop's servants: the Court Book of Wiveliscombe is thought to have been written by him. Certainly the income from Wells jumped immediately on his appointment in 1573, and by 1577 he was handling not only the revenues of the township of Wells, but also those of the manor. On 20 September that year he had been promoted to the post of under-steward, without prejudice, of course, to the grant to Sir Amyas Paulet; the dean and chapter gave a double ratification on 1 October 1580 and 15 June 1581.[1]

The income from the town of Wells came largely from the four annual fairs and the perquisites of the court, and assiduous supervision could improve it. The tolls were just about doubled by Bishop Berkeley from his meagre takings in 1566,[2] but the market tolls could not be increased, being farmed to the bailiff at 6s. 8d. a year; there were also a few rents worth about £8. Charged on this revenue were repairs, such as those to the Guild Hall and to the prison called 'Le Cage', and the loss of rents and fines through default, for 'some are dead, some have fled, others are poor and have nothing in goods or chattels which the bailiff could distrain'. Other charges were the fee of the auditor, 8s., and of the bailiff of the liberty, 6s. 8d., and an annual retaining fee of £1. 6. 8d. to Thomas Greke and Richard Durant, 'attorneys of the Lord Bishop in suit to the Lady Queen at Westminster', who must have been well occupied with the many disputes then proceeding between town and bishop. The income from Wells Forum, under the care of that enduring deputy-bailiff John Wensley, consisted of the tolls from the fairs at Binegar and Priddy, usually about 7s. 6d. together, and the perquisites of the two hundred courts at Michaelmas and Hocktide and the sixteen three-weeks courts; set against it were the expenses of the under-steward in holding the sixteen courts, which had become formalized at 5s. 4d., and of parchment for the auditor's office at 6s. 8d., and bad debts.

The more pliant bishop coming after Berkeley was, of course, Godwin, whose eldest son Thomas was elected one of the two members for Wells in the parliament of 1586. In 1588 he used his influence, for which he was handsomely paid by the city,

---

[1] S.R.O. DD/CC/31523; P.R.O. S.C.6/Eliz./2011; Wells Chapter Acts, Bk. H, fos. 15, 17.   [2] See Appendix A.

in helping to procure their new liberties, which included two new fairs presumably free of episcopal tolls.[1] The chapter of the cathedral must have viewed this encroachment of civic power with alarm. In 1590 they tried to veto the appointment of Thomas Purfey, the bishop's son-in-law, as bailiff of the bishop's liberty, for he had replaced Godwin as one of the city's members of parliament, and they saw his becoming a tool of the city fathers. Unable to prevent his appointment, they insisted on his giving a heavy bond to uphold the liberties and privileges of the bishop and not to assign his office to any burgess of the city of Wells.[2]

Bishop Still, taking over in 1593, was less amenable, although the city, mindful of the previous bishop's compliance, was prepared to give him cordial welcome. As early as 14 January the corporation arranged that a piece of plate or a cup of silver, to the value of £8 and engraved with the arms of the city, should be presented to him on arrival, and on 20 February they agreed to give the bishop an official reception. One obstreperous member, Edward Smythe, a master, was ordered to wear his scarlet gown and to be fined £10 if he refused. It was also resolved that if the mayor invited the bishop and canons to a dinner he should be allowed £2. 13. 4d. towards the cost.[3] This cordiality was soon to be strained. Acting through his steward, Robert Eyre, the bishop showed himself jealous of his rights and apt to interfere in city affairs. When he made a claim against the three-weekly borough court and questioned its legality, the corporation decided in January 1599 to send John Colles to show him the *Quo Warranto* allowed by the attorney general. Again, on 15 August 1603 Robert Eyre wrote to the mayor that it was the bishop's wish that John Saer and Edward Elliot should be nominated as vintners and that he commanded the city to confirm their appointment; he added, by way of postscript, 'I pray Mr Mayor let there be due regard of my lord's right in his liberties touching this nomination'. This was both peremptory and self-interested, for John Saer was none other than the steward of the bishop's household.[4]

---

[1] See above, pp. 34, 159.   [2] See above p. 164–5.
[3] C. W. Goodall's Book, fo. 166.
[4] C.W. Act Book 1553–1623, fos. 240d–241, 264; P.R.O. S.C.6/Eliz./2008.

FIVE BRIEF STUART EPISCOPATES

Still's successor was Dr James Montague, the fifth son of Sir Edward Montague of Boughton in Northamptonshire and 'a hard student and a general scholar', in other words, not an intellectual. Bred up at Christ's College, Cambridge, he rose to be the first master of Sidney Sussex College, and also dean of Lichfield and of Worcester and dean of the chapel to James I. He held the king's confidence, for in his will he left his royal master a cup of gold worth £100 with dutiful thanks for high favours; he also enjoyed the protection of the Duke of Buckingham, the king's favourite, to whom he left 'a diamond ring of seventeen diamonds in token of my unfeigned love to him: having been the most faithful friend that ever I had'.[1] Fuller confirms that Bishop Montague stood high in favour with King James, although he was hardly an impartial observer: the Montagues were among his patrons, and Volume VI of his *Church History* is dedicated to Edward Montague, the bishop's nephew.[2]

Bishop Still had died on 26 February 1608; Montague was elected on 29 March and installed on 14 May—a marked change from the Elizabethan timetable. Once more the city of Wells prepared to greet a new bishop. On 18 July 1608 the corporation agreed to attend the mayor in their best apparel to receive the bishop at the High Cross on his entry. Perhaps it was through the king's favour towards Montague that the city was honoured by a royal visit during this episcopate. In July 1613 the mayor, William Bull, heard that Queen Anne proposed to visit Wells. When the corporation met on the 19th he read a letter from the bishop giving notice of the intended visit and desiring 'that there shall be a silver bowl given to her Majesty of the price of £20: that the streets should be made handsome, and the town rid of beggars and rogues'.[3] The town records describe the pageantry of the occasion, which included

The Third Company—The Tanners, Chandlers and Butchers and they presented a cart of old Virgins, the cart covered with hides

[1] P.C.C. 71 Meade.   [2] Fuller, *Worthies*, II, 506.
[3] C. W. Goodall's Book, fo. 183.

and horns, and the virgins with their attires made of cow tails, and bracelets for their necks of horns, sawed and hanged about their necks for rich jewels. Their chariot was drawn by men and boys in ox skins and calves' skins, and other skins. Saint Clement, their saint, rode also with his book and his friar rode also, who dealt his alms out of his master's bag, which he carried very full of grains, very plentifully. Acteon with his huntsmen.[1]

Professor Trevor Roper sees the period from 1610 to 1628, which he calls the true 'Jacobean era', as of special significance in the history of the episcopacy. It was then, he argues, that the bench of bishops, most of them indifferent, negligent and secularist, sold the pass to the puritan opposition, so that the Laudian attempt to recover authority for the bishops came too late. They, the Jacobean bishops, were 'courtiers in clerical clothes', who had little conviction or sense of vocation.[2] One is inclined to agree that the inadequacy of this particular generation of bishops contributed to the destruction of episcopacy. Certainly at Wells the period between the death of Still in 1608 and the appointment of Peirs, a strong Laudian supporter, in 1632 gives an impression of stagnation. Five bishops passed through the palace at Wells during this period, but none of them remained as long as Berkeley and Still, or as long as Peirs who succeeded them, and they did not leave the same impress on the diocese or estate arrangements. Their energies were usually directed elsewhere: Montague and Laud were drawn to ecclesiastical politics at the centre, Mawe was a sick man, and Curll in his third year was given preferment; only Lake stands out as a sincere and pious, but unassuming, scholar.

There are hints of Bishop Montague's arbitrary and intimidating behaviour, which could only exacerbate the puritan opposition. Sitting in his palace at Wells on 27 September 1609 as a justice of peace to deal with a case of assault and riotous behaviour in Chewton mineries, he heard it alleged that the defendant John Leman, a Priddy yeoman, had said that there was 'no justice but justling' in those parts and that he would 'tell such a lesson to the king that never the like would be told him'.[3]

[1] H.M.C. 1st Report, p. 107.
[2] H. R. Trevor Roper, *Historical Essays*, pp. 130 ff.   [3] P.R.O. St. Ch. 8/159/10.

A conflict in which the bishop himself was involved concerned his right to take tolls in the market at Wells. Richard Crosse, who had taken over the post of bishop's bailiff of the liberty and clerk of the market from his father, Leonard Crosse, claimed a toll of one pint from every bushel of grain sold in the markets on Wednesdays and Saturdays, the only sellers exempt being persons dwelling in Glastonbury and within the twelve hides of Glaston. On several days in November 1612 John Davye of Chewton, John Mogg and James Plumpton of Bruton, who were all yeomen, and John Glover, a Somerton innkeeper, none of them qualifying as exempt, refused to pay, on the ground that the market in grain was free and the toll illegal.[1] Since the profits concerned were let to the bailiff at a rent which had now become standardized at 10s. a year, the bishop himself had nothing to gain by adding to the extra tolls, and it is clear that the defendants regarded Crosse as the real offender. It was nevertheless the bishop's rights which were at stake, and this at a time when episcopal authority in general was being called in question. Whether Richard Crosse was successful in his action is unknown, but the affair certainly made no difference to the Crosse family's tenure of the office.

The bishop himself intervened in the Somerset election of 1614, curiously enough in favour of Robert Phelips, son of a famous father, Sir Edward Phelips, who had been Speaker in the parliament of 1604–11 and who was now out of favour with the king because of his attitude to monopolies. It is odd that the bishop should have supported Phelips against the two successful candidates, Sir Maurice Berkeley and Sir John Paulet, because Sir Maurice's uncle, Robert Berkeley, was the bishop's auditor and Sir John was his chief steward.[2] The bishop wrote to Sir Edward Phelips:

I will send down upon Monday to my chancellor and send my servants to all my tenants, that if they go not with your son and where he will dispose of them, I will never acknowledge them, and they shall smart for it soundly.

Sir Edward, writing to his son on 20 March 1614, reported that

[1] P.R.O. C3/262/7.
[2] Bates Harbin, *Members for Somerset*, pp. 134–6, 140.

the bishop had promised 'three hundred freeholders besides the vestry'.[1]

Montague was the bishop who according to Fuller had the gleanings of the lead mines, and large gleanings they must have been to judge by the scale of his philanthropic and other activities. Phelps quotes Chyles as saying that the lead receipts amounted to £100–£140 weekly,[2] and although these must have been exaggerated gross amounts on which the royalty of 10 per cent was taken, the resulting income is far in excess of any for which there is documentary evidence either before or after Montague's time and must have conduced to his munificence. At Cambridge he helped the college of which he had been master, Sidney Sussex; he bestowed £13. 6. 8d. a year on it, wainscoted the lower part of the chapel and brought the water-course through the college and to the town. He was also associated, although not perhaps financially, in the foundation of Wadham College, Oxford; he wrote to Sir Thomas Lake, clerk of the signet, on 18 March 1610 seeking his help for a college at Oxford and saying that Mrs Wadham would bestow £6,000 to build a new one.[3] At Wells Montague increased the maintenance of the almsmen and incurred 'great charges' in expanding and beautifying the palace, especially Joceline's Chapel and the gallery; he also repaired the manor-house at Banwell. But his great achievement was the completion of the abbey church at Bath. The story goes that Sir John Harington of Kelston took him into the roofless abbey to shelter from the rain one day and thereby impressed on him the need to repair the neglected building. He is supposed to have contributed £1,000 for the purpose, and Fuller attributes this directly to the profits from the lead mines; 'he did but remove the lead from the bowels of the earth to the roof of the church'.[4]

There is the bishop's own word for his generosity in his lifetime, for in excusing the paucity of his bequests in his will he wrote: 'If any shall think I have given too little for good uses in my death: I answer I have bestowed much in my life: I am sure

[1] E. Farnham 'The Somerset Election of 1614', E.H.R., XLVI, 590.
[2] Phelps, II, 128 n.
[3] Cal. S.P.D. Add. 1580–1625, p. 523.
[4] B.M. Add. MS 21,089, fo. 63; D.N.B.; Worthies, III, 89.

not so little as five thousand pounds upon my two bishoprics'.[1] The second bishopric was the rich see of Winchester to which Montague was transferred on 4 October 1616. It was fitting, however, that when he died of jaundice and dropsy at Greenwich on 20 July 1618 at the age of fifty, he should have been brought back to the abbey at Bath, which he had so richly adorned, as he had provided in his will:

my body to be buried without cutting or mangling if it be possible in the great church of Bath in some convenient place in the body of that church to stir up some more benefactors to that place.

The bishop's tomb with his effigy, for which he left £300, is on the north side of the nave. Montague could better afford to indulge his charitable instincts in that, unlike the two preceding bishops, he was presumably unmarried; the only relatives mentioned in his will are his brothers Sir Edward, Sir Henry the lord chief justice, Sir Sidney the master of requests, and Sir Charles.

The next bishop, Arthur Lake (1616–26), also had close connexions with the court, being the brother of Sir Thomas Lake, now secretary of state; but Fuller is insistent that he owed his promotion to his own deserts and not to his brother's influence. Born in St Michael's parish in Southampton he was bred up at Winchester College, where his portrait by Richard Greenbury still hangs in the dining-hall, and he retained links with that city: he was rector of Stoke Charity (1605–8) and master of St Cross Hospital (1603–17).[2] From Winchester he passed in the usual tradition to New College, where he became a fellow and also warden, and where there is again a portrait of him in the hall. By 1616 he was vice-chancellor of Oxford, and he became dean of Worcester before being consecrated bishop of Bath and Wells at Lambeth on 8 December 1616.[3]

Exemplary in his life, Lake was diligent in preaching in the cathedral and the adjacent parishes, and he showed a paternal interest in his clergy. Fuller says that he was also liberal and

[1] P.C.C. 71 Meade. The will is dated 25 May 1618.

[2] Lists in Stoke Charity Church and in the north transept of the Church of S. Cross.

[3] *D.N.B.*; B.M. Add. MS 21,089, fo. 1156. There is also a portrait of him in the palace at Wells.

hospitable: 'when bishop, he kept fifty servants in his family, not so much for state or attendance on his person, but pure charity, in regard of their private need.' The puritans may have questioned this explanation of the bishop's large establishment, but his care of his servants emerges from his will. He bequeathed to them one-third of his goods (except his books), mentioning especially Richard Phillips, the steward of his household, Ezechiel Barkham his receiver, and Barnard More his gentleman of horse. The servants of his chamber were not included in this share

because I will that they have my apparel both linen and woollen (saving my episcopal robes and parliament robes and my best gown and cassock) . . . my executors to dispose of the latter as they think best.

He apologized for not having provided better for his servants 'because God hath not so far blessed my temporal or rather I have not been so provident as I should'.[1] Yet, according to Fuller, he had not permitted extravagance and had lived austerely himself:

such was his austerity in diet that he generally fed but on one (and that no dainty) dish, and fasted four times a week from supper. . . . The rankness of housekeeping break not out into any riot; and a chapter was constantly read every meal, by one kept for that purpose. Every night (besides cathedral and chapel prayers) he prayed in his own person with his family in his dining-room.

There is no mention of a wife or children in Lake's will, but he had a 'mother-in-law', possibly a step-mother, alive, and he hoped that his statesman-brother Sir Thomas would care for her and his brother John 'for the remainder of their life considering it cannot be long and it will be no great charge to him to keep them at his country house'. His favourite relative seems to have been his cousin Philip Mahat to whom he left a share of his books and the fair copies of his sermons, with the command to burn the rest of the imperfect papers in his study. Mahat honoured these instructions by procuring the immediate publication of a selection of these sermons and it was from a preface to this book, 'A Short View of the Author's

[1] *Worthies*, II, 11–12; P.C.C. 99 Skynner.

Life' by John Harris D.D., that Thomas Fuller probably took his eulogistic account of Lake, since there are distinct resemblances of fact and style between the two. Harris praises Lake's humility, tranquillity and temperance, his integrity in handling college and church leases, and his generosity and hospitality, which were the only reason why he left no greater estate:

I am verily persuaded, if he had attained to that wealth which some of our English prelates heretofore have done: he would have built churches and colleges. But his forwardness in this kind could never stay till his purse was full: therefore he never attained to the doing of any pompous work . . . He was a Solomon to his household servants, to the city where he lived an Oracle, to any scholar that resorted to him a living library.[1]

On Lake's accession to the see the city again honoured the new bishop; on 26 July 1617 the corporation sent him a silver bowl and a gilt cover costing £10 10s. The city fathers seem to have been deferential to Bishop Lake. Thus they sought his mediation on 26 March 1618 in hearing the case concerning libellous speeches spoken against the mayor and common council. At the parliamentary election of 1625 the corporation, the elective body, actually delegated the choice of one member to the bishop:

It is agreed that the mayor, with two or three of the rest of his brethren shall go unto my Lord Bishop and certify that his lordship shall command one discreet and sufficient worthy burgess to serve in the next parliament.

The bishop nominated his brother Sir Thomas—no longer secretary of state for he had fallen from power in 1619—who was sworn as a burgess on 22 April and elected as one of the M.Ps. the following day.[2]

If the magistrates thus followed the bishop's lead, other citizens of Wells flouted his authority in the person of Robert Powell, who claimed that he had been appointed bailiff of his liberties in 1618. How it was that Powell was exercising this office, the monopoly of the Crosse family, is hard to explain,

[1] *Bishop Lake's Sermons*, pp. 1–21. Printed by W. Stansby for Nathaniel Butter, London, 1629. Copy in Wells Cathedral Library.

[2] C. W. Goodall's Book, fo. 188; *Cal. S.P.D. 1619–23*, p. 39; C.W. Serel MSS, Recorders, Mayors and Clerks, Thomas Southworth.

especially since a Mr Crosse was acting as bailiff and collecting the Green Wax in Bishop Peirs' time. In any case the action which Powell brought into the star chamber in 1620 against William Galhampton and his confederates illustrates very well how bishops were then having to fight to preserve their rights. Powell claimed that the bishop enjoyed by charter, as his predecessors had done, the return of all writs and processes within the city of Wells and the hundred of Wells Forum free from the interference of the king's sheriff or of his bailiff; the return and execution of such writs were the responsibility of the bishop's bailiff. William Galhampton, against whom he raised the complaint, was active under the authority of another, spurious, bailiff, William Marshall, himself an upstart who had raised an estate of £500 out of nothing. Galhampton had drawn various poor men into debt and with the aid of 'other loose and disordered persons' had had them arrested and carried to obscure alehouses, where they were imprisoned for very small debts until they entered into bonds with him. Clearly Galhampton was measuring the authority of William Marshall against that of the legitimate bailiff Powell, although on what ground Marshall claimed does not appear either from the case or elsewhere. Galhampton had been so far successful as to have procured writs and warrants directed to Marshall both out of the court of kings bench and from Sir Theodore Newton, sheriff of Somerset.

When a citizen of Wells, Thomas Sweate, challenged the pair's right to arrest him and said that Powell was the only bailiff whom he recognized, they replied that they knew nothing of the bishop's liberties and that they would not be deterred from arresting Sweate either by Powell or by the bishop. Eventually they forged a warrant for Sweate's arrest, and then, one day in October, the fun began. William Marshall and his cronies sallied forth armed with staves, daggers and other weapons, and near the Guild Hall, where a crowd of about two hundred had collected for a lottery to promote the king's plantation in Virginia, they arrested Sweate with such violence as to draw blood and to arouse a tumult. When Powell, having hastened there to preserve the king's peace, demanded of Marshall, Galhampton and their companions the reason for the uproar, they replied that they had a warrant against Sweate and that they would carry him away; William Marshall had a hatchet in his hand and would have struck Powell if several bystanders had not called upon the constables to keep the peace. What happened after that is not recorded, and there is no means of telling who was in the right, although Galhampton's feeble defence that the allegations were 'petty and trivial' suggests that he and Marshall were at fault. Certainly, the extensive liberties which the bishop enjoyed had been renewed as recently as November 1582 by charter from Elizabeth I to Bishop Godwin.[1]

Some changes about this time in the official establishment are worthy of note. One was the appointment in 1621 of Ezechiel Barkham as the receiver-general in the place of Bishop Still's sons. Barkham is not a west country name and Ezechiel may have been imported by Bishop Lake from Sunbury-on-Thames, Middlesex, where his brother Sir Thomas Lake was lessee of the rectory from the dean and chapter of St Paul's; several members of the Lake family lived at Sunbury in early Stuart times, as did at least one Barkham—on 22 February 1609 'Old John Barkham' was buried there.[2] Ezechiel Barkham stayed on in Wells and eventually died there, but he did not establish a dynasty in the office of receiver-general which in 1640 passed to Arthur Mattock. A family which had by now become established in office was that of the Lundes. In 1611 the veteran John Lunde had been given a fresh grant of the keeper-ship of the bishop's palace, with the attendant offices of bailiff of the stock and of the bishop's woods at Wells, for the lives of himself, his son Maurice and Sir Edward Perham. In Bishop Lake's time a new name, that of Walter Bushell, became assoc-iated with theirs, and in 1625 the office was granted anew to Bushell and his assigns for the lives of himself, John Lunde and Edward Bushell. The Bushells were not outsiders; there is evidence of the family's being in Wells in the 1590's. The Hoptons, too, had been confirmed in the surveyorship: in 1616

[1] S.R.O. DD/CC/13324, fos. 252, 367 ff, DD/CC/14263/4/5, fo. 15 ff.; P.R.O. St. Ch. 8/Jas.I/241/17.
[2] S.R.O. DD/CC/13324, fo. 341; Sunbury Parish Register; D. Lysons, *Middle-sex Parishes*, p. 280.

the office had been granted to Robert Hopton for the lives of himself and of Ralph and William his sons. A new official made his appearance, however, in John Riesley, appointed for life as keeper of the mansion and park of Banwell and bailiff of the hundred of Winterstoke by Bishop Montague in 1611.[1]

Bishop Lake made his will on 27 December 1625, when he was fifty-nine, 'weak in body but of good and perfect memory'. He died on 4 May 1626,[2] and was buried in his own cathedral. In his will he had laid it down:

for the place of my burial I desire it may be in the cathedral church of Wells (if I die bishop there) just behind the bishop's seat in the chancel . . . in the aisle through which I used to pass to my seat . . . Only I would have a plain stone laid on my body even with the ground having this epitaph engraven on it. 'A Lake I was by nature barren, bitter, dead, I lived, waxed sweet, bare fruit, by streams from Gods well head, and Ezekiel c.47 graven over it. Under it, Here lies Arthur sometime Bishop of Bath and Wells where he sat years etc. died anno domini etc. and in the year of his age etc.'[3]

Ezekiel, chapter 47, describes the life-giving properties of water, and the play on his name and on the abundant streams of Wells shows a nice conceit on the bishop's part. In fact, the present inscription on his flat gravestone falls far short of his requirements: it reads, 'Arthur Lake, Lord Bishop of Bath and Wells who died 1626'. Among his chief beneficiaries was his godson, Launcelot Lake, to whom he left one-third of his property (excepting his books, which went to Winchester College and New College, Oxford) and also his seal of arms, his 'watch with a clock on it' and his bible covered with green velvet and silver clasps.

The tenure of the next bishop, William Laud, was but a fleeting one (1626–8), procured by the influence of the king's favourite, the Duke of Buckingham: a mere stepping stone from St Davids to London and then in 1633 to Canterbury. Bath and Wells had little interest for this king's minister: he is supposed never to have visited his diocese, and he had little influence on the administration of the estates.[4] In his absence a

---

[1] *Wells*, II, 335, 360–1, 371, 383.   [2] Phelps, II, 128.
[3] P.C.C. 99 Skynner.
[4] *Cal. S.P.D. 1625–26, App.*, p. 570; H. R. Trevor Roper, *Archbishop Laud*, p. 92.

dispute arose about who was to be the keeper of the bishop's palace, and Laud succeeded in ousting Walter Bushell in favour of his own nominees, Adam Torrles and Richard Robinson. He sent Adam Torrles with letters to explain the case to the chapter on 1 October 1627: if Bushell would surrender the patent of the office which he held for three lives the bishop would allow him to keep it for his life only. After Bushell had refused to agree and had 'done many ill offices' to the bishop, the offer was withdrawn and the post given to Torrles and Robinson for their lives, a subservient dean and chapter confirming the grant.[1]

That Laud was interested in the management of episcopal estates is shown by a document in his hand, dating perhaps from 1626, which concerns the status of bishops' stewards in dealing with episcopal lands. The paper discusses the powers of a steward during a vacancy and may well have been prompted by the handling of the Bath and Wells estates between the death of Bishop Lake in May and the appointment of Laud in August. The steward then was still Robert Eyre, Bishop Still's son-in-law. Some of Laud's conclusions were that the king could dismiss the steward of a bishopric, but only as long as it remained void; that a lease by the steward for lives or years was not good in law unless the succeeding bishop confirmed it or the lands concerned were copyhold according to custom; and that the steward could not on his own authority sell church lands. During their terms of office bishops, being owners of their lands, may do all lawful things with them, but the king is not their owner and has only the right to bestow them; even the bishops may not let by common law for longer than three lives without the confirmation of the dean and chapter.[2]

In the summer of 1628 Laud was translated to London and a Cambridge scholar, Leonard Mawe, took his place in the West. Mawe was the son of Simon Mawe, a gentleman of Rendlesham in Suffolk; he had been bred up in Cambridge, where he rose to be master of Peterhouse and then, after accompanying the Prince of Wales to Spain as his chaplain in 1623, master of Trinity in 1625. He gave Peterhouse £300 for covering the chapel roof with lead and he helped to free Trinity from debt.

[1] *Wells*, ii, 387. [2] Ibid., 385; P.R.O. S.P.16/43/21; *Cal. S.P.D. 1625–26*, p. 514.

'A good scholar, a grave preacher, a mild man, and one of gentle deportment', he obviously preferred the academic quiet of Cambridge to the more public cares of a bishopric, and it was with reluctance that he prepared for Wells. Elected on 24 July 1628 and consecrated at Croydon on 7 September, he appeared to cling to his establishment at Trinity. On 11 August 1629 he wrote to Henry, Earl of Holland, chancellor of Cambridge, acknowledging letters which conveyed the king's wish that he should quit Cambridge by a fixed date but also gave him leave to reside elsewhere than in one of his episcopal houses, so that he might recover his health. He probably never reached Wells, for less than a month after writing to Lord Holland, on 2 September, he died at Chiswick, and was buried there in the riverside church of St Nicholas. His presence at Chiswick is explained by his will made on 31 May 1629: a sister had married William Smith, a gentleman of Chiswick, and Mawe left monetary bequests to three of their children, Lewes, Elizabeth and Kinborough Smith, and all his books of Hebrew, Greek, Latin, English, French, Spanish, Divinity, Philosophy and History to a fourth, Simon Smith. He was not wealthy and had not seized the opportunity to profit from his episcopal estates in Somersetshire: 'my worldly goods . . . are not many (for I never had, nor cared to have much).' Family property in Suffolk and Lincolnshire bequeathed to him by his father and his brother Charles now reverted to the next heir. The bishop had presumably not married.[1]

Two absentee bachelor bishops, Laud and Mawe, were succeeded by a married man, Dr Walter Curll, who as bishop (1629–32) certainly resided at Wells. Curll probably originated from the official hierarchy centred on the court: his father is thought to have been William Curll, auditor of the court of wards under Elizabeth I, who lived at Hatfield and enjoyed Cecil's patronage. Like Mawe, Curll was a Cambridge scholar, a fellow of Peterhouse before he became chaplain to James I, dean of Lichfield and, in 1628, bishop of Rochester. His election to Bath and Wells on 29 October 1629 caused a minor contretemps. The common or chapter seal was kept in a chest in the treasury and the key was in the keeping of the dean, Dr

[1] *Wells*, II, 388, 414; *D.N.B.*; P.R.O. S.P.16/148/41; P.C.C. 78 Ridley.

Barlow, but he was away from home and it could not be found. Mrs Barlow denied having the key and so the chest had to be forced open. Fortunately for the chapter Dr Barlow wrote signifying his consent on 6 November. The new bishop was installed on Christmas Eve.[1]

Curll is reputed to have been a man of very great charity to the poor, but of his administration almost nothing is known. There is a glimpse of his wife involved in a dispute with one Joan Pope, who used irreverent and unmannerly words to her in the cloister of the palace in January 1632.[2] The bishop had one son, William, and in 1632 the office of registrar of the archdeaconry of Wells was granted to William Androwse of Shipham for the lives of Mark Tabor, Francis Keene and William Curll; since Francis Keene seems to have been specially favoured by Bishop Curll, this arrangement may have been in the nature of a trust for the bishop's son.[3] Keene himself did well; in 1631 he was made keeper of the manor, mansion and park of Banwell for life with a fee of £10, although with a special note that, unlike other episcopal offices, this was not a grant to Keene and his assigns and that he was therefore precluded from granting it to another. He had no rights of pasture or wood, but in Bishop Peirs' time he was claiming to graze ten beasts and a horse as well as to take wood, and perhaps that was why his fee was two years in arrear in 1634. Four years later he was paying 20s. for the right of fowling there. Keene's other gains were a lease of the rectory of Glastonbury and West Pennard for twenty-one years and another of the manor of Chard, both in 1631. His Chard lease is peculiar because the Paulets still held that manor, but there were to be other attempts to get it away from them during the next episcopate. Thus comfortably supported Keene lived in Wells to 1661 when he died leaving his wealth to his wife Jane. A further change in Curll's time was that the Bushell family retrieved the keepership of the bishop's household at Wells from those who had annexed it in Laud's time: in 1632 the office was granted by the bishop to William Bushell for life.[4]

---

[1] *D.N.B.*; *Wells*, II, 391.   [2] *Wells*, II, 394.   [3] Ibid., 395; *D.N.B.*
[4] *Wells*, II, 394–5; S.R.O. DD/CC/13324, fo. 341; Wells Chapter Acts 1621–35, fos. 106, 108d; Keene's will P.C.C. 98 May.

In November 1632 Bishop Curll was promoted to Winchester, and Bishop William Peirs of Peterborough was elected to Bath and Wells in his place. Some information about Curll's administration of the temporalities is given by the dispute which subsequently arose between the two: it was the old story of an outgoing bishop leaving liabilities for the incoming one. The suit between Peirs and Curll which came into the court of arches for arbitration by Archbishop Laud on 12 May 1636 concerned both the ruin and dilapidation of the episcopal houses and controversy over fines for leases made by Bishop Curll. The case must have been of interest to Laud since it concerned a diocese so recently his. His verdict was that Curll should pay Peirs £160 for the dilapidations and £80 in lieu of fines for leases and copyholds; that the cost of bringing the case before the court was to be born by Bishop Peirs, and that all suits and controversies between the Right Reverend Fathers were to 'utterly cease and determine'.[1] Steps were also to be taken to reduce the future liabilities for fabric of the bishops of Bath and Wells; a commission was to recommend the pulling down of such parts of the buildings of Banwell House and of the old stable at Wells as should be judged useless. This commission apparently got to work. Among the Wells consistory records is a series of letters of the late 1630's from a London correspondent, William Bellarmine, to James Huish, the bishop's registrar at Wells. On 2 July Bellarmine wrote to Huish: 'my Master desires that . . . you would deliver the box to my Lord Bishop wherein is a commission to visit Banwell house for the pulling down so much of it as is burdensome to the bishopric'.[2] What a find the report of this commission would be!

Amidst all the preparations for his departure for Winchester, Bishop Curll saw to the making on 7 January 1623 of an inventory of all the furniture which he had inherited in the thirty-six rooms of the palace, excluding the chapel and the brewhouse, and which he was now leaving for Bishop Peirs. This inventory shows that there was a basic stock of household goods there (and some refinements such as the twenty-five pictures in

[1] P.R.O. S.P.16/221/4; *Wells*, II, 396.
[2] Wells Diocesan Registry, Miscellaneous Letters 1589–1639 (uncatalogued).

the long gallery) for every bishop's use. The incoming bishop brought his own luxuries, such as the draped bedsteads, hangings, cushions and stools, and the plate, pewter and linen which figure in the wills. The stock furniture consisted chiefly of square, round and long tables and of bedsteads, cupboards and cushioned forms, but there were also 'boxes for writings' in the secretary's chamber, and a bin for bread and a glass cupboard in the pantry. The brewhouse, obviously an important part of the episcopal economy, was well-equipped with a great copper furnace, two wooden hooped vats, a leaden cooler, a trough lined with lead, a wooden spout and a wooden horse to set the hogsheads on.

The new bishop, Peirs, took a notebook and copied all this out, two pages of it, and then he made a careful list of all the locks and keys, and the doors to which they fitted in the palace and in various outhouses such as the bottle house and the butter house, both in the cloisters. There were keys to the cellar, the camery,[1] the great garden, 'Mistress Curll's garden', and the coalhouse by the hall. The principal rooms (apart from the various chambers allocated to the chaplain, the secretary, the steward and the auditor) were the long gallery, two other galleries (one of them the matted gallery), three dining-rooms (known as the 'ordinary', the 'best' and the 'old' dining-room), the famous cracking chamber where Bishop Godwin had held his fateful audiences, and the study, the wardrobe, and (shades of Bishop Still!) two nurseries. This survey of the palace on the eve of the civil war is the more interesting because the building was genuinely one of the ruins that Cromwell, or rather his men, damaged extensively.[2]

---

[1] Camery, 'a piece of ground within the precincts of the bishop's palace'.
[2] S.R.O. DD/CC/13324, fo. 348 ff.

CHAPTER VIII

Bishop Peirs: Victim and Victor

LOCAL ADMINISTRATION

His action in sending a claim for damages after Bishop Curll illustrates the character of the new bishop; meticulous, orderly, a little mercenary, Peirs was a good example of the Laudian episcopate as described by Dr Mathew, when the bench of bishops included the occasional cadet of a good house, a number of sons of clergy, and a sprinkling of those who had worked their way with city connexions, mostly from the privileged wealthy burgess group—Peirs' father was a hatter. Such men had respect for authority, realism where money was concerned, and driving energy. At the same time they were influenced by the universities, bred in the community of high tables, appreciative of learning if not scholarly themselves, skilled rather in academic administration, which became a training school for prelates: 'the headship of certain colleges seems to have led on naturally to the episcopate.'[1] All this was true of Peirs. No one credits him with ability as a preacher, there is no mention of his piety, he left no volumes of learned sermons or catalogues of bishops. More so even than Still, he seems to have been just an administrator: an administrator with dogmatic ideas on doctrine.

William Peirs was very much an Oxford man moving in ecclesiastical circles. He was born in Oxford in 1580 and his father was related to John Peirs, archbishop of York. He went to Christ Church, where he became a doctor of divinity in 1614, and continued to reside mostly at Oxford, although he acquired

---

[1] D. Mathew, *The Social Structure of Caroline England*, p. 69 ff; Hunt, *Bath and Wells*, p. 198.

posts elsewhere, several of which he held in plurality. He was rector of Grafton Regis in Northants (1609–11) and of Northolt in Middlesex until 1632, chaplain to Bishop King of London, rector of St Christopher-Le-Stocks (1615–20), canon of Christ Church Cathedral (1616–32), and a prebendary of St Paul's and a divinity reader from 1618. His first administrative post of importance was the vice-chancellorship of Oxford (1621–4). His propagation of high church doctrine soon earned him the favour of Laud, and so 'the great Creature of Canterbury's', as he was called, made a typical transfer from academic to ecclesiastical administration. As dean of Peterborough from 1622 he is reputed to have shown 'a good secular understanding' in the management of the estates but also to have served his own interest well; as late as 1642 his successor, Cosin, had to call him to account for money which should have been spent on the repair of the cathedral. In 1630 Peirs had (most unusually) become bishop of the same diocese, but his interests still lay in Oxfordshire where he had acquired a mansion and an estate at Denton in the parish of Cuddesdon. He was staying there, and not in Peterborough, when on 4 December 1631 he wrote to Philip King, the auditor of Christ Church, urging him to pay a visit although travelling was so difficult in mid-winter:

I have sent mine own nag to carry you and my footman to wait upon you hither; and if my coachman had been at home I would have sent my coach for you because the ways are so foul.[1]

The same coach presumably brought him to Wells when, on Curll's translation to Winchester, he was promoted to Bath and Wells.

Peirs married twice. His first wife, Anne, died during the civil war and was buried at Sunbury in Middlesex where Peirs had a house and where he was perhaps encouraged to seek asylum by the Lakes and the Barkhams.[2] While Anne was the bishop's lady at Wells the dean and chapter ordered that special seats should be constructed in the choir of the cathedral

---

[1] Bodleian Library, Tanner MSS, lxix, fo. 202.

[2] Peirs' will P.C.C. Penn 63. There is no entry of her burial in the Sunbury Parish Register, which I was allowed to search through the kindness of the Rev. E. M. Johnson, but the burials for 1655–60 inclusive are not recorded.

for her and the canons' wives; later they ruled that a portable desk in the choir should be reserved for the sole use of these wives.[1] After the death of his first wife the bishop seems to have moved from Sunbury back to Denton, and there he married a second wife, Mary, who is reputed to have been young and cunning and to have wheedled away from him the greater part of his estates, to the detriment of his first wife's sons. There was some substance in these charges.

By his first wife Peirs had two sons, William and John. William followed his father into the church and also became a doctor of divinity. As usual in these episcopal families, his father smoothed his path to preferment. In 1638 he was given a prebend at Wells, that of Cudworth and Knowle, and was also made archdeacon of Bath; the next year, again on his father's instructions, he acquired another prebend, Whitchurch, but did not resign the Cudworth one for over two months. Later, in 1643, when the chapter at Wells were debating the election of one of the king's nominees, Dr Watts, as a canon residentiary, the whole question of pre-election and of interference with the liberties and customs of the chapter was raised, and reference was made to the circumstances in which Bishop Peirs' son had become archdeacon of Bath. Dr Creighton, who was obviously one of his supporters, was driven to protest that 'when he had formerly given his consent to the pre-election of Mr Peirs he was ignorant of the laws and customs of this church'; he did it neither for fear nor favour. This rumpus did not prevent the translation of William Peirs to the archdeaconry of Taunton in 1643, and the question of pre-election was not settled until 1644 when, episcopal authority being almost in abeyance, the chapter ruled that since all pre-elections were contrary to the charter of the church and freedom of election, that of Mr Peirs, now described as 'late archdeacon of Bath', was annulled. Dr Godwin alone disagreed, holding himself bound by his previous promise; himself the son of a former bishop, Paul Godwin perhaps felt that episcopal sons should stand together.[2]

William Peirs the son married into a local family, the Cowards of Wells. His wife's christian name is not known, but

---

[1] *Wells*, II, 400, 422.   [2] *Wells*, II, 418, 421, 428–9.

she had two brothers, Thomas and Francis, the latter of whom left some lands to his brother-in-law the archdeacon in 1665. William Peirs had two sons, William and Thomas, and at least two daughters. The eldest daughter, Anne, married Dr Henry Deane; the other, referred to as 'my daughter Creighton' was the wife of the Dr Creighton (son of Bishop Robert Creighton) who was to be one of his executors.[1]

Needless to say, the archdeacon was deprived when the Presbyterians seized power: he was also rector of Kingsbury at that time. His sufferings and those of his family must have been as great as those of any of the clergy, as he was reduced to working as a day-labourer doing threshing and carrying cheeses to Taunton and Ilminster markets. He and the other royalist clergy could be seen sitting together on market-days eating bread and salt, lacking even a penny to buy a glass of ale.[2] It may be wondered why he did not join his father on his private estate in Oxfordshire. One can imagine the joy when in 1660 father and son were restored to their dignities in Wells, although the archdeacon was to find that his canonical house had been destroyed and converted into public premises for the reception of people attending the assizes and sessions. Having repaired it and made it habitable, he found to his dismay that the town was to build a great market-house nearby which would bring the clamour of the market.[3] This was the market-house built by the corporation in 1663 on waste land of the manor of Wells obtained from the bishop.[4] The archdeacon's troubles did not end there. After his father's death he became involved in a dispute with Bishop Robert Creighton; the bishop suspended him and complained to Archbishop Sheldon that Peirs had let out his canonical house. Peirs died, still archdeacon of Taunton, in 1682: he bequeathed to his two sons the lands which he had inherited from his father.[5]

The bishop's second son, John, settled on the estate that his father left him at Denton in Oxfordshire: a mansion house and

---

[1] Jewers, *Wells Cathedral*, p. 134; Brown, *Wills*, II, 27, and IV, 81; Bishop Peirs' will P.C.C. Penn 63; Matthews, *Walker Revised*, p. 317.

[2] Hunt, *Bath and Wells*, p. 212.

[3] *Wells*, II, 431.

[4] I am grateful to Dr R. D. Reid for this information.

[5] Tanner MSS, cxl, fo. 23; Brown, *Wills*, IV, 81.

land. This son had at least one daughter, Mary, and he was still living at Denton in 1665.[1]

One is bound to agree that the appointment of Peirs to the diocese of Bath and Wells in 1632, at a time when the episcopacy was subject to general attack, was an ill-judged one. Many of the important county families, such as the Paulets and the Hoptons, were Anglican and royalist, perhaps because they had an interest in the episcopal estates. Presbyterianism had important adherents, the Pophams, Horners and Strodes, none of whom held episcopal office, while many of the lower clergy were of a radical way of thinking. Yet it was probably Peirs' uncompromising attitude, more than issues of principle, which was to provoke so much of the considerable opposition which he had to face. There were three grounds of dispute. The first was that, after sounding the opinions of seventy-two of his clergy, Peirs came out with a pronouncement in favour of wakes and ales of which the puritans disapproved:

if people should not have their honest and lawful recreation upon Sundays after evening prayers, they would gather into tippling houses, and there, upon their ale benches, talk of matters of the Church and State, or else into conventicles.[2]

After Charles I's order that his father's Declaration of Sports should be read in the churches, disciplinary action, in some cases amounting to imprisonment, was taken against several of the clergy of Somerset. Peirs incurred further odium by his war against lectures by puritan ministers. Following the king's Instruction of 1629 the bishop went beyond the mere enforcement of conformity; he attempted to suppress all lectures, even when given by the parish priest, ordering that a catechism should take the place of a lecture on Sunday afternoons. His enemies reported that he was shortly able to boast, 'I thank God that I have not one lecture left in my diocese'.

The dispute productive of the most serious results was that arising from the order of 1633 to set communion-tables against the east wall and to rail them in. Peirs attempted to enforce this

---

[1] Bishop Peirs' will; *Hearth Tax Returns, Oxfordshire, 1665* (Oxford Rec. Soc. XXI), p. 57.
[2] Hunt, pp. 198, 201 ff.

order, but he was resisted in many parishes, notably in Beckington, where his authority was flouted for many years. The churchwardens, Wheeler and Fry, were excommunicated and the
parishioners sent fruitless appeals to Archbishop Laud and the
king. Only later was their petition acted upon; in December
1640, when after eleven years' interval parliament was again
sitting, the Commons requested the Lords to take security
for Bishop Peirs' coming to answer criminal charges about the
corruption and subversion of religion in the diocese of Bath and
Wells.[1] At this point the attack on Peirs was caught up in the
general onslaught on the bishops, but that was only a part of
his troubles. In the spring of 1640 he was involved in acrimonious debate with the body to which in normal circumstances he would have looked for most support, the dean and
chapter. The opposition to him was led by Dr Gerard Wood
and Dr Paul Godwin, and the chapter alleged that the bishop
was seeking to infringe their liberties and jurisdiction, to claim
the disposition of seats, and to cite canons residentiary before
his consistory court. Eventually perhaps common peril brought
them together: on 24 October the chapter agreed to forget their
various differences with the bishop and to seal leases as he
wished.[2] This did not, as has been seen, prevent trouble from
breaking out over pre-election in 1643, but by then Dr Godwin
was a bishop's man.

As long as the authority of the Crown was not materially
reduced Peirs was safe, for he obviously had the confidence
of the court party. His ability as an administrator is reflected
in the number of commissions he was given in local government.
Many were the ship-money disputes referred to him for settlement in the hundred of Bath Forum and seven other hundreds.
He was asked to examine allegations that in time of plague
people had come from London without health certificates, that
a William Bicknell had used indecent language, and that a son
of William Gilbert, who was claimed to be a seventh child, was
doing cures by touching every Monday.[3] Particularly trouble-
some was the case of William Strode who in 1637 complained

[1] *V.C.H. Somerset.*, II, 44–6.
[2] *Cal. S.P.D. 1640*, p. 454; *Wells*, II, 422–4.
[3] *Cal. S.P.D. 1636–37*, pp. 31, 150, 169; *1637*, pp. 165–6, 169, 450, 548.

that he had been overcharged for ship-money and wrote several times to Secretary Nicholas about it, even when the case was under hearing by the bishop. Strode was ordered by the star chamber to apologize to the bishop for 'inconsiderate words'. Although by 1 August Strode claimed to have given the bishop full satisfaction, it was not until 18 November that Peirs certified this to the council.[1]

Symptomatic of the tension of the time is the long report that Peirs sent to Secretary Windebank from Wells on 20 May 1639 about two strange Scots who had appeared there. On examination by the bishop and another of the justices, Sir Thomas Wroth, these modestly-clad men in scarlet cloaks turned out to be Lord Angus, son of the Marquis of Douglas, and William Cockburn, who had come not long since from Scotland by way of the court at York, where attempts were being made to raise troops for Charles I against the covenanting Scots, and so to the western parts. What they were doing there is not clear: the people of Wells would have arrested these men with their outlandish speech as spies, but the bishop, satisfied that they had a passport from the secretary of state, let them go their way.[2]

Such were the minutiae of local government in which a bishop, as a justice of the peace, became entangled. The details of estate administration received no less attention, as Peirs' surviving notebook, an *aide mémoire* about his temporalities, attests. Here, in addition to the survey of the rooms and furniture of the palace, the bishop proceeded to list all the officers of his estate, the rents due to the crown, a rental of 1635 of all the leasehold and copyhold tenants on the manors which he still had in hand, and other useful information. This invaluable book supplies some of the missing facts for the previous five brief episcopates and provides a picture of the state of the temporalities which may be compared with that of Bishop Still's day.[3]

The list of officers and their fees shows dynasties well established. John Lord Paulet was still monopolizing the chief stewardship, although now at the reduced fee of £11. 6. 8d., instead of the original £13. 6. 8d. Robert Hopton and his sons Ralph and William were holding the surveyorship by virtue

---

[1] *Cal. S.P.D. 1636–37*, pp. 401, 522; *1637*, pp. 61, 140, 348, 549.
[2] *Cal. S.P.D. 1639*, p. 199.   [3] S.R.O. DD/CC/13324.

of their grant from Bishop Montague in 1616, and a Crosse (no christian name is given) was still acting as the bailiff of the liberty. The grants made by Bishop Curll, of the office of keeper at Wells Palace to William Bushell, and of the keepership of Banwell to Francis Keene, still held good. The most significant change concerned a new favourite, Arthur Mattock, who was almost certainly an importation of Bishop Peirs, for Mattock is not a west country name. The coat of arms which he used resembled that of the Matokes or Matticks of Hertfordshire and Yorkshire.[1] When Peirs came to the diocese Richard Hicks, Laud's appointee, was still acting as auditor under a life grant, and Robert Eyre, Bishop Still's son-in-law, as the steward, although obviously an ageing one. They were both performing these duties in 1635, but Eyre probably retired in that year, for on 4 October Hicks received his post for life and he was acting as steward at a smaller fee on 27 April of the next year.[2] The auditorship which Hicks had vacated was given to Arthur Mattock. More was to follow. The manor of Chard was still apparently on lease to the Paulets, for although no name is given in the accounts, the usual rent of £50 a year, less the Paulet fee of £11. 6. 8d. for the chief stewardship, was being paid regularly during the years 1634–9, and in 1635 the lease of Edward VI still held good.[3] Yet on 1 July 1631 the chapter had confirmed a lease of the manor by the bishop to Francis Keene, his Banwell keeper, and on 1 October they ratified this for twenty-one years; one can only suppose that it was a sub-lease from the Paulets. More strangely still, only three years later, on 1 April 1634, Chard manor and the rectory there were leased to Arthur Mattock for twenty-one years.[4] Although the full story is not given, there is every indication that this transaction did not go through easily and that the bishop was trying to deflect something to a favourite, presumably at the expense of the Paulets or of Francis Keene, and in the face of the opposition of the chapter. Two years later, on 4 March 1636, the confirmation of a lease of Chard manor for twenty-one years was

[1] T. Serel, *Historical Notes on the Church of St. Cuthbert, Wells*, p. 83.
[2] Wells Cath. Chapter Acts 1635–44, fo. 1; S.R.O. Banwell Court Roll 1636; see p. 292 above.
[3] S.R.O. DD/CC/13324, fo. 363 ff.
[4] Chapter Acts 1621–35, fos. 108d, 114d, 157d.

reiterated by the chapter, though no names were given. When on 24 October 1640 the bishop and the chapter tried to compose their quarrels about jurisdiction and lands, the chapter agreed to confirm a lease of the manor and borough of Chard to Arthur Mattock and his assigns, for twenty-one years, and further pledged their readiness in future to confirm all other patents and leases of the bishop, 'as shall be according to the laws of this kingdom and customs of this and other churches'.[1]

That was not the end of the story. In 1643, when the bishop's authority had been smashed, Alexander Jett, his registrar, whose letters indicate that he was trying to keep some grip on affairs when all was in danger of dissolution, managed to wrest the Chard lease from Mattock. The lease of the manor was confirmed to him on 29 December, and at the same time Mattock was compensated with land in Banwell. The final act of the chapter before its interregnum was, on 28 January 1645, to confirm these leases jointly to Jett and Mattock for a fine of £2. 13. 4d. Although Mattock had been given the prebend of Wanstrow on 31 December 1642, there is no other indication that he was a cleric, and he may have held it as an impropriation.[2] In that case both he and Jett were lay servants of the bishop whose ruin by the impending destruction of the church was not so certain as that of the clerics: it was obvious that they would try to salvage something from the wreckage. In this Mattock at least was successful. When Peirs came to Wells Ezechiel Barkham still held the office of receiver-general, to which he had been appointed by Bishop Lake in 1621, and he was performing his duties, receiving money for lot lead and paying it over to the bishop, as late as the spring of 1640.[3] But he died in the following autumn and was buried in St Cuthbert's, Wells, on 5 October 1641.[4] Four days earlier, on 1 October, and probably within hours of Barkham's death, Arthur Mattock was appointed to his vacant post, at the usual fee of £10. Capitular distrust of Mattock once more delayed the affixing

---

[1] Chapter Acts 1635–44, fo. 15; *Wells*, II, 424; see above, p. 231.

[2] Chapter Acts 1635–44, fos. 112, 116; *Wells*, II, 422, 426.

[3] S.R.O. DD/CC/13324, fos. 244, 357.

[4] St Cuthbert Wells Parish Register. St Cuthbert's has two silver flagons inscribed with the date 1637 presented by Barkham. He was one of the founders of the Blue Coat School at Wells. Dr R. D. Reid has kindly confirmed the date.

of the chapter seal to this grant, a life one, until 28 January 1645.[1]

Mattock stayed on at Wells after the dissolution of the bishopric, living with his wife Elizabeth at Milton. Between 1644 and 1651 six of their children were baptized at St Cuthbert's, three of whom, and another son, were buried there while still young. The loyal Mattock must have been there to greet his old master on his return in 1660, and the bishop showed his affection for him when he drew up his will on 21 December 1668: 'to Mr. Arthur Mattock a ring and his wife another having formerly given him a cupboard of plate which cost me an hundred pounds.' Mattock just outlived the bishop and was buried in St Cuthbert's on 2 January 1674. In his will he left all the plate which Peirs had given him equally among his four sons, Arthur, Charles, Thomas and George. He left 20s. each to buy a ring to 'My Lady Peirs' and to Dr Peirs, presumably the bishop's eldest son. Half of his household goods and chattels and Milton Farm were left to his wife for life, but she was to pay his son Arthur a rent of £40 for Milton. To his other three sons he left £300 each, and the other half of his goods were to be divided between them. Service with a bishop could obviously provide a sufficient fortune.[2]

So much for the bishop's officers. Information about the episcopal estates in the early Stuart period is meagre. The Stuarts did not follow Elizabeth's example of keeping bishoprics vacant when death gave the opportunity, and so there are no accounts of temporalities, at least of Bath and Wells, for this period among the central records, nor with the exception of some court rolls for Banwell have any manorial records come to light elsewhere. One is dependent on scraps of information from various sources, and the net result is not very illuminating, but it may well be that this was an uneventful period in the administration of the estates. Bishop Still had obviously just accomplished a very thorough overhaul of his lands and his successors probably kept to his arrangements: they certainly employed the same officers. When accounts become available again in 1634, they show quite clearly that there were no

[1] *Wells*, II, 425, 429.
[2] Jewers, *Wells Cathedral*, pp. 138–9; P.C.C. 22 Bunce.

important territorial changes in this period: no more manors were filched by Crown or courtier and no more leases went to rapacious relatives, although episcopal servants, Francis Keene under Bishop Curll and Arthur Mattock under Bishop Peirs, were served well. All was stable: estate administration had become routine, and because, this was, to judge from the accounts of the 1590's, a flourishing period in the history of the bishopric, there would be little incentive to alteration. One thing is certain: the renewal of leases for fines was being pressed as actively as in Bishop Still's day, but then Robert Eyre, Still's son-in-law, was still serving as the steward of the estates, at least until 7 October 1635 when he attended the Banwell manor court for the last time.

The manor court rolls for Banwell, running for a series of years from 1625, reveal that the bishops were now as enterprising as any in extracting the equivalent of improved rents from their tenants to match the rise in prices.[1] An interesting development was taking place at Banwell. Although most of the tenants who came into the court baron, held usually four or five times a year, were customary tenants and there was a brisk insistence on the payment of heriots, their tenures were, on payment of fines, being turned into tenures for lives. What was happening was that during the lifetime of the holder he surrendered his tenement to the lord and, on payment of a fine, received it back for himself and the lives of others; the customary tenant was thus effecting an insurance for his family and the bishop was doing well out of times which were obviously profitable for the small farmer. There seems to be no relation between the number of lives added in this way and the amount of the fine. For example, at the court held on 5 October 1627 it was recorded that John Kencott had died and that his heirs had paid a black cow, valued at £5, as a heriot; his wife Elizabeth and John Jeffreys were to be the next tenants. At the next court, on 16 October, Elizabeth Jeffreys, wife of John Jeffreys, surrendered a holding and half a virgate of land in Puttingthorpe and on payment of £60 received it for herself and her husband. At yet the next court on 3 November 1627, John and Elizabeth, on payment of another £60, had the 'lease' extended to include

[1] S.R.O. Banwell Court Rolls 1625–30.

the lives of Marie Jeffreys, their daughter, and Elizabeth Pether and Thomas Pether, the son and daughter of Elizabeth Jeffreys. There may, of course, have been two Elizabeths whose land transactions were carried on with John Jeffreys, otherwise Elizabeth would seem to have married three times, but that is not the point. What is important is that on one small piece of land in Puttingthorpe the bishop made £120 in one year. By comparison, on 5 May 1628 William Gooderidge and Henry Gooderidge surrendered a small holding, and on their payment of a fine of only £4 possession was given to them and also to George and Agnes, the son and daughter of William, for their lives. At four courts held in 1627 the bishop made £271 by this method alone. Customary rents might be fixed, but if the bishop was following the same practice on all his manors he was drawing an income which allowed him to ride inflation. The Banwell rolls also reveal a good state of manorial discipline. There are frequent references to fines for failing to maintain the water-courses, for example, on 9 April 1630: 'The ditch of Thomas Swayne against Parkfield is not properly scoured and must be done on pain of 3s. 4d.' It will be remembered that the water-courses were particularly important in this low-lying manor.

THE CROWN'S CONCERN ABOUT EPISCOPAL ESTATES

When Peirs took over in 1632 the character of his régime in estate administration was conservative. As in Still's episcopate, there were no innovations and no exceptional leases or grants, and no attempt, as there had been under Henry VIII, to buy off the enemy. In his effort to preserve the endowment the bishop was now supported by the Crown. More than any other monarch, Charles I was adamant that bishops and chapters should not weaken themselves by ill-considered grants and leases. The dignity of the episcopate would be undermined even more than it was already by puritan attack unless its economic resources were husbanded. This was a point which Elizabeth I had not appreciated; James I showed more concern for the bishops, but even he was not guiltless of raiding their estates.[1]

---

[1] Hill, *Economic Problems of the Church*, p. 34.

Yet it was in James's lifetime, in 1622, and while Bishop
Lake was still alive, that instructions were issued by the Crown
to Abbot, archbishop of Canterbury, for the observance
of the bishops of his province. Three of these instructions
concerned the care of their estates. Bishops were to keep
residence in their sees unless their attendance at court was necessary. They were not to reside on property which they had purchased or leased, but in one of their episcopal houses, and they
were not to waste woods. Any bishop nominated to another
bishopric was not to make any further leases or renew any
estates or cut any wood or timber, but merely to receive the
rents due and quit the place, 'for we think it a hateful thing
that any man leaving the bishopric should almost undo the
successor, and if any man shall presume to break this order we
will refuse our royal assent and keep him at the place which he
hath so abused'.[1]

Under Charles I even more forceful instructions on the
conservation of estates were sent to all the bishops, as in the
king's letter to Peirs of 22 June 1634: 'We have of late taken
the state of our several bishoprics into our princely consideration, that we may be the better able to preserve that livelihood
which as yet is left unto them.' Of recent times, the letter proceeded, no greater inconvenience had arisen than the practice
of turning leases of one-and-twenty years into lives. By that
means the present bishop puts a great fine into his own purse,
to the enrichment of himself, his wife and children, and leaves
succeeding bishops destitute of the increment that should come
to them. Should this practice continue, hardly any bishop
would be able to live and keep house according to his rank and
calling. Although it was lawful for bishops to let for either
twenty-one years or three lives, time and experience had shown
that there was a great difference between them, especially in
church leases where men were usually advanced in years
before they entered their endowment. Accordingly 'upon peril
of our utmost displeasure and what shall follow thereon', the
bishop was commanded not to convert any leases into lives
that were not in lives already, and where opportunity offered
existing leases for lives were to be turned into years. The bishop's

[1] P.R.O. S.P.15/42/88(ii).

registrar and the dean and chapter were to register copies of this letter and they were to see that succeeding bishops knew of these instructions. A letter in identical terms was sent to the dean and chapter on the same date, and it referred to the instructions of 1622 that bishops were to make no new leases after promotion: this command now applied equally to deans. These letters from the king were duly read to the dean and chapter at Wells and entered in their register.[1]

No doubt it was these instructions of the king which prompted Bishop Peirs to draw up, at the front of his new notebook, a comprehensive rental of the copyholders and leaseholders in those four manors, Banwell, Huish, Wells and Westbury, and the part of Buckland which he still had in hand. He noted the names of those jointly holding a lease or copy for lives, their ages, the land held, the date of the grant, the number of heriots paid, the rent, and—most revealing—the actual value per annum, which it must be supposed represented the improved value. Only by study of such a detailed survey could the bishop decide how the new instructions would bear upon his particular case. At length in consternation he must have written to the king, and perhaps to Laud as well since he had once held the bishopric. Not until 20 March 1640 did Charles reply and his letter reveals the gist of Peirs' request, although Peirs' letter is not extant.[2] The bishop reminded the king that he had only four manors and a part of a fifth where, for the present, he could make fines. This was correct. All of these manors, the bishop pleaded, consisted of small copyholds, and he asked leave of the king to demise the smaller leaseholds (he seems to have been using the term leasehold and copyhold loosely) for three lives, as his predecessors had done and as had been the custom of the see. The king referred the petition to Archbishop Laud, the bishop of London, and the lord treasurer, and they confirmed that the number of small leaseholders on the bishop's estates was between three and four hundred, so that a large part of the revenue was derived from fines for the

---

[1] *Wells*, ii, 407–9.

[2] There are two versions of the king's letter to Peirs, one in S.R.O. DD/CC/13324, fo. 185, and a draft among the State Papers, *Cal. S.P.D. 1640–41*, p. 340. In main points they are identical, but there are some differences of wording which suggest bad copying.

renewal of leases. These would be much reduced if the bishop
were restrained in the making of leases. The king replied
graciously that he was pleased to allow Peirs and his successors
in the see to let the smaller leaseholds for three lives as before,
but he was adamant that his previous order—that leases were
to be for twenty-one years only—still applied to manors, to
demesnes of entire farms, and to impropriations. Whenever the
bishop had opportunity to reduce any that were in lives into
years, he should do so, so that such leases should yield him and
his successors an annual increase of income.

Not only did the bishop draw up a rental of those tenants,
leasehold and copyhold, who paid their rents directly to the
reeves in Wells, Westbury, Banwell, Huish, and the part of
Buckland which was not leased out, but he proceeded to make a
survey of all the rest of his endowment which was let out in
large leases. The survey, dated about 1635,[1] and the only one
of its kind for the bishopric in this period, shows the position
virtually unaltered since Bishop Still's day, except that even
more of the estates were leased out, for now the Banwell
demesnes, 281 acres, were granted to Francis Keene, the keeper
of Banwell Palace, at a rent of £57. Peirs did not share the
former bishops' fondness for Banwell: he spent his time either
in Wells or London. The only other change is that the rectory
of Westdown in Devon seems to have been dropped, but this
comparatively small item (it was worth only £10) may be
an omission from the accounts. The leased properties under-
line the changelessness of the position: Wiveliscombe was
held by (John?) Colles under Bishop Godwin's lease to the
queen of 1586 and hers to Sir George Bond for £80; Chard
was held by John Lord Paulet for 99 years by the lease of
1550 at £50 a year; and Compton Parva by Thomas Smith by a
lease of 28 October 1624 for £2. 13. 4d. a year.

The position about Buckland manor is not so clear. A large
part of it, the demesne, was leased out in several small tenancies.
The other half had been intended in Bishop Still's time for his

---

[1] S.R.O. DD/CC/13324, fo. 23ff. There is a copy of the 1635 Survey in the Wells
Museum Notebook, but it has omissions which suggest that it was copied from the
more complete first one. The Parliamentary Surveys of the bishop's manors cannot
be found, although those for the impropriated rectories survive: Lambeth Palace
MSS, Parliamentary Surveys, I, 1648.

son Nathaniel, but it must have been his for only a short time.[1] On 25 April 1627 Laud leased it to John Warre for three lives at a slightly higher rent than previously, £49. 3. 4d. There seems to have been trouble over this lease, for there is a statement by Laud on 21 September that he had received a surrender of a former lease of Buckland and that at the request of the copyhold tenants of the manor he granted a new one, the demesne lands still excepted, to Anthony Paulet, David Slocombe and Edward Thurston for the lives of Peter Cordwent and two others. Peirs for some reason did not allow this lease to stand, and in turn, perhaps tempted by the prospect of the large fine of 100 marks, conceded an entirely new lease to William Every of Othay and two associates on 29 April 1634, still at the old rent of £49. 3. 4d. When he was restored in December 1662 he had to return the lease to Laud's grantees, Anthony Paulet and his cronies.

The position with regard to the leased rectories was that Glastonbury and West Pennard was held by Bernard and William Strode from an unknown date for £42. 13. 4d. a year, Weston Zoyland by Thomas Dyer from 29 September 1600 for 99 years at £70, Northlode by Andrew Bowerman from 17 September 1608 for £2 15s., East Brent by Agnes Cook from 12 April 1632 for £18. 5. 4d., Corston by John Harington from 26 July 1631 for £2. 2. 6d., Compton Dando by Thomas Milner clerk (or Richard Harvey) from 3 January 1627 for £2, Castle Cary by James Kirton from 26 March 1611 for £12, and East Pennard by an unnamed person for £19 10s. Leaving the rectory of Westdown, Devon, out of account, these eight rectories were still leased at approximately the same total rent £169. 17. 7¾d., as in Bishop Still's time. It is significant that although five of the families who had been leaseholders in Still's time continued in possession, the leases in operation had been made within the last thirty years: the family interest had been maintained only at the cost of lease renewal. Moreover they were all, except Dyer's lease of Weston Zoyland, leases for lives, and they had doubtless been procured at the cost of large fines. There is evidence of this in one case; the renewal of the Castle Cary lease in 1611 had cost James Kirton of Ansford £80.

[1] See above p. 196.

No doubt the bishops were prepared to forgo a little rent in order to persuade their tenants to take a fresh lease. They could be more generous in the Weston Zoyland case, allowing a lease for 99 years, because the annual rent was so much higher than the others, £70.[1]

The policy of the bishops of Bath and Wells in leasing their rectories indeed amply justifies the criticisms of Charles I: they were undoubtedly letting property to their immediate advantage without thought of their successors. Perhaps that was why Bishop Peirs, ruefully surveying all these recent leases for lives yet to run, with no prospect of a rewarding fine to come his way, tried to unseat the tenant of Compton Dando. On 3 January 1627 Laud had let the rectory of Compton Dando to Thomas Milner, clerk, of Corston, for the lives of his sons Samuel, Richard and Nathaniel at the usual rent of £2. In June 1635 Milner sold his interest in it to one Jerome Harvey for £250; Harvey was to hold it for three lives, but which three are not specified. On Harvey's death his title was claimed by his nephew, Richard, by will, and it was Richard Harvey's right that Bishop Peirs denied in 1638. In October of that year, Nicholas Martin, an agent or servant of Harvey, wrote to his master that he had been to Wells with the rent of Compton Dando (the accounts show that it was then two-and-a-half years in arrear) and had offered it to the bishop's steward, Richard Hicks, since he had been unable to see the bishop himself. The steward refused the rent and told Martin that the bishop proposed to bring Harvey to trial over his claim to Compton Dando. Harvey's defence in January 1640, in an unnamed court, was based on the will of Jerome Harvey, a copy of which it was alleged the bishop had received, together with other relevant deeds. The bishop must have lost the case for in June 1640 he received five years' arrears of rent, £10, from Mr Harvey, and when the parliamentary survey was drawn up in 1648 'one Harvey' was recorded as holding the rectory tithes of Compton Dando: there was no glebe land.[2]

---

[1] Wells Museum Notebook, fo. 236ff.; S.R.O. DD/CC/13324, fo. 363ff. Where there is a slight discrepancy in the figures from these two sources the latter has been preferred.

[2] Lambeth MSS. Parliamentary Surveys, I, 1648; *Cal. S.P.D. 1638–39*, p. 56; *1639–40*, p. 415.

The net result of all the meticulous attention that Peirs paid to the accounting of his estates was that the endowment was remarkably stable and resembled that of Still's time. Within a few pounds all the properties were producing, during the years 1634–40 for which accounts exist, roughly the same income as in late Elizabethan times.[1] The income from the manor of Wells had in fact dropped from an average of about £200 to one of £145, because the demesne lands, about which Thomas Emylie had been so concerned, had been taken in hand again and were no longer let out: in 1635 they were worth £110. 13. 4d. Perquisites of the court averaged about £24 and show no relaxation of the bishop's control towards the end: 1639 was, in fact, a good year, bringing in £28. 11. 1d. The Banwell demesnes, including the deer park of 200 acres, a third of which was covered with trees or copsewood, were let to Francis Keene for £57, against which were charged expenses such as building and repairs. One must remember that Keene was also the keeper of the old mansion house at Banwell in which there were still certain goods and utensils. Another cost allowed to him was £1 a year for a court dinner, and in 1637, because there had been a dry summer, his rent was abated by £2. The Towerhead lease of 364 acres granted by Bishop Godwin to Elizabeth I still held good, and the rent for it was included in the reeve's general account for Banwell manor. The Westbury part of the lease, approximately 110½ acres, now in the hands of the Rodney family, was dealt with in the same way.

All the other properties yielded almost exactly the same rents as in Still's episcopate. The Green Wax was still farmed out to the Crosse family for a nominal £40 a year, but in fact they usually found excuses for allowances which brought it down to £30. By 1640 the bishop seems to have become resigned to this position, for he noted in his accounts 'pays but £30 now'. The bishop's gross income from all these sources, including his allowances for tenths under the Kingsbury arrangement, was in the region of £960. Expenses had come down since Bishop Still's day. There were the old-established crown rents, £115 from Banwell and £10 from Wells to pay to the sheriff, but the charge on the rectories had, unaccountably, been reduced from

[1] S.R.O. DD/CC/13324.

£11 to £8. 3. 5d. The annuities to Lord Henry Seymour and to William Grilles had also ceased, a saving of £46. 13. 4d. a year. The net yield to the bishop was about £760 a year, to which there were added the royalties from the lead mines amounting to about £125. His total net income was thus approximately £885.[1]

THE CATACLYSM

Nemesis threatened, but the bishops went about their daily business, each the centre of a small world of agents and dependants. Peirs was not the only one concerned with economic security. The bishop of Lichfield was deforesting his land to get the profit of the timber with little thought for the future. Bishop Skinner of Bristol was involved in a dispute about temporalities with the bishop of Hereford.[2] The small routines of life continued. One of the episcopal circle, William Bellarmine, was in London with his master, Ezechiel Barkham, in March 1636, and on the 15th he wrote to James Huish, the bishop's registrar at Wells:

Good Mr. Huish, on Saturday last I wrote by the carrier that my master desired your wife to speak with Mistress Barkham about buying and baking a bushell of wheat against his coming down, for the poor, and to buy 200 or 300 herrings for them; and to send to Alice Parker to starch 2 ruff bands for him against his coming which will be on Saturday sevennight.

Bellarmine was a useful friend to have in London: in January 1637 he sent Huish two pounds of the best tobacco by Green the carrier: 'I got it cut and dried: it is made up in paper directed to you: when you receive it you were best to keep it in a glass bottle and stop it: the price is 12s. the pound.' James Huish, the busy notary, also had time to write gossipy letters. He reported from Wells on 3 February 1637 that the bishop had been ill of an ague and fever, the result of taking cold at the sessions, but now the fever had left him and he could walk a little in his chamber.[3] Their letters soon became devoted to more serious affairs.

[1] See Appendix D.
[2] C. V. Wedgwood, *The King's Peace 1637–41*, p. 98; *Cal. S.P.D. 1639–40*, pp. 71–2.
[3] Wells Diocesan Registry, Miscellaneous Letters 1589–1639.

The calling of parliament in 1640 after the eleven years' interval was fatal for the bishops in general, and for Peirs in particular. Peirs's enemies now had the opportunity to appeal against his handling of the Beckington case, and they did so by petition to the Commons.[1] On 21 November 1640 one Flamsted wrote at the bishop's command ('my Lord hath no leisure to write to you now') to Alexander Jett, who appears to have shared James Huish's duties. The bishop, he said, had already sent two letters to Jett by the Wells carrier a fortnight ago, in which he had told Jett that he, the bishop, had been commanded not to receive any more contribution money from the clergy of the diocese or to send out any censures of the church.[2] On 11 December the first great organized demonstration against the bishops, the 'root and branch' petition, was presented to parliament by Alderman Isaac Pennington of London. The petition bore 15,000 signatures and called for the entire abolition of the government of archbishops and bishops. A few days afterwards Laud was committed to the Tower, and Peirs, with Bishop Wren, was impeached before the House of Lords and bound over on a heavy bail to appear to hear the charges against him. The articles of impeachment violently denounced him, and much emphasis was put on his having urged his clergy to contribute to the Scottish wars. The committee appointed to investigate the charges became known as the 'Bishop of Bath's Committee' even when its terms of reference were widened to cover the clergy generally, since he was regarded as the chief offender. At Christmas 1640 William Bellarmine wrote to Jett that he feared that the bishop would be sent to the Tower; there was a great plot laid against him and unless he gave bail by Tuesday next he would certainly be committed.[3]

Meanwhile some of the other bishops were in conference with the Presbyterians at the dean of Westminster's house about the reform of the church, but it was clear that the episcopate was divided. Some, the 'moderate cathedral men', hoped to find a compromise; others, the court prelates, were not prepared to concede any of their power. But the radicals were

---

[1] *V.C.H. Somerset.*, II, 46.   [2] Wells Diocesan Letters 1640–1759.
[3] Wedgwood, *King's Peace*, p. 98; *D.N.B.*; Wells Diocesan Letters 1640–1759.

getting impatient. In May 1641 Sir Edward Dering presented his bill to abolish deans and chapters, and then began that battle over the episcopacy which lasted, with mighty and acrimonious speeches on either side, for about a year. On the whole the bishops' defence was weak, except for the lucid and well-argued speech of Dr John Hacket, a prebendary of St Paul's, who was put up as their chief speaker. His arguments included the economic one that it was only just to let the clergy retain their endowments so that they could share the general improvement in living which every knight, gentleman and yeoman enjoyed. Further, he reminded his audience that ecclesiastics paid a higher proportion of taxes than any other bodies or estates in the kingdom.[1] Yet the adherents of episcopacy were shaken. William Bellarmine wrote to Alexander Jett at Wells from London on 29 May 1641: 'I can write you no good news: 'tis very doubtful whether bishops shall continue or not, or what government we shall have; the parliament are now very hot upon it.'[2] Hacket's defence had made a good impression, and if a vote had been taken then, thought Fuller, the bishops' lands might have been saved. But the critics would not be silenced and one in particular, Cornelius Burgess, vehemently urged the conversion of episcopal endowments to private persons' use. He and his following were able to get a bill through the Commons curbing the bishops' political power, abolishing their votes in parliament and their temporal jurisdiction. This bill was thrown out by the Lords on 8 June, but the bill to repeal the court of high commission went through on 5 July, and with it the power of the church consistories went down.[3]

William Bellarmine informed Alexander Jett of the disaster from London on 10 July 1641:

Yesterday was a fatal day for the bishops. They are voted down, and their lands to be seized into the King's hands. . . . What will become of ecclesiastical jurisdiction is yet uncertain; some report we shall have some doings, though not as we have had; others that the

[1] T. Fuller, *Church History of Britain*, VI, 198 ff.
[2] Wells Diocesan Letters 1640–1759.
[3] Godfrey Davies, *The Early Stuarts 1603–60*, p. 102; S. R. Gardiner, *Constitutional Documents of the Puritan Revolution 1625–60* (3rd edn 1906), p. 186.

causes of our courts and probates of wills shall be turned to the common laws. What to think of it I know not, but in the Act of suppressing the High Commission Court, which is now in print, there is a clause which most concerns to reach to the suppressing of all ecclesiastical judges after the first of August next.

Alexander Jett's moans were written to a James Samford in London on the 19th. He had lately invested much money in an office which, for ought he could perceive, was likely to come to an end. He referred, of course, to his office as registrar. 'God give me patience', he added, 'and that all things may work for the best: I shall heartily rejoice to hear good news from London, especially from you.' Five days later Jett wrote with more vehemence:

we daily hear of our downfall, and it is reported here for credit [that] ecclesiastical jurisdiction will utterly be taken away, which if it be, my loss you know will be very great. God almighty give me patiently to endure it, which I trust of his mercy he will.[1]

Jett was related in some way to Ezechiel Barkham: he referred to 'my uncle Barkham'. All of them, all the officers forming the bishop's circle whose fortunes depended on the maintenance of episcopacy, must have been in despair.

The bishop of Lincoln was now trying to save the day by voluntarily introducing a bill for the regulation of bishops. This included ten points, one of which was that all archbishops, bishops and collegiate churches should donate a fourth of their fines and improved rents to buy out impropriations of livings. This would have met one of the main puritan complaints that the clergy were impoverished and depressed by the laity's taking the profits from impropriated benefices. The bishop of Lincoln however had little support, and the bill was read but once. All this time the bishops were also fighting to save their votes in parliament. An attempt was made to impeach them, but it was dropped. By Christmas-time feeling against them was expressed in apprentices' riots and stone-throwing, so that they dared not land from the barges which had brought them by water to Westminster to attend parliament. Laud was by now in the Tower, but the twelve bishops who were in town,

[1] Wells Diocesan Letters 1640–1759.

including Peirs, drew up a petition to the king begging security, and claiming that all legislation passed in their absence from the Lords was void. The next day, 30 December, the twelve subscribers to the petition were committed to the Tower and there, Peirs among them, they languished for eighteen weeks. On 4 March 1642 Peirs wrote in his own hand from there to Alexander Jett signing himself 'your very assured friend'.[1]

And so, with twelve bishops in the Tower, five so newly appointed that they dared not utter in the Lords, and the rest negligent of their duty, in a speech of Dr John Warner, bishop of Rochester 'dying episcopacy gave the last groan', and early in February 1642 the bill depriving the bishops of their votes in parliament was passed. The Lords now agreed to the release of the bishops from the Tower, but the Commons objected and back the bishops went. Perhaps the Commons could not feel secure of episcopal plotting until the king gave his assent to the bill. This was not easily obtained, but at last Charles gave his reluctant assent at St Augustine's, Canterbury, through which he was passing while escorting the queen to Dover. From there on 19 February 1642 Secretary Nicholas reported the acceptance of the bill to Sir Thomas Roe. But the bishops remained in the Tower blaming the archbishop of York for their troubles. On 31 March they sent a petition to the Lords that they might be released on bail, since the Commons had decided not to proceed against them by impeachment. Their pleas were renewed on 5 April and 5 May.[2] The next year, 1643, after war had begun, ordinances were issued by parliament abolishing bishops, deans and chapters and, on 27 March, sequestrating their estates. But the liquidation of these estates did not get under way until 1647, when the first sales were made by the trustees for the sale of the bishops' lands acting by virtue of the ordinance of 17 November 1646.[3]

A study of the disposal of the lands of the bishopric of Bath and Wells is outside the scope of this book. Two summaries of

---

[1] *Cal. S.P.D. 1641–43*, p. 217; Wells Diocesan Letters 1640–1759.

[2] *Cal. S.P.D. 1641–43*, pp. 286, 288; H.M.C. 5th Report, pp. 15, 16, 18.

[3] C. H. Firth and R. S. Rait, *Acts and Ordinances of the Interregnum 1642–60*, I, 106, 887.

this process have previously been made and neither is accurate. The first includes sales of the Bath and Wells lands from March 1647 to December 1650 and is obviously copied from the close rolls;[1] but a check of four of these entries against the originals revealed errors in each one of them.[2] This summary records twenty-one sales worth £24,433. 9. 6½d. The second estimate, also based on the close rolls, records twenty-seven entries of sales relating to the bishopric of Bath and Wells between 1648 and 1658 totalling £22,176. 9. 8½d.; but it misses the sale of the Westbury and Wells lands on 5 March 1647 to John Casebeard and others, and its total is obviously incompatible with that of the first summary.[3]

One would like to know more of the life of the bishops who shared Peirs' disasters during the Interregnum and how they contrived to live on their private resources. Laud had hidden a trunk of plate in the stable at Lambeth and later he had it secretly buried by Nicholas Smith, his groom. Morgan Owen, bishop of Landaff, while a prisoner in the Tower in October 1641, made a lease of his whole estate for 100 years to Owen Peirs, his servant, reserving only 40s. rent a year; this was probably in the nature of a trust arrangement.[4] With the utter loss of all his goods and personal estate, the broken Bishop Peirs retired to Sunbury-on-Thames where he lived for many years, and where his first wife, Anne, was buried. Later he moved to the family estate at Denton where he was the neighbour of the bishop of Oxford at Cuddesdon and where he married his second wife, Mary.[5]

[1] B.M. Add. MS 9049.
[2] P.R.O. Close Rolls:

  (i) March 1647, Casebeard etc.—C54/3385.
  (ii) July 1648, Taylor—C54/3413.
  (iii) September 1648, Parker—C54/3413.
  (iv) January 1649, Averye—C54/3415.

[3] G. B. Tatham 'The Sale of Episcopal Lands during the Civil Wars and Commonwealth', *E.H.R.*, XXIII, 91; P.R.O. C54/3385. See D. Underdown 'A Case Concerning Bishops' Lands: Cornelius Burges and the Corporation of Wells', *E.H.R.*, LXXVIII, for an account of the prolonged conflict arising out of the bishop's property rights in Wells.

[4] *Cal. S.P.D. 1648–49*, p. 341; *1650*, p. 343.

[5] Peirs' will P.C.C. 63 Penn; *D.N.B.*

THE RESTORATION

Peirs lived to see episcopacy restored when he was already eighty-four, and the revenues from his restored estates must have been large, for he left a considerable personal fortune when he made his will on 21 December 1668. On reinstatement at the Restoration his opportunities for the renewal of offices and leases for large fines were, of course, considerable, and he spent lavishly of the proceeds, not solely for his personal profit. In the work of resettlement and restoration he expended £400 on ornaments and utensils in Wells Cathedral. According to Christopher Clement, his bailiff, who had charge of the work, he laid out £5,000 on rebuilding his palace at Wells and the house at Banwell. He gave the king £200 and donated £100 towards the redemption of captives. A schedule of these expenses was drawn up after the bishop's death, and Arthur Mattock, who was now acting as steward of the episcopal estates, also certified that the bishop had made abatements of rent to his tenants—to some because they had been purchasers in the late ill times, and to others for their loyalty and suffering in the king's cause—to the tune of £6,000. The full cost to the bishop of all this generosity was £11,700.[1]

Peirs died in 1670 and was buried on 19 May at Walthamstow, Essex. He was then ninety-four, the oldest bishop in Christendom. He obviously expected trouble over his will for in it he urged his two sons not to 'sue, molest or trouble my faithful and dearly beloved wife Mary Peirs'. One can understand the acrimony generated by the will when one studies its terms. Mary, the second wife, did indeed benefit to the detriment of Anne's children: according to Wood she was too young and too cunning for Bishop Peirs and she wheedled the greater part of his estates from him. It was at her persuasion that, at the close of his life, he left Wells and settled at Walthamstow.[2]

The will begins frankly:

By reason of my great age being now in my fourscore and tenth year and for having one foot already in the grave . . . if I die in London or thereabout I desire my body may be buried either in the

---

[1] Bodleian Library, Tanner MSS. cxl, fo. 2.
[2] D. Lysons, *Environs of London*, IV, 214, 224; P.C.C. 63 Penn; *D.N.B.*

chancel of the Church of Sunbury, Middlesex where the body of
my first wife Anne Peirs lieth . . . or else in the chancel of Walthamstow in Essex.[1]

For Sunbury he seems to have had a special affection: it is the
only place which benefited by the will. He left that parish £20 to
buy a silver flagon, a silver chalice and a paten for communion,
and £10 for the poor. The silver paten at least still belongs to the
church of St Mary, Sunbury, and it is inscribed: 'A Legacy of
Wm Peirs late Ld Bpp of Bath and Wells to ye parish Church
of Sunbury 1670.'[2] Then followed the long list of bequests to
Mary Peirs. He left her a choice of five homes. There was
first the new house in Sternal Street in Walthamstow recently
built on ground which Peirs had purchased: it had gardens
compassed with brick walls, an orchard, a wash-house, stables,
a coach-house, outhouses and yards. All this and the goods and
household stuff there went to Mary and her heirs. Also left to
Mary in Walthamstow was the dwelling-house and farm occupied by William Colvin, husbandman, who rented them for
£30 a year; Mary was given a life-interest in them, and after
her they went to Anne, the eldest daughter of his son William,
as a marriage portion.

Mary was also given a life-interest in a fair mansion house
called Whynns (its locality is not given), with all the lands,
orchards, gardens and outhouses, which again the bishop had
recently purchased. After her it was to go to William Peirs, the
son. The goods and household stuff in Whynns went to Mary.
In Sunbury Mary already held a house and copyhold land,
doubtless the bishop's home in the time of the troubles. Now he
left to her and her heirs all the household goods there. Another
dwelling house in Mile End, Stepney, with its backyards and
stable which the bishop had lately built, again with the household stuff, was left to Mary, with remainder at her death to
his son William. There were two other tenements out on lease
in Mile End left to Mary, and then one to each son, William and
John. Somersetshire lands left to Mary were a farm in East

---

[1] The church of St Mary, Sunbury-on-Thames, was entirely rebuilt temp.
George II and there is no trace of this grave in the chancel.
[2] I was able to see this paten through the kindness of the Rev. E. M. Johnson,
but not all the church plate was available for inspection.

Street, West Pennard, lately purchased with her money, two closes containing six acres in Henstridge left to her and her two sisters as coheirs, and a farm in Baltonsborough which Peirs had recently bought. She also had a farm at Denton in Oxfordshire leased for £34. It is significant that so many of these lands and buildings were recent purchases: more evidence of the bishop's sudden accession of wealth after the Restoration.

The bishop's two sons were given but one estate each. William, the elder, inherited a mansion house and lands in West Bradley, Somerset. John was endowed with a mansion house, its contents, outhouses and orchards in Denton, together with some freehold lands there and some leases in Bicester and Town Langford(?) in Oxfordshire. Of the movable goods, Mary again had the pick. She was to have the bishop's best coach, his new chariot, a pair of his best coach-horses, which she was to choose, and a pair of his best coach-harnesses; the other coach-horses and harnesses went to William. Mary had his biggest horse litter: the other went to William. She had all his English books: the others passed to William and John. The silver indeed was shared between William and Mary, but she had the 'tuff taffety' window cushions and the organ which the bishop had recently purchased for £30: another, bigger organ went to William.

There was a long list of bequests of household goods in the palace at Wells, and here again Mary had the cream: the bishop's purple cloth bed lined with aurora-coloured sarsnet, the purple bays hanging in the chamber over the parlour, landscapes over the chimneys in the chamber and the parlour, a red cloth bed, all the linen, pewter and iron household goods, and the virginals and harpsichord bought with her own money. William and John had but a few of these household goods.

Lastly there was a provision in the will which was incredibly foolish and bound to create trouble: the whim of an aged, near-witless bishop. This concerned the joint occupation of a house within the liberties at Wells, on the north side of the cathedral, which the bishop had purchased on lease from Humphrey Walrond for sixty years for £1,000. The lease was in the name of Peirs' sons William and John, but the house was intended for the sole use of William. The bishop now cancelled that arrangement and instructed William to make his stepmother Mary a lease of a part of the premises for her own and her family's use for fifty years. There was to be the use in common of the kitchen, hall, great gardens, coach-house and yards. There was a specific list of the rooms in the west part to be reserved for Mary: the wainscot parlour at the west end of the hall, the chamber over it and the closet near that, three ground rooms, the great dining-room and chambers over it, the little buttery or wine-cellar, the two little studies which the bishop had built in the yard, four yards, and the lesser garden.

The interest of the will lies, however, not in the family squabbles, but in the evidence of the wealth of a restored bishop, which would seem to be much more than that of other Tudor or Stuart bishops of Bath and Wells. Bishop Godwin had a well-provided household but his standard of living was not such that he could afford more than one coach: Peirs had at least two. Bishop Still invested in land for his family, but not on the scale of Bishop Peirs. Yet Peirs ended his will pathetically saying that what he had left could not be much after all his losses in the time of the troubles and the great expenses which he had incurred in rebuilding the palace at Wells and the court house at Banwell.

Conclusion

THE post-Reformation bishopric of Bath and Wells appears to have lost some status in the hierarchy of bishoprics. In 1535, in the *Valor Ecclesiasticus*, it had been valued at £1,899. A more realistic survey of its income in 1539 put it a little higher, at £2,202. Against this, by Elizabethan times it was valued for tenths in the crown records at only £533, in the same class as Carlisle at £531 and Exeter at £500, while the great rewards were in another flight altogether: Canterbury £3,903, York £2,609, Winchester £2,400 and London £1,219. There were bishoprics like the Welsh ones which were more miserable than Bath and Wells: St Asaph was worth a mere £187.[1]

This assessment of Bath and Wells at £533 for purposes of tenths was slightly on the low side, for the Elizabethan bishops, by efficient, even ruthless, management of their much depleted estates, usually succeeded in extracting a higher income. The gross figure between 1566 and 1575 fluctuated from £747 to £989, but fees, annuities and costs of administration reduced it to a net sum between £522 and £764. By 1595 Bishop Still had raised the net income to about £843,[2] and in Bishop Peirs' time, by when it was relieved of some annuities, it was a fraction higher, at £885. The bishop's purse had indeed become a lean one by pre-Reformation standards and this in a period of inflation.

It is possible that while all bishoprics suffered by the upheavals of the mid-sixteenth century and the depredations of Elizabethan courtiers, Bath and Wells lost more than most. The Protector Somerset's interest in building up his west

---

[1] B.M. Add. MS 18, 666, fo. 2; Stowe MSS 572, fo. 51.
[2] This figure allows for an adjustment of the Green Wax profits, three years of which were included in the account for 1595.

country holding had made the Wells bishopric particularly vulnerable. Certainly it seems to have become less attractive to the careerist. Of the thirteen bishops there between 1363 and 1523, eight had been bishops before they came to Wells and six passed on to greater bishoprics. Of those—the same number—reviewed in this book, only four had attained episcopal rank before Wells and only four passed on, to Chichester and London, and two to Winchester. Wells seems to have become a dumping ground for aged deans (four of them), archdeacons and academic administrators (two of each), while one of its bishops, Berkeley, had been merely rector of a Norfolk parish and royal chaplain. Some of them were primarily statesmen and after years of harassed travel as diplomats semi-retirement at Wells was no doubt a reward.

Semi-retirement brought, as it often does, its financial problems. These men were used to moving in court circles and had a proper appreciation of the style of living which a bishop should support: open house for the locality, a staff of forty or fifty servants, and alms for the poor at the gates. Several of them faced the additional problem of meeting the demands of wives and families. Estates must be built up for sons and offices found for them, but this brought conflict with the local gentry, or alternatively sons must have cathedral prebends or benefices, but this raised the jealousy of the clergy. Daughters needed dowries. Inevitably tensions arose. Money must be found, the estates must be made more remunerative.

The bishops examined their accounts and called their officials to book: the quarrels of Bishop Berkeley with his auditor John Rawlins and of Bishop Still with Leonard Crosse, his bailiff at Wells, are two examples. The tenants were harried, customary tenures turned into leases for lives, fines for renewal of leases and even heriots levied mercilessly, the markets and fairs supervised and the productivity of the lead mines doubled. None of this added to the popularity of the bishops. It is not surprising that their estates, with those of the Crown and of royalist delinquents, came onto the market in the mid-seventeenth century in a great land revolution like that of the Norman Conquest or of the Tudor monastic lands.

Permission for clerical marriage raised new social questions for the bishops. There was much advantage in having a bishop's lady to supervise the domestic arrangements of the episcopal palace, but the new régime cannot have been altogether welcomed by stewards and servants who were accustomed to an all-male, celibate household. More problematical was the social status of these new phenomena, the bishops' wives and children. To which social group could a bishop legitimately look for a marriage partner?

Of the ten bishops included in this study for whom marriage was an official possibility six took wives, if one includes the doubtful case of Bishop Berkeley, and at least two outlived their wives to marry a second time. This suggests that to the bishops personally marriage was a blessing which they accepted gratefully, but the uncertainty which surrounds Bishop Berkeley's wife and the malicious rumours about Bishop Godwin's second one suggest that episcopal marriage was not well received and that the early Elizabethan bishops were rather hesitant to own it. Their archbishop of Canterbury, Matthew Parker, had to keep his wife in the background at Lambeth.

Episcopal marriage had its disadvantages, and bishops' wives seem to have come from minor gentry or trade or even lower. Bishop Barlow's wife was a former nun; Bishop Berkeley, if he married his Anne Smarthwett, acquired a servant as a father-in-law; Bishop Godwin married into the Buckinghamshire gentry; but Bishop Still's first wife was a clothier's daughter. It was only after he had become established at Wells that Still made the advantageous second marriage which brought him into the circle of the Somerset gentry who revolved round Sir John Popham, the lord chief justice. That was in 1594 and by then marriage with a bishop had apparently become more usual. The origins of the wives of Bishop Curll and Bishop Peirs cannot be determined.

The consequence of all this was that episcopal families were forced back onto themselves and tended to make a new cohesive group in society, like the Quakers. Marriages within or between the cathedral closes were common: the Barlow ramifications at Chichester and Salisbury are a case in point. Again, Francis Godwin, second son of Bishop Godwin, married a daughter of the bishop of Exeter, and when he went to Hereford as bishop his daughter married the archdeacon there. Bishop Peirs' eldest son was an archdeacon whose daughter in turn married Dr Creighton, himself the son of a bishop. Nevertheless, the fact that none of Bishop Still's four daughters married clerics suggests, again, that by early Stuart times episcopal families had become an accepted fact and had a wider field of choice in marriage. All twelve of the bishops' daughters covered by this study found husbands: further evidence that episcopal families came to be socially integrated.

In their standard of living the bishops certainly aped the leaders of society, as their large households of servants, their coaches, and their abundance of fine furniture, tapestries, cushions, linen and domestic utensils show. In learning, too, they kept up a standard and their families shared their books. Of the bishops themselves seven had been to Oxford and five to Cambridge: only one, William Barlow, started life as a monk and had not been through the university. Even two of the three sons of Bishop Peirs who settled down as country gentry had been first to Trinity College Cambridge.

Bishops tended to have large families. Barlow had seven children, Godwin eight and Still ten, of whom three died young. Of the thirteen sons six went into the church, five settled down as country gentry, and the careers of two are unknown. Bishop Godwin's sons had, with one exception, crowded into the church. Was it symptomatic of the times that Bishop Peirs' three sons growing up under Charles I chose the ampler and more secure rôle of country gentry?

When the monks had been turned out of their monasteries in the 1530's there had undoubtedly been hardship, above all among the lay servants of the communities. The social readjustment for monks and nuns was difficult; but these religious were celibate and had no family responsibilities, and they received pensions and in many cases benefices. The dissolution of the bishoprics and cathedral chapters in the mid-seventeenth century, if it could be fully documented, would reveal a tale of hardship on a far greater scale in terms of individual human suffering. The bishops were each the centre of a little world of relatives and dependants in episcopal administration. They were suddenly ejected with meagre compensation: the families of these clergy received only one-fifth of their former parochial revenues, at the expense of their successors.[1] Penury and near-starvation were their lot.

Even in normal times the bishop's family was none too secure, for the revenues of his estates came to him as the adjuncts of office, not as his personal property. When the bishop died both his income and his homes, the episcopal palaces, went to his successor; his wife and children became destitute unless he had made private provision for them. It is not surprising that the bishops tried to build up private estates for themselves and their sons and sons-in-law: it was the prudent thing to do. Those who like Bishop Peirs had private resources could retire into obscurity during the civil wars until the storm passed. One can understand, too, that men who had jobs such as stewards, auditors, and registrars in episcopal administration, which they often purchased and came to regard almost as inheritable family property, were dismayed at the abolition of their community. For them there was no redress or compensation. Perhaps one day an historian will be found to write the full story of the suffering of the clergy and their dependants of which Walker's study is but the preface.

[1] C. Hill, *Century of Revolution*, p. 163; J. Stoughton, *Ecclesiastical History of England*, II, 109.

APPENDICES

A. The Bishops' Income in Tolls from Markets and Fairs

Date	Source	Cal.	St. A.	Holy X	J.B.	W.M.*	Bin.	Pr.	Total
1535	A	56s. 9d.	44s. 6d.	9s. 5d.	6s. 7d.	6s. 8d.	3s. 4d.	4s. 1d.	131s. 4d.
1548	B	12s.	28s. 2d.	16s.	6s.	6s. 8d.	3s. 6d.	3s.	75s. 4d.
1549	B	11s. 8d.	18s.	8s.	18s. 10d.	6s. 8d.	3s. 4d.	3s. 4d.	69s. 10d.
1555	C	25s. 8d.	26s. 2d.	5s.	4s. 4d.	6s. 8d.	5s.	3s.	75s. 10d.
1566	D	8s. 6d.	9s.	3s. 8d.	2s. 3d.	6s. 8d.	7s. 10d.	2s. 4d.	39s. 7d.
1567	D	10s. 4d.	10s.	2s. 8d.	3s.	6s. 8d.	6s.	2s. 6d.	41s. 2d.
1568	D	{	{	{	{	6s. 8d.	5s. 4d.	2s.	?
1569	D	16s.	20s.	3s. 6d.	2s. 4d.	6s. 8d.	5s. 4d.	2s.	55s. 10d.
1570	D	42s. 8d.	17s.	19s.	2s. 8d.	6s. 8d.	5s. 4d.	{	?
1571	D	39s. 8d.	18s.	16s.	2s. 8d.	6s. 8d.	5s. 4d.	2s. 5d.	58s. 11d.
1572	D	{	{	{	{	{	5s. 6d.	2s.	?
1573	D	17s.	19s.	3s. 8d.	2s. 3d.	6s. 8d.	5s. 8d.	2s. 4d.	56s. 7d.
1574	D	18s.	18s.	3s. 8d.	3s. 5d.	6s. 8d.	5s. 10d.	2s. 3d.	57s. 10d.
1575	D	17s. 3d.	19s.	3s. 8d.	2s. 3d.	6s. 8d.	5s. 2d.	2s.	56s. 10d.
1578	D					6s. 8d.			
1594	E	20s.	20s.	5s.	5s.	10s.	{	{	?
1595	F	20s.	20s.	5s.	5s.	10s.	{	{	?
1596	F	20s.	20s.	5s.	5s.	10s.	{	{	?

The formalized figures for 1594–6 probably arose out of the settlement with Leonard Crosse. See above p. 197.

Sources

A   P.R.O. S.C.6/Hen. VIII/3075
B   P.R.O. S.C.6/Ed. VI/420
C   P.R.O. S.C.6/P. & M./263
D   S.R.O. DD/CC/31523
E   P.R.O. S.C.6/Eliz./2008
F   P.R.O. S.C.6/Add./3545/84

Abbreviations

*	tolls let to the bailiff
Cal.	St Calixtus Fair
St A.	St Andrews Fair
Holy X	The Invention of the Holy Cross Fair
J.B.	St John the Baptist Fair
W.M.	Wells Market
Bin.	Binegar Fair
Pr.	Priddy Fair

B. Proposal to Confiscate Episcopal Wealth

(Précis of text modernized and punctuated, from P.R.O. S.P. 1/152, fos. 11–13)

When I behold . . . my most dear sovereign lord's continual study and painful travail . . . for the advancement of Christ's faith and true religion . . . I judge the duty of every true subject . . . to bear part of the burden and to devise ways and means whereby your gracious intent and enterprise may take effect . . . for my part not forgetting but taking example of a good physician touching the cure of his sick patient I searched diligently . . . to find out the root, the foundation and the original cause of the sore disease in Christ's church and what thing it might be that caused the ministers of the same . . . now to swerve from the straight rule and line. Considering the primitive church with the church present: I find that then poverty did take place: and that now riches with possessions be superabundant—now pleasant ease, pride, glossing, incontinency, avarice, arrogance in prosperity. . . . Wherefore to cure the disease that is engendered needs must the original cause of the same be removed and taken away which is great possessions and superfluous riches. The naughty tree is not mortified by lopping of the boughs: but only by the cruel plucking up of the roots. . . . Of this tree your excellent majesty hath already extirped and pulled up certain roots rank and noisome beyond measure: Nevertheless some yet still remain full deep and fast in the ground. I mean some part of the feigned religion hath been partly abolished, party (*sic*) [fo. 11 *d*] altered changed and converted by your Grace's industry and your noble discreet counsel to good uses and to the common profit of this your realm. But the high priests, the bishops with their deans, archdeacons, officials, commissaries and other their substitutes be yet untouched. Many colleges many chapels and chantries have not yet tasted of the wholesome medicine and treacle which your grace prepareth for their souls' health bitter at the first receipt, but at length sweet and pleasant. The church remaineth as yet monstrous, partly reformed, partly incorrect. . . . Which reformation to make perfect through your grace's assistance, sufferance and will, I have drawn out a short act in this your high court of parliament to be established in manner and form as hereafter followeth:

[fo. 12] . . . Be it established ordained and enacted that the king . . . shall have full power and authority to assign to every bishop now being instituted or hereafter by him to be instituted . . . such convenient lands, tenements, rents, benefices, colleges or any other temporal lands or spiritual provisions of what nature or kinds soever they be as shall be thought by his highness or his most honourable council, sufficient and meet for [fo. 12 *d*] the reasonable finding of a christian bishop, & for the reasonable maintenance of a preacher of God's word without superfluity, and the rest of all such manors, lands, tenements, rents, reversions . . . profits and emoluments . . . which they heretofore have occupied and enjoyed or of right ought to enjoy . . . the same to retain in his own hands or else to assign to other bishops of new to be instituted in every diocese or shire of this his realm of England . . . from time to time or otherwise to order, distribute, sell, change, alter, give, grant or alien under his grace's letters patent as well for the help and commodity of his poor subjects as for the maintenance of this his realm or otherwise as shall seem best to his grace's majesty and his most noble Council. . . .

All possessions of any cathedral church or minister [fo. 13] or governor of the same e.g. dean, subdean, chanter or other officer, or belonging to any collegiate free chapel, prebend, hospital, chantry or other cathedral place shall also be at the king's will to retain in his own hands or to assign to whomsoever it shall please.

And for that great pollings and exactions have been taken by the archdeacons, commissars, officials, scribes and other the bishop's officers by colour of their office . . . be it enacted . . . that the king's majesty supreme head of this church . . . shall have power to grant out commissions into all dioceses to survey, try and enquire as well by the oath of 12 honest men of every county, as well by the oaths of other that can inform them of the same, what lands, tenements, fees, annuities, prebends or other profits, exactions or emoluments the archdeacons, commissaries, officials, scribes or other officers under the bishop of the same diocese hath been used to have, receive or take . . . the commissioners to certify the same to the king's council. The king shall have authority to assign to every such officer such lands as shall be thought expedient for them & what fees every one of them shall receive by virtue of their office as shall seem to His Majesty and His Council most expedient. Every commissary or official exacting more than the amount specified shall suffer imprisonment for one year & pay a fine at the king's pleasure. The king shall have authority to grant away the surplus to any person.
[*Endorsed*]

1540

A bill drawn and not put up for the parliament house, to give power to the king to assign to bishops and deans and to colleges such livings as he should think fit and to help the rest of his people.

C. Bishop Berkeley's Leased-out Properties

(Account Book of 1566–78: S.R.O. DD/CC/31523)

Property	Lessee	Rent
Manors		
Buckland	(i) Humphrey Colles	£47. 18. 5d.
	(ii) from 1573, John Colles	
Wiveliscombe	Richard Bourne	£75. 18. 3½d.
Westbury	Richard Bourne	£42. 8. 5d.
Chard	(i) Hugh Paulet, Kt	£50
	(ii) Amyas Paulet from 1574	
Compton Parva	(i) Thomas Smythe	£2. 13. 4d.
	(ii) From 1573, Richard Smith	
	(iii) From 1577 (?) John Smith	
Rectories		
Glaston and		
West Pennard	?	£42. 13. 4d.
Weston Zoyland	(i) Thomas Dyer, Kt	£70
	(ii) From 1571, Edward Dyer	
Northlode	(i) Richard Browning	£2. 11. 8d.
	(ii) From 1577, John Browning	
	and others	
East Pennard	(i) Cicilie Haggatt	£18. 6. 8d.
	(ii) From 1577, her assignees	
East Brent	(i) Alice Haggatt	£17. 6. 8d.
	(ii) From 1573, her assignee	
Corston	(i) William Horsington	£2
	(ii) From 1577(?), his assignee	
Compton Dando	Thomas Kelbe—not clear	£2
	for how long	
Castle Cary	William Crowche	£12
Westdown, Devon	Richard Roberts	£10
	Total	£395. 16. 9½d.

D. Lead Royalties of the Bishops of Bath and Wells

Year[1]	Source	Amount			Price per ton	Gross value	Expenses	Net Value
		tons	cwt	lb				
1567	A	2	8	37	—	—		
1570	A	3	10	4	—	—		
1572	A	3	14	21	£6. 10s.	£24. 2. 4½d.		
1573	A	4	2	14	—	—		
1574	A	5		87	£8	£40. 6. 8½d.[3]		
1575	A	5			—	—		
1577	A	9	7	44	—	—		
1578	A	9	12	7	—	—		
1583	B							£33. 1s.
1584	C							£20. 4. 8d.[2]
1591	D							(annual rate)
								£8. 3. 8d.
1592	E	6	15	40	—	—		£26. 1. 10d.
1593	F	5	10	91	—	—	£1. 10s.	
1634	G	17			(i) £10. 14s.	£182. 6. 11d.	£5	£177. 6. 11d.
					(ii) £10. 15s.			
					(iii) £10. 12s.			
					(iv) —			
1635[4]	G	13 annual rate			(i) —	£138	£4. 19. 8d.	£123. 0. 4d.
					(ii) —	(annual rate)	(annual rate)	(annual rate)
					(iii) £11			
					(iv) £10			
1636	G	10½			(i) £9. 12s.	£105. 9. 0d.	£6. 18. 8d.	£98. 10. 4d.
					(ii) £9. 12s.			
					(iii) £10. 5s.			
					(iv) £10. 13s.			
1637	G	14½			(i) £10. 15s.	£165. 14. 6d.	£13. 15. 6d.	£151. 19. 0d.
					(ii) £10. 14s.			
					(iii) £11. 13. 4d.			
					(iv) £11. 13. 4d.			
1638	G	13			(i) —	£141. 14s.	£12. 5. 5d.	£134. 8. 7d.
					(ii) £11. 5s.			
					(iii) £11. 11s.			
					(iv) £11			
1639[5]	G	11 (annual rate)			(i) £10	£107. 7s.	£10. 2. 6d.	£97. 4. 6d.
					(ii) —	(annual rate)	(annual rate)	(annual rate)
					(iii) £9. 8s.			
					(iv) £9. 10s.			
1640[6]	G	11			(i) —	£79. 9s.	£8. 10. 2d.	£69. 18. 10d.
					(ii) £9. 5s.	(annual rate)	(annual rate)	(annual rate)
					(iii) £9. 12s.			
					(iv) —			

Notes

[1] Accounts were made up annually at Michaelmas, so the first item on the tables is for Michaelmas, 1567.
[2] This is the figure given in the account: £40. 6. 9d. is arithmetically correct.
[3] This account runs for only half a year, viz. 29 September 1583 to 25 March 1583–4.
[4] The figures given are for the second half of the year only. They have been doubled in the table.
[5] These figures are partly estimated. The account is not complete.
[6] Two quarters only are given. The figures have been doubled.

Sources

A S.R.O. DD/CC/31523
B P.R.O. S.C.6/Eliz./2011
C P.R.O. S.C.6/Eliz./2012
D P.R.O. S.C.6/Eliz./2013
E P.R.O. S.C.6/Eliz./2014 and S.C.12/38/46
F P.R.O. S.C.6/Add./3545/84
G S.R.O. DD/CC/13324

BIBLIOGRAPHY

Primary Sources

I. MANUSCRIPT

British Museum
Additional MSS (various).
Cotton MS Cleo. E. vi.
Egerton MS 2350.
Stowe MS 572.

Public Record Office
C1, C2, C3 series   Chancery Proceedings.
C54 series,   Chancery, Close Rolls.
E 134 series   Exchequer: Depositions by Commission.
E 178 series   Echequer, King's Remembrancer, Special Commissions of Enquiry.
E 318 series   Exchequer, Augmentation Office, Particulars for Grants of Crown Lands.
Rental and Surveys.
Req.   Court of Requests, Proceedings.
S.C.6. series   Special Collections, Ministers' Accounts.
S.P.   State Papers.
St. Ch.   Star Chamber, Proceedings.

Somerset House
Prerogative Court of Canterbury, Wills.

Bodleian Library
Tanner MSS.

Canterbury Cathedral Library
Bishops' Transcripts, No. 86 Chartham.
F. W. Tyler, Transcripts of Chartham Parish Register, 1558–1740 (1937, typescript).

Institute of Historical Research
Price History Material, P.8/No. 19080.

Lambeth Palace Library
Parliamentary Surveys, 1, 1648.

Somerset Record Office, Taunton

MSS of the bishopric of Bath and Wills recently moved from the Church Commissioners' Office, Millbank:

DD/CC/12357 Mendip Mining Laws, Code and Orders (to 1675).
DD/CC/13324 Book of fines, leases and heriots etc. 1634.
DD/CC/13331 Mendip Mining Laws, Code and Orders (to 1749).
DD/CC/31523 Compotus of Bishop Berkeley 1566–78.
DD/CC/14263/4/5 Charter of Elizabeth I to Bishop Godwin 1582.
DD/CC/28225 18th century copy of Banwell lease of 1590.
Banwell Court Rolls (early 17th century).

Taunton Castle

Banwell lease of 1590 PR 436.
G. Bennett 'The History of Banwell, Somerset' (1825), typescript.
Nathaniel Chyles, 'The History of the Cathedral Church of St. Andrews in Wells' (c.1680) CH 22.
General Audit of the bishopric of Bath and Wells 1541–2.
Wiveliscombe Transcripts and Court Book, given by T. V. Pearce 1928 PR 37.

Wells Cathedral Library

Chapter Act Books Book H 1571–99
April 1591–Dec. 1607
1607–21
1621–35
1635–44

Town Clerk's Office, Wells
City of Wells MSS

Act Books of Convocation 1450–1553, no. 241.
1553–1623, no. 242.
Goodall's Book (mostly transcripts from the Act Books).
Serel MSS, Recorders, Mayors and Clerks (transcripts and notes by T. Serel).

Wells Museum

An uncatalogued manuscript notebook, probably Bishop Hooper's c. 1703, referred to as Wells Museum Notebook.
Transcripts of Documents, 2 vols.

Wells Diocesan Registry

Marriage Licences (Phipps transcripts, 1946).
Miscellaneous Letters 1589–1639, 1640–1759.

Parish Registers

Banwell, Somerset.
Helmdon, Northants.
Sunbury-on-Thames, Middx.
Wells (St. Cuthbert), Somerset.
Youghal, Co. Cork, Ireland.

MSS of the Marquess of Bath

Seymour Papers (transcripts).

2. PRINTED

Acts and Ordinances of the Interregnum 1642–60, ed. C. H. Firth and R. S. Rait, i (1911).

Abstracts of Somersetshire Wills, ed. F. Brown, 6 vols. (1887–90).

Acts of the Privy Council, ed. J. R. Dasent (1890–1907).

Bishop Lake's Sermons. Printed by W. Stansby for Nathaniel Butter (London, 1629).

Calendar of Letters and Papers of Henry VIII.

Calendar of Patent Rolls.

Calendar of State Papers Domestic.

Calendar of State Papers, Spanish.

Correspondence of Matthew Parker 1535–75, ed. J. Bruce and T.T. Perowne (1853).

D'EWES, S., *Journals of Parliaments of Queen Elizabeth* (1682).

Forfeited Lands of the Duke of Somerset, ed. D. T. Phillips (1866).

FULLER, T., *The History of the Worthies of England* (1840 edn.).

GARDINER, S., *Constitutional Documents of the Puritan Revolution 1625–60* (3rd edn. 1906).

HARINGTON J., *Nugae Antiquae* (Parks edn. 1804).

HARLEIAN SOCIETY, *Visitation of Somersetshire 1623*, xi (1876).

Historical Manuscripts Commission:

    1st Report (1870), 5th Report (1876), 10th Report (1885).

    Calendar of the MSS of the Dean and Chapter of Wells, 2 vols. (1941).

JEWERS, A. J., *Wells Cathedral: Its Monumental Inscriptions and Heraldry* (1892).

Leland's Itinerary 1535–43, ed. L. T. Smith, ii (1907).

Letters and Epigrams of Sir John Harington, ed N. McClure (1930).

LINCOLN RECORD SOCIETY, *Chapter Acts of Lincoln 1547–59*, xv (1917).

NORTHANTS RECORD SOCIETY, *Musters, Beacons and Subsidies in Northampton 1586–1623*, iii (1926).

Official Returns of Members of Parliament 1213–1702, (1878).

OXFORD RECORD SOCIETY, *Hearth Tax Returns, Oxfordshire, 1665*, xxi (1940).

Correspondence of Matthew Parker 1535–75, ed. J. Bruce and T. T. Perowne (1853).

Somerset Record Society:

    The Particular Description of Somerset by T. Gerard, 1633, xv (1900).

    Somerset Medieval Wills, 1531–58, xxi (1905).

    Quarter Sessions Records, James I, xxiii (1907).

    Mendip Mining Laws and Forest Bounds, xlv (1931).

    Wells City Charters, xlvi (1931).

    Register of Bishop Beckynton, xlix (1934).

    Somerset Enrolled Deeds, li (1936).

    Registers of Bishops King and de Castello, liv (1939).

    Registers of Bishops Wolsey, Clerk, Knight and Bourne, lv (1940).

    Somerset Assize Orders 1629–40, lxv (1959).

RYMER, T. *Foedera* (3rd edn. 1741).

Syllabus of Rymer's Foedera, ed. T. D. Hardy (1869–85).

Valor Ecclesiasticus, i (1810).

Statutes of the Realm 1509–47, (1810–24).

Walker Revised, ed. A. G. Matthews (1948).

Letters Relative to the Suppression of the Monasteries, ed. T. Wright. Camden Society, xxvi (1843).

Secondary Sources

I. GENERAL

BALDWIN SMITH, L., *Tudor Prelates and Politics 1536–58* (1953).

BARNES, A. S., *Bishop Barlow and the Anglican Orders* (1922).

BASKERVILLE, G., *English Monks and the Suppression of the Monasteries* (1937).

BATES HARBIN, S. W., *Members of Parliament for Somerset* (1939).

BURNET, G., *The History of the Reformation of the Church of England*, ed. Pocock (1865).

CAM, H. M., *Liberties and Communities in Medieval England* (1944).

COWPER, J. M., *Lives of the Deans of Canterbury* (1900).

DAVIES, GODFREY, *The Early Stuarts 1603–60* (1st edn. 1937).

DICKENS, A. G., *Thomas Cromwell and the English Reformation* (1959).

DICKENS, A. G., *The English Reformation* (1964).

Dictionary of National Biography.

DIXON, R. W., *History of the Church of England* (1902).

ELTON, G. R., *The Tudor Revolution in Government* (1953).

FULLER, T., *Church History of Britain*, vi, ed. J. S. Brewer (1845).

GARRETT, C. H., *The Marian Exiles 1553–59* (1938).

GEE H. and HARDY, W. J., *Documents Illustrative of English Church History* (1896).

HILL, C., *Century of Revolution 1603–1714* (1961).

HILL, C., *Economic Problems of the Church from Archbishop Whitgift to the Long Parliament* (1956).

LEWIS, S., *Topogaphical Dictionary of England* (1840).

MACKIE, J. D., *The Earlier Tudors* (1952).

MATHEW, D., *The Social Structure of Caroline England* (1948).

MATTINGLY, G., *Catharine of Aragon* (1950)

NEALE, J. E., *Elizabeth I and her Parliaments 1559–81* (1953).

NEALE, J. E. *Elizabeth I and her Parliaments 1584–1601* (1957).

NEALE, J. E., 'The Elizabethan Political Scene', *Essays in Elizabethan History* (1958).

OLLARD, S. L., CROSSE, G. and BOND, M. F., *Dictionary of English Church History* (1948 edn.).

PARKER, T. M., *The English Reformation to 1558* (1950).

POLLARD, A. F., *England Under the Protector Somerset* (1900).

RAMSEY, P., *Tudor Economic Problems* (1963).

TREVOR ROPER, H. R., *Archbishop Laud* (1940).

TREVOR ROPER, H. R., *Historical Essays* (1957).
RIDLEY, J. *Thomas Cranmer* (1962).
ROWSE, A. L., *The England of Elizabeth* (1950).
ROWSE, A. L., *The Expansion of Elizabethan England* (1955).
ROWSE, A. L., *Tudor Cornwall* (1941).
RUPP, E. G., *The English Protestant Tradition* (1949).
SKEEL, C. *The Council in the Marches of Wales* (1904).
SOUTHGATE, W. M., *John Jewel* (1962).
STRYPE, J., *Annals of the Reformation* (1824 edn.).
WEDGWOOD, C. V., *The King's Peace 1637–41* (1955).
WHITE, F. O., *Lives of the Elizabethan Bishops* (1898).

2. LOCAL

Proceedings of the Somersetshire Archaeological and Natural History Society.
BRIDGES, J., *History of Northamptonshire* (1791).
BROWNE WILLIS, *History of Buckinghamshire* (1791).
CASSAN, S. H., *The Lives of the Bishops of Bath and Wells* (1829).
COLLINSON, J. *History of Somersetshire* (1791).
DUNCUMB, J., *County of Hereford*, i (1804).
DUNNING, R. W., The Administration of the Diocese of Bath and Wells, 1401–91 (unpublished Ph.D. thesis, Bristol, 1963).
Easton and its Church, Anonymous Local Guide (1952).
GOUGH, J. W., *The Mines of Mendip* (1930).
HANCOCK, F. A., *Wifela's Combe* (1911).
HASTED, E., *History of Kent* (1798).
HUNT, W., *The Somerset Diocese, Bath and Wells* (1885).
KNIGHT, F. A., *The Sea-board of Mendip* (1902).
LONG, B., *Records of the Parish Church and Parish of Wokingham* (1937).
LYSONS, D., *Environs of London* (1792).
LYSONS, D., *Middlesex Parishes* (1800).
MALDEN, R. H., *The Story of Wells Cathedral* (1934).
Murray's Handbook for Somersetshire (1899).
PEVSNER, N., *The Buildings of England. South and West Somerset* (1958).
PHELPS, W., *The History and Antiquities of Somersetshire* (1839).
PIGOT, H., *Hadleigh* (1860).
RUTTER, J., *Delineations of N.W. Somerset* (1829).
SCOTT HOLMES, T., *The History of the Parish and Manor of Wookey* (1886?).
SEREL, T., *Historical Notes on the Church of St. Cuthbert, Wells* (1875).
Somerset and Dorset Notes and Queries, xii.
TOMLINSON, E. M., *History of the Minories* (1907).
Victoria County Histories:
    Somersetshire, ii (1911).
    Worcestershire, ii (1906).
WEAVER, F. W., *Somerset Incumbents* (1889).
A Guide to Whitbourne Church, Anonymous (1963).
WOOD, F. A., *Collections for the Parochial History of Chew Magna* (1903).

3. ARTICLES

DU BOULAY, F. R., 'Archbishop Cranmer and the Canterbury Temporalities', *E.H.R.*, lxvii (1952).

ELTON, G. R., 'Parliamentary Drafts, 1529–40', *Bull. Inst. H.R.*, xxv (1952), 'A Further Note on Parliamentary Drafts in the Reign of Henry VIII', *Bull. Inst. H.R.*, xxvii (1954).

FARNHAM, E., 'The Somerset Election of 1614', *E.H.R.*, xlvi (1931).

FARNHAM G. F. and HERBERT, A., 'Fenny Drayton and the Purfey Monuments', *Trans. Leics. Arch. Soc.*, xiv (1925).

FAULKNER, P. A., 'Domestic Planning from the Twelfth to the Fourteenth Centuries', *The Archaeological Journal*, cxv (1958).

HEMBRY, P. M., 'The Death of Thomas Godwin, Bishop of Bath and Wells (1584–90)', *Proc. Som. Arch. Soc.*, xcvi (1951).

JENKINS, C., 'Bishop Barlow's Consecration and Archbishop Parker's Register', *Journal of Theological Studies* (1922) reprinted by the Church Historical Society (1935).

STONE, L., 'The Political Programme of Thomas Cromwell', *Bull. Inst. H.R.*, xxiv (1951).

TATHAM, G. B., 'The Sale of Episcopal Lands during the Civil Wars and Commonwealth', *E.H.R.*, xxiii (1908).

UNDERDOWN, D., 'A Case Concerning Bishops' Lands: Cornelius Burges and the Corporation of Wells' *E.H.R.*, lxxviii (1963).

WILLIAMS, GLANMOR,. 'The Protestant Experiment in the Diocese of St. Davids', *Bulletin of Celtic Studies*, xiv (1952), xv (1953).

INDEX

Bourne, Gilbert—*contd.*
the Waldegraves, 126–7; president of the council of Wales, 98; deprivation, 99–100, 129
his brother Richard, 90, 91–8, 100, 127, 134, 138, 139, 140, 142, 143, 148, 165, 208; sons of Richard, John, 90, 94, other sons, Gilbert, William, Thomas, Roger, 90, 94, 97–8
Bourne, John, 24, 144
Bourne, Sir John, 89, 91, 126; son Anthony, 91
Bourne, Philip, 89
Bowerman, William, 158, 169; son Andrew, 158, 199, 241; wife Elizabeth, 161n.; daughter Margaret, 157, 158
Boys, John, 163, 204–5
Brackley, Northants., 152, 155, 165
Bridge, John, 208
Bright, Geoffrey, 38
Bristol, Glos., 145; bishopric of, 2, 244
Bruton, Somt., 50, 101, 104, 179, 213
Brugge, John, 39
Bryckley, Roger, 124
Buckingham, Duke of, *see* Villiers
Bull, William, 211
Bullingham, Nicholas, bishop of Lincoln, 100, 154, 155
Burgess, Cornelius, 246
Burnham-on-Sea, Somt., 163
Bushell, Edward, 219
Bushell, Walter, 152, 218, 221
Bushell, William, 223, 233
Butcher, John, 149–50
Bysse, James, 131

Cambridge, university of, 52; chancellor of, 222; Christ's College, 183, 211; Peterhouse, 221, 222; St John's, 183; Sidney Sussex, 211, 214; Trinity, 183, 192, 193, 221, 222, 257

Camden, William, 160
Came, Joan, 177
Campeggio, Lorenzo, cardinal, bishop of Salisbury, 54, 58
Cannington, Somt., 127
Canterbury, archbishops of, *see* Abbot, Cranmer, Laud, Parker, Pole, Sheldon, Whitgift
—, archbishopric of, 16, 60, 74, 130, 131, 154, 220, 238, 254; province of, 130; deanery of, 154, 155, 156, 162, 164
—, St Augustine, monastery of, later royal palace, 248
Carew, Pemb., 83
Carew, George, dean of Exeter, 100
Carlisle, bishopric of, 129, 254
Carr, John, 115
Cartwright, Thomas, 183
Casebeard, John, 249
Cassan, S. H., 151, 158
Castle Cary, Somt., 114, 199, 241
Catharine of Aragon, queen of England, 28, 54, 59
Catherine Parr, queen of England, 76
Cecil, Sir William, Lord Burghley, 91, 98, 101, 102, 113, 130, 147, 160, 174, 176, 222
Champernowne, Sir Richard, 185
Champernowne, Bridget, 193
Chapel Royal, 53, 141
Chapuys, Eustache, 60
Chard, Somt., manor and borough of, 5, 23, 24, 78, 107, 112, 116, 129, 132, 145, 201, 223, 233–4, 240
Charles I, king of England, 52, 221, 230, 232, 237, 238, 239, 242, 248, 257
Charles V, emperor, 2, 60, 72
Chartham, Kent, 155, 162
Cheddar, Somt., manor of, 5, 17, 18, 29, 43, 78, 107, 108–9
Cheke, Sir John, 117